THE
EXECUTION OF
BHAGAT SINGH

THE
EXECUTION OF
BHAGAT SINGH

LEGAL HERESIES OF THE RAJ

SATVINDER SINGH JUSS

AMBERLEY

To my parents

First published 2020

Amberley Publishing
The Hill, Stroud
Gloucestershire, GL5 4EP

www.amberley-books.com

British Library Cataloguing in Publication Data.
A catalogue record for this book is available from the British Library.

ISBN 978 1 4456 8976 0 (hardback)
ISBN 978 1 4456 8977 7 (ebook)

1 2 3 4 5 6 7 8 9 10

Typeset in 10.5pt on 14pt Sabon.
Typesetting by Aura Technology and Software Services, India.
Printed in the UK.

We are sorry to admit [that] we who attach so great a
sanctity to human life, we who dream of a glorious future,
when man will be enjoying perfect peace and full liberty,
have been forced to shed human blood.

The Hindustan Socialist Republican Association
4 June 1929

Contents

Khush Raho Ahle Watan,
Hum toh Safar Karte Hain

Stay contented,
And pay no attention to my plight, my countrymen,
for I am but a traveller in this world,
Who now leaves you to pass on to the next.

Bhagat Singh, shortly before his death

Prologue

Zulm rehay aur Amn bhi ho! /
Kyaa mumkin hay? Tumm hi kaho

Will there be Repression? Or will there be Peace?
What is possible? Only the powerful can decide.

Habib Jalib

The Bhagat Singh archive lies in the heart of historic Lahore within the tree-lined precincts of the Central Punjab Secretariat compound. With its well-manicured gardens and neatly laid-out lanes and pathways surrounding its forty-eight departments, it is not easy to access. The noted travel writer William Dalrymple has remarked that, '[t]o get to its gate is a difficult task, leave alone accessing the archives'.[1] Being the bureaucratic nerve centre of the city, the place is heavily fortified. Prior written permission is required to enter. Once one is inside the compound, however, one is richly rewarded with the sight of the highly atmospheric 400-year-old 'Tomb of Anarkali', where the papers are carefully held. Here important exhibitions of these documents are now beginning to take place for the benefit of local Lahoris and others who care to visit.

The tomb itself reeks with the mystique of a past splendour. One reason for this is the legend associated with the grave inside. It is said to be that of one of Emperor Akbar's wives, who was supposedly bricked alive following a death sentence over an illicit affair with the Crown Prince. Whether the grave contains the remains of the Emperor's wife is a question that continues to beguile everyone because it bears no name. The British tourist and trader William Finch, in his travelogue, mentions how when he came to Lahore in August 1608, Anarkali was one of the wives of Emperor

Akbar, and the mother of his favourite son, Daniel Shah. Akbar developed suspicions that Anarkali had an incestuous relationship with Prince Saleem (who later went on to become Emperor Jahangir), and so Akbar had her buried in the Lahore Fort. When Jahangir later ascended the throne, he had the tomb constructed in her memory. Eighteenth-century historian and architect Abdullah Chugtai, however, has a different view. He maintains that the tomb was built in the centre of a pomegranate (*anarkali*) garden, and contains the grave of Jahangir's wife, Saheb Jamal, who was very dear to him. Whatever the truth, one would have to agree that the Persian inscription on the tomb – 'If I could only behold the face of my beloved one last time / I would be beholden to my God to the day of my resurrection' – is a most endearing one from a wife to her Lord Emperor.

Inside the Punjab Civil Secretariat grounds, located within the Anarkali precincts, one can find some of the earliest buildings dating back to the Sikh reign. They are still functional and well maintained. In the midday Lahore sun their gleaming white radiance is a spectacle to behold. General Jean Baptiste Ventura, of Maharajah Ranjit Singh's army, built his 'Anarkali House' next to what was then the Anarkali Garden. A parapet of cornices beautifully brings together the simple Doric columns on which is placed the deep-fronted verandah. General Jean Francois Allard, another French adventurer, who helped build Maharajah Ranjit Singh's army into the most powerful fighting force in Asia, also had his residence there. It is constructed on the ruins of a Mughal palace with a half-European and half-Persian ambience to it. It had once been decorated magnificently with Persian and Kashmiri rugs, allowing the general to live in European comfort whilst enjoying the trappings of Eastern grandeur. The buildings still stand in all their sumptuous magnificence, though when later acquired by the British they were modified to suit British tastes, making them the oldest British buildings in Lahore.

It is possible to discern remnants of what would have been the broad, leafy avenues lined with white colonial bungalows featuring porticoes and arches, high ceilings, spacious rooms and forbidding perimeter walls. There is a garden the size of a public park. There is the occasional splash of the fountain water nearby. The large trees are fragrant. It was against this background that in its time the Mughal tomb of Anarkali came to serve many purposes. It was occupied by Ventura's wife as her residence. The British used it as a church, and one can still see the immaculately maintained and darkly polished pews from that time. Today, it is increasingly used to showcase the wealth of the priceless documentation that is held within its vaults. Only a fraction has so far been seen. The wooden vaults stand 6 inches from the floor, preventing book lice from creeping up and eating away at the paper. In carefully wrapped white sheets, bound with solid brown tape, are the long-preserved records of past times. For most historical periods the record is complete.

The people of Lahore are slowly growing accustomed to the exhibitions in the Tomb of Anarkali. They are learning to escape the narrow rumbustious lanes of the city outside, which fan out from Anarkali, where the residents live cheek by jowl, and daily stand witness to the city's raucous, joyous events. There is a gradual realisation that the Tomb of Anarkali is a beacon calling out to them. Here they can leave behind the deafening cacophony of modern Lahore. The city of sounds and smells and dilapidated buildings gives way upon entry to a lost world of past riches as one comes face to face with large maps, photographs, paintings and documents encased in glass frames. All this is there to see just by entering through the tomb's large medieval doorway. The people eagerly eying the exhibitions, many barely remembering the illustrious past of the great city of Lahore, are a sight to behold. Every visitor stunned with awe. Every visiting family enraptured. Every discussion that follows invigorating. The Tomb of Anarkali deserves to stand as the symbol of unity that has bound the community for so long. This is exactly what happened when, not long after this writer had himself visited to undertake research into the Bhagat Singh archive, the Punjab government decided, for the first time in its history in 2018, to exhibit the contents of the case file of the trial of Bhagat Singh, Sukhdev and Rajguru, hanged together on 23 March 1931.

The exhibition was inaugurated at the Tomb of Anarkali, referred to as 'the main storehouse of the Punjab archives department',[2] by the Additional Chief Secretary Umar Rasool. The documents displayed included the paperwork for the arrests by the British Indian police of some twenty-five members of the Hindustan Socialist Republican Association and the Naujawan Bharat Sabha from right across India. There were also documents relating to the parties, their manifestos and literature. For the first time, the addresses of places where Bhagat Singh and his comrades stayed were also disclosed – namely, a factory on Ravi Road, a rented house in Gowalmandi, another house in Mozang, and an address in Kashmir Building on McLeod Road. Such is the detailed nature of the Anarkali repository that it also includes such minutiae as the admission register of one of Bhagat Singh's associates, who was at the time studying at D. A. V. College in Lahore (now Islamia College Civil Lines). There is also a detailed list of Bhagat Singh's own reading material, including those books which he requested while detained in jail. This ranges across non-fiction works, novels and other revolutionary literature, all of which was displayed, revealingly disclosing references to the 'Punjab Tragedy, Zakhmi Punjab, Ganga Das Dakoo,

Sultana Dakoo, the Evolution of Sinn Fein and History of the Sinn Fein Movement',[3] giving an insight into the workings of Bhagat Singh's mind.

My good fortune from the outset was to meet with two people in Lahore soon after my arrival there. One was the highly accomplished and urbane Fakir Syed Aijazuddin. He is the seventh descendant of Fakir Nuruddin, who served as a Vizier under Maharajah Ranjit Singh. If there is one person who can speak with authority about the Sikh presence in Lahore from that time it is Mr Aijazuddin. He was always my first port of call in Lahore. The other person was the Director of the Lahore Archives, Mr Abbas Chugtai, a man who is professional in his work to his fingertips and who displays an unrivalled knowledge of the materials that he is tasked with protecting in this treasure trove. I owe him my unstinting gratitude. A quietly spoken, unassuming and serious man who was always immaculately dressed, he saw everyone who came to his office. Whether it was students wishing to carry out research on archival materials to whom he patiently listened and advised, or individuals who came in search of identity documents for family members from remote outlying villages, or officials from within the government departments itself who wished to take his advice on matters of the day, they came to his office. Seated at a large desk with a glass top, Mr Chugtai would see them all, and was unfailingly polite as they walked in one after the other, often at the cost of missing his lunch in a city which loves its food. He would not infrequently take his lunch at around 3 p.m.

Despite all the calls on his time I was fortunate to have been able to sit in his office and talk with him as the weather sizzled outside, working in comfort and sipping traditional Punjabi tea across the room from him. I found him an immensely engaging, sprightly and talkative director, always willing to share his knowledge of the archival materials. Being dedicated to his work, and having a good memory, he would beam with pleasure if the documents I was reading threw up a new historical fact. Through such efforts I was able to reconstruct the vanished outlines of a much overlooked insurgency, with its intrigue, its conspiracy, and its intelligence- and counterintelligence-led operations. There are still many gaps. Many individuals are unaccounted for. What is lost to posterity may yet be uncovered one day. Many questions remain. Others have been answered. My main purpose was to ensure that this book saw the light of day in time for the ninetieth anniversary of the execution of Bhagat Singh, Sukhdev and Rajguru, under the Lahore Ordinance No. III of 1930. The life of the Tribunal was six months. Three weeks before the Tribunal was to cease to exist, Bhagat Singh, Sukhdev and Rajguru were convicted and sentenced to death. This was on 7 October 1930. The execution by hanging was carried out on 23 March 1931.

1

Coercive Colonial Legalism

Mujh se insaaf ki ummeed na rakh, aye saa'il
Jis adaalat ka maiyn qaazi hoon vo deewaani hai

Be under no illusion of Justice, O' friend,
For the court of which I am a judge is a Court of Clowns
Akbar Allahabadi

The time for execution was unusual. It was not at dawn but at 7.30 p.m. in the cool, crisp evening of 23 March 1931, just as twilight was setting in. This was when the Chief Superintendent of Central Lahore Jail, Major P. D. Chopra, escorted a lean, sinewy young man of twenty-three years to the raised scaffold in the grounds of the jail. Looking on, a bewildered Deputy Jail Superintendent, Khan Sahib Mohammad Akbar Khan, struggled in vain to choke back his tears. The lush green trees outside the jail swayed in the gentle wind. Bhagat Singh was the condemned man. The most famous man in India. He grasped at the rope as it was brought near. Despite the deprivations of prison life, his face was still handsome. Undaunted and undeterred by the fate that awaited him, his hands dug deep into the fibrous strands of the braided, twisted piles of yarn which were about to extinguish his life. Bhagat Singh kissed the hangman's noose. It was an occasion he had longed for, waited upon, and even planned. Calmly, assuredly, and with a wry smile on his face, he took a quick glance sideways in both directions. He then airily placed the noose around his neck. Before he knew it, the noose drew in and fastened tight around his throat. The trapdoor fell open under his feet. His body cascaded. The plunge snapped his neck in two. Bhagat Singh was hanged.

Two of his comrades, Sukhdev and Rajguru, met with a similar fate at the same time in what became known as the Lahore Conspiracy Case. They too went to their deaths defiantly. All three had requested that they be executed by firing squad due to their status as political prisoners, and not hanged by the neck as common criminals; this had gone unheeded. Bhagat Singh had walked in the middle, with Sukhdev on his left and Rajguru on his right. It was not too difficult to see why they felt so elated, because as they had walked the path to the gallows Bhagat Singh sang out a verse. The other two joined in: '*Dil se niklegi na marker bhi watan ki ulfat / Meri mittee se bhi Khushbue watan aegi*' ('When we are dead there would be still patriotism left in us / Even my corpse will emit the fragrance of my motherland').[1] On the scaffold, Sukhdev and Rajguru also kissed the hangman's noose. They too tumbled down the trapdoor with a heavy thud, dying instantly. It was all over so quickly. Afterwards, their bodies were hurriedly taken down from the gallows. They were dragged along the dirty passageway, chopped into pieces and stuffed into sacks, which were then whisked out of the jail compound surreptitiously. Outside the jail, the remains were unceremoniously stacked on a truck. The truck made haste, speeding northwards from Lahore to Kasur, some two hours' drive away. There, on the banks of the River Sutlej, two holy men awaited. The harried men, dressed in full priestly garb, clutched their prayer books for solace. One was Sikh and the other Hindu. The priests read out the final prayers over the dismembered bodies, which were quickly loaded onto a funeral pyre to burn fiercely in the eerie silence of the night. Before the pyre had fully burnt out, and as dawn threatened to break over the silent waters of the Sutlej, the roaring fires were hastily put out. The charred remains were then hurled into the river. The precise spot was to be later identified as Post No. 201. Once the priests and the policemen had departed, villagers who had been looking on with suspicion went into the water. They retrieved the body parts and set about cremating them properly.[2] Having always been of the people, it was the people who gave Bhagat Singh, Sukhdev and Rajguru the dignity in death they already had in life.

Public outrage erupted on the streets as news of the hangings swept the country like wildfire the next day. Unbeknown to everyone, the time of the execution had been secretly brought forward by eleven hours. The three young men had been due to be hanged the next day, at dawn on 24 March 1931. The public, which had expected a commutation of the death sentence, felt doubly cheated. The result was immense anger everywhere. In New York, on the other side of the world, the *Daily*

Worker denounced Bhagat Singh's hanging as 'one of the bloodiest deeds ever undertaken by the British Labour Government'.[3] Gandhi, visiting Karachi at the time, was blamed for not intervening. As his train slowly shunted in at the railway station and he disembarked, inflamed protesters thrust clusters of black flowers into his hands – not the usual red or white flowers used to commemorate the arrival of a much awaited dignitary. He was branded with ignominy for not demanding commutation of the sentence of death from the Governor-General, Lord Irwin, as a condition of any further talks on the future of India. This ultimate stain of dishonour was one Gandhi never succeeded in removing during his lifetime.

In faraway London, a month earlier, a tenacious forty-four-year-old British lawyer by the name of Dennis Nowell Pritt had taken a taxi to Downing Street on a dank, misty February morning. He had gone there to argue the appeal against the sentence and conviction of Bhagat Singh and his two comrades. It was the last straw. All else had failed in India before then. The appeal was made before the Judicial Committee of the Privy Council, the highest court in the realm. The Privy Council was used to hearing appeals from thousands of miles away in the far-flung corners of the British Empire, from the Caribbean to Australia. It was the British Empire's court of last resort. Situated just off Whitehall, and a few minutes' walk from the Houses of Parliament, it was within shouting distance of the Prime Minister's office at 10 Downing Street, where Ramsay MacDonald, the first Labour Party politician to become Prime Minister, now resided.

When Pritt strode into Downing Street he knew what was at stake. If he could not persuade the Judicial Committee of the Privy Council that Bhagat Singh, Sukhdev and Rajguru had been wrongly tried and convicted, they would most certainly hang in India. Pritt knew he faced an uphill struggle. The judges were not going to be sympathetic. Their demeanour before him vacillated from giving the appearance of apoplectic outrage at the temerity of Pritt's audacious submissions to falling asleep. In the Privy Council (as with what was then the Judicial Committee of the House of Lords but is now Britain's Supreme Court), a single lawyer must face five judges who may interrupt, harangue or cajole him at any time to throw him off balance. He must possess immense lawyerly legal skill and presence of mind to have any chance of winning on his arguments. In *Bhagat Singh v. The King-Emperor*[4] the Judicial Committee of the Privy Council did everything in its power to break Pritt's resolve as he heroically attempted to defend what the judges considered to be the indefensible. Together with Sukhdev and Rajguru,

Bhagat Singh had been charged with conspiracy against the King. Pritt was not yet a veteran of defending conspiracy trials, but this case ensured that he would soon become one. His reputation would span the length and breadth of the British Empire. Bhagat Singh's case was going to be his baptism of fire.

Tall, patrician in outlook and with intelligent eyes, Pritt had a long face, a square chin and a high forehead. Atop his slender nose sat tortoiseshell glasses, through which he peered coldly and piercingly. Renowned for his dry wit and photographic memory, he only read a document once but could recall it with effortless ease at any given moment. In 1929 he had started to defend the Meerut Conspiracy Case. This ended in 1933, two years after the case of Bhagat Singh, but so grateful were his clients in India for his services that they had honoured him with the gift of a silk gown, which he took pride in displaying in his chambers in the Inner Temple. The Meerut Conspiracy Case had been reported in *The Manchester Guardian*, which unabashedly expressed solidarity with fellow socialists abroad. There had even been a theatrical play that immortalised the trial. But this was different.

Pritt was defending someone who had shot a twenty-one-year-old probationary police officer, John Saunders, as he came out of a police station in Lahore. He had been mistaken for James Scott, the police superintendent whom the alleged conspirators blamed for the beating to death of Lala Lajpat Rai on 17 November 1928 after he led a protest march against the Simon Commission in Lahore barely three weeks earlier. The cold-blooded assassination of the young Saunders was hard to defend. As fate would now have it, Pritt's name was to be forgotten. Bhagat Singh was to be forgotten. That there was ever such a case in the heyday of the British Empire, testing its commitment to the rule of law, was to be forgotten. Almost everyone associated with the case has been forgotten. There were a myriad other lawyers of great renown and legal acumen in the defence of Bhagat Singh, Sukhdev and Rajguru, in what became known as the Lahore Conspiracy Case, and they too were consigned to the dustbin of history. They all lie forgotten. Yet, the truth is that they have been unjustly robbed of what is their due. The recognition of their dauntless gallantry in the defence of those accused in this, the most unjust of all trials, is long overdue in circumstances where many have conspired to ensure that the trial remains forgotten.

The death of Lala Rajpat Rai on 17 November 1928 saw Bhagat Singh, together with B. K. Dutt, move into action. The two of them set out to disrupt the passage of the Public Safety Bill and the Trade

Disputes Bill, which were currently before the Central Legislative Assembly in New Delhi. These bills would reduce the civil liberties of citizens, and the young men believed action had to be taken. They travelled to Delhi, and on 8 April 1929 threw two smoke bombs from the balcony of the assembly 'to make the deaf hear'.[5] Pandemonium ensued. Both of them were immediately arrested. They were sent for committal proceedings before a regular magistrate, which took place in Lahore Central Jail, before Rai Sahib Pandit Sri Kishen from 10 July 1929 onwards. Proceedings were slow, with the hapless magistrate struggling to keep things under control, so on 1 May 1930 the trial was transferred under the executive authority of Governor-General Irwin to a 'Special Tribunal' constituted under a special government Ordinance known as Lahore Ordinance No. III of 1930.

It was highly irregular to transfer a hearing that was already committed to trial before the regular courts, so the transfer had to be done by an executive act of the Governor-General. For this to happen, it had to be shown that there was an 'emergency' which threatened the peace, order and good government of British India, justifying a suspension of the normal procedures of a criminal trial before the regular courts even where the hearing was being held in Lahore Central Jail. The lawyers in Lahore soon latched onto the government's distinct inability to point to such an 'emergency'. They made it clear that there was nothing which threatened the life of the nation. They quickly challenged the jurisdiction of the Tribunal to try the case on 5 May 1930 under the name of one of the accused in the Lahore Conspiracy Case of 1930, which included twenty-four defendants. The name chosen was *Des Raj*. His name appeared as the fourth accused in the Schedule to the Lahore Ordinance No. III of 1930, the emergency legislation which the government had enacted by way of an executive act. *Des Raj* argued that Lahore Ordinance No. III of 1930 was devoid of all constitutional authority. The Lahore Bar Association supported him. Surprisingly, the Indian Bar Association in Delhi did not. Remarkably, they failed to register a strong protest, even though they had counsel of national renown and notability in their ranks. The Lahore Bar Association alone issued a thorough and detailed report, dated 19 June 1930, against the Lahore Ordinance No. III of 1930. This was passed by a resolution of the High Court Bar Association Sub-Committee. It was signed off by two Muslims, Barkat Ali and Mohammed Iqbal, and two Hindus, Gokal Chand Narang and Nanak Chand.[6] Hardly any trace exists to commemorate these lawyers today. No one talks of them or knows anything of them.

When D. N. Pritt stood before the Judicial Committee of the Privy Council, his purpose was to challenge the existence of any jurisdiction in the Special Tribunal to try the Lahore Conspiracy defendants, who had been transferred from the ordinary courts of the land, namely, the Magistrates' Court in Lahore. In doing so, Pritt was building upon arguments which had already been raised in Lahore on 5 May 1930. What was new in his argument was that the particular Ordinance used to convict Bhagat Singh and his comrades was '*a priviligium of a very terrible description*'. Just like the Indian lawyers before him at the Lahore Bar, he was clear that whether the Ordinance used to convict the accused 'could possibly conduce to peace is a matter of some difficulty; that it could conduce either to good government *or to government at all*', such was the extent of his condemnation of the law being used to put these three young men to death.

Pritt argued that the ordinance 'is a priviligium' because '[i]t makes no law that any man has to obey, except the civil service of the Crown and the members of the Tribunal. It lays down no liberty to any man to do anything; it lays down no provision by way of criminal law or anything else that any man shall not do anything.' Given that Lahore Ordinance No. III of 1930 was a piece of delegated legislation passed under an imperial statute, Pritt submitted that 'all that the Governor-General can do is to make and promulgate Ordinances for the peace and good government of British India or any part thereof, which are to have the force of law for six months. That is a *priviligium*, and I submit that cannot in any view be called legislation at all for peace, order and good government.' The question, of course, is why so soon after the end of the First World War, when facing an unprecedented revolt against imperial rule, it was felt necessary for the government to act through such draconian measures. This book considers the reasons for this kind of legislation or 'priviligium' and argues that it was in order for the government of the day to justify the propagation of a form of 'colonial legal violence' through the medium of the law. In the words of Professor Chaman Lal, 'Rajguru, Sukhdev and Bhagat Singh's hanging was nothing but judicial murder – and that too performed in a hurry, with the colonial state clearly in a state of panic'.[7] It is worse than that. The three were executed under an Act of Attainder, something which has gone unremarked upon in almost a century since his trial. They were executed unlawfully because, entirely on account of their wanton abuse by both King and Parliament, by the nineteenth century all forms of Act of Attainder had been abolished in England. Yet, here was a case from

India, of a trial of twenty-four alleged conspirators against the King, all
of whom were undergoing an ordinary criminal trial before a magistrate,
when suddenly they were prised away from it and subjected to the very
process which had been banned for at least a hundred years and not used
since 1798.

The neglect of lawyers who took up unpopular causes during the
most repressive periods of British colonial rule is most lamentable. Many
lawyers provided advice and assistance in the cases of revolutionaries
who were fighting to wrest their freedom from their colonial masters.
They often did so for free. Many a time they were poorly remunerated.
They did this work at great personal and professional sacrifice to
themselves. Yet today, not one of them is a household name. Largely
forgotten, most of their names reach out to us from the faded light-brown
pages of officially recorded trial proceedings. The trailblazing works of
A. G. Noorani, Malvinder Jit Singh Waraich and Chaman Lal mention
some of them, but we know almost nothing about their lives. Asaf Ali,
Pran Nath Mehta, Rai Bahadur Badri Das, Amolak Ram Kapoor and
Baljeet Singh were some such lawyers who remained in active practice in
Delhi, Chandigarh, Shimla, and Ambala following the Partition of India
in 1947. Today they are lost to public memory. Amolak Ram Kapoor
is one lawyer, however, who has been brought back to life in this book.
This is largely due to the help given to the author by his granddaughter,
Sunaina Suneja, who presently lives in Delhi. The other lawyers, it is to
be earnestly hoped, will also one day be resurrected and rescued from
oblivion. They deserve better if Amolak Ram Kapoor's defence of Bhagat
Singh is anything to go by. His achievement is that, very early on, he
contested the jurisdiction of the Special Tribunal to have any power to
try Bhagat Singh and his comrades. The sheer clarity and incisiveness
of his legal mind is something to behold, as is his use of precise legal
language.

In the end, however, Amolak Ram Kapoor too had to withdraw from
the case. He was forced to do so just six months before Bhagat Singh
and his comrades were hanged. The trial before the Special Tribunal,
with which he had strong disagreement, was coming to its inevitable
end because the Lahore Ordinance No. III of 1930, which established
the Special Tribunal to try the three accused, only had a lifespan of six
months. Proceedings had to be cut short. Witnesses waiting to be called
had to be abandoned, and the cross-examination of Crown witnesses
had to be aborted. It was a remarkable feature of the trial that, as Binda
Preet Sahni has observed, 'the legal proceedings were marked by denial

of counsel for the defendants, unreliable witnesses, and arbitrary legal standards'.[8] Amolak Ram Kapoor had nevertheless made an unsuccessful last-ditch application for an adjournment given the circumstances. This had followed upon the denial of his request that he be allowed to cross-examine witnesses for the prosecution. When this was refused, he had withdrawn from court on 1 September 1930. With him gone, the trial came to a close just over a week later on 10 September 1930. Government advocate Carden Noad had risen imperiously to deliver his closing speech before an obliging colonial judiciary. It was clear that all was now lost. As the law fell away, raw human emotions took over. Kishen Singh, the father of Bhagat Singh, made a desperate and pitiful attempt to save his son from the gallows. On 20 September 1930, he petitioned the Tribunal in a draft written by a lawyer that identified issues of some considerable significance which in turn raised questions about the fairness of the trial.

First, he questioned the testimony of the witnesses who had identified Bhagat Singh as the assailant on the scene during the murder of John Saunders in Lahore, on grounds that,

> There is no manner of doubt that Mr. Fearn, European gentleman and Traffic Inspector of Police, who had plenty of opportunity to see the real criminal, could not identify the culprits. This man being a Traffic Inspector had developed his sense of identifying the natives by virtue of his profession and calling in life. He could not pick out Bhagat Singh but it is curious that Ganda Singh, Head Constable, and a Naib Court Police Constable and other witnesses, who were accidentally present on the spot, could spot Bhagat Singh. *It means that accused was shown to those witnesses before the identification parade.*

This is significant, because it does suggest that had the trial not been conducted through 'special procedure' under a government Ordinance, and before a specially constituted tribunal, there was every reason that the court would have given the benefit of the doubt to the accused. This being so, it could have concluded that the accused had not been properly identified as the murderers of John Saunders. Second, there was the emotional torment of Kishen Singh, who had watched the trial closely for so many difficult months, which he could evidently no longer suppress. He went so far as to plead an alibi for his son which was manifestly false:

> Bhagat was in Calcutta on the day of the occurrence and he actually wrote and dispatched a letter to one, Ram Lal, manager of the Khaddar

Bhandar, Pari Mahal, Lahore, which was duly received by him. There are respectable gentlemen to swear that Bhagat Singh was in Calcutta on the day of the occurrence. I can produce them if I'm given an opportunity.

With these words, Kishen Singh implored the Tribunal that 'Bhagat Singh may be given an opportunity to produce his defence'.[9] What is remarkable here is the reaction of Bhagat Singh to his father's desperate attempts to save him from the gallows. Without mincing his words, and infuriated by the steps that his father had just taken to save his life, Bhagat Singh wrote a letter chiding him. This was a tantalising three days before the Tribunal was to pronounce its sentence of death on the three young men. The letter demonstrated Bhagat Singh's determination to stand uncompromisingly steadfast in the face of the hangman's noose:

I was astounded to learn that you submitted a petition to the members of the Special Tribunal in connection with my defence. This intelligence proved to be too severe a blow to be borne with equanimity. It has upset the whole equilibrium of my mind. I have not been able to understand how you could think it proper to submit such a petition at this stage and in the circumstances. *In spite of all the sentiments and feelings of a father, I don't think you were at all entitled to make such a move on my behalf without even consulting me.*

Bhagat Singh was relentlessly unforgiving in upbraiding his father:

Father, I'm quite perplexed, I fear I might overlook the ordinary principles of etiquette, and my language may become a little bit harsh while criticising or rather censoring this move on your part. Let me be candid. I feel as though I had been stabbed in the back. Had any other person done it, I would have considered it to be nothing short of treachery. But, in your case, let me say that it has been a weakness – a weakness of the worst type... I want that the public should know all the details about this complication and, therefore, I request you to publish this letter.[10]

Bhagat Singh, however, need not have been so intolerant of his father's entreaties on his behalf because they were to count for nothing. They fell on stony ground. On 7 October 1930, the Special Tribunal gave its judgment. Of the fifteen arraigned before it, twelve were convicted, and given harsh sentences ranging from transportation for life to several years of rigorous imprisonment. Bhagat Singh, Sukhdev and Rajguru were sentenced to death.

Within a week, Jawaharlal Nehru had angrily denounced the judgment. In a speech in Allahabad on 12 October 1930 he was excoriating in his criticism, not just of the Special Tribunal but also of the Viceroy and Governor-General of India (who held office between 1926 and 1931). This was a most turbulent and tempestuous period of time in India, because between 1930 and 1932 three Round Table Conferences were organised by the British government with the Indian National Congress. The purpose had been to discuss constitutional reform in India. The three conferences were to no avail. In fact, the stakes in India's struggle for independence had been raised during this time when in 1928 India saw the visit of the Simon Commission to Lahore, the death of Lala Rajpat Rai at the hands of the police, the avenging of his death with Bhagat Singh's murder of John Saunders, and the founding of the Hindustan Socialist Republican Association ('HSRA') by Chandrasekhar Azad and Bhagat Singh. Then in 1929 there was the throwing of smoke bombs in the Delhi Legislative Assembly Hall by Bhagat Singh and B. K. Dutt. Mahatma Gandhi's Civil Disobedience Movement was by comparison a tame affair at this time. At its height, it had only achieved his defiant 1930 'salt march' to the sea in protest at the British monopoly on salt. This paled into insignificance next to the violent climax of Bhagat Singh's movement in 1931 with the rushed, clandestine execution of these three young revolutionaries who had become household names. It was Bhagat Singh, Sukhdev and Rajguru whom the authorities feared, not Mahatma Gandhi. Despite their attempts to hurry along the execution and keep it quiet, the inevitable backlash arrived.

This was the febrile atmosphere in which Nehru openly defended the actions of the three young men. In words that are rarely recalled today, he quite simply demanded an answer to one question:

If England were invaded by Germany or Russia, would Lord Irwin go about advising the people to refrain from violence against invaders? If he is not prepared to do that, let him not raise the issue. It is for Mahatma Gandhi and others, who believe with him, to do so ... But let there be no mistake about it. Whether I agree with him or not, my heart is full of admiration for the courage and self-sacrifice of a man like Bhagat Singh. Courage of the Bhagat Singh type is exceedingly rare. If the Viceroy expects us to refrain from admiring this wonderful courage and high purpose behind it, he is mistaken. Let him ask his own heart what he would have felt if Bhagat Singh had been an Englishman and acted for England.[11]

This exemplary speech brings out two points. First, that the debonair Harrow- and Cambridge-educated Nehru himself could not resist justifying the use of 'violence against the invader' in just the same way as the Indian revolutionaries then fighting for Indian freedom. Second, that Nehru was obliquely aware that Mahatma Gandhi himself, notwithstanding his Civil Disobedience Movement, was not necessarily of the same mind.

Jawaharlal Nehru, who would later become India's first Prime Minister, was a close confidant of Mahatma Gandhi, who was said to have failed to save Bhagat Singh from the gallows in 1931 when he alone had the influence to do so. Most people felt that the full story of Bhagat Singh – who he was, what he did, and how he came to die at the tender age of just twenty-three years – was yet to be told. Over the decades that followed, a belief persisted that moth-eaten documents awaited discovery in Lahore, containing hidden secrets and lost answers to these questions. The Partition of India in 1947 meant that Indians would thereafter find it next to impossible to obtain a visa to go and trawl through these hidden archives. Within the Islamic Republic of Pakistan itself, meanwhile, it was anathema to ascribe the fruits of independence to anyone other than Quaid-e-Azam Muhammad Ali Jinnah. So Bhagat Singh is forgotten.

Today, if one makes a Google inquiry into any of the big names who contributed to the independence of India, one fails to come up with the name of Bhagat Singh. If one undertakes a search on social media for any of these names, nothing connects them to the name of Bhagat Singh. Whether it is in the lives of India's imperial masters, such as Governor-General Irwin, or in the lives of India's founding fathers of independence, such as Mohandas Karamchand Gandhi, there is not a trace of Bhagat Singh. Nor is there any such trace in the histories of any of the big lawyers, such as D. N. Pritt, who defended him – nor in anything associated with distinguished judges of the realm such as Viscount Dunedin, who heard Bhagat Singh's appeal in the Privy Council. Nothing connects anyone anywhere to Bhagat Singh. It is as if his name has been erased from any connection with the build-up to India's independence. To survive, Bhagat Singh has had to find a home in the vivid memorialisation of great men in common Indian folklore, propagated by men like my grandfather, who told stories by the fireside in the evenings after a day's work. Bhagat Singh's life has thus become one of myth and fable.

One reason for this is how competing national narratives of the Congress Party in India have squeezed out Bhagat Singh. These narratives seek to portray Gandhi's non-violent brand of politics as the thing that finally triumphed, not a violent revolutionary creed of socialism. In Pakistan, too, he was easily squeezed out of official narratives that credited the Muslim League and Jinnah's far-sightedness with bringing the Muslim people to their 'promised land'. These are not, however, the only reasons for Bhagat Singh's consignment to oblivion. Just as important is the fact of Partition itself. The Partition of 1947 was brutal. It destroyed lives. Communities were shattered. With that shattering went the shared memories of places and people. Entire villages, towns, cities and even regions were torn asunder in a flash. Those who could do so packed up hurriedly and fled for their lives across a new border and into a new country. Their sense of a close-knit community disintegrated before their very eyes as they tried to find new homes in new societies. They learnt to think in terms of the feverish tensions that characterised their ethnic groups. Bhagat Singh was relegated to an unmerited mental backwater. This is because Bhagat Singh lived and fought for the people's freedom in what was to become the new country of Pakistan.

The distinguished Lahore-based writer and historian Fakir Syed Aijazuddin has encapsulated the cataclysmic suddenness and completeness of India's Partition by Sir Cyril Radcliffe, a British lawyer who had never before set foot in India, in words which will be noted for years to come: '[India's Partition] was an unconscionable act of imperial arrogance. History would be revenged were Theresa May [the British Prime Minister at the time] to allow a Pakistani or Indian or Bangladeshi lawyer to decide Brexit in five weeks.'[12] India's Partition into two competing countries, born in the furnace of fire, meant that the telling of its history broke up into different disjointed fragments, which suited particular ethno-nationalist interests in both countries. Neither country will recognize Bhagat Singh so long as its political narratives are driven by ethno-nationalism. Paradoxically, the popular narrative in both countries has not followed suit. However, the state-driven narrative has done, and this is why there has been a divergence in truth-telling at the state level. The result is that Bhagat Singh and the Hindustan Socialist Republican Association, which was the vehicle that he and Ashfaqullah Khan used to promote their ideals, has not been part of the official historiography of India's freedom struggle. Even within Western scholarship, Bhagat Singh has traditionally been little more than a footnote in the road to freedom. He and others like him have largely been overlooked by historians.

This is extraordinary. Long before Frantz Fanon published his *The Wretched of the Earth*[13] in 1961 and made a case for the necessary role of violence by the oppressed against their colonial masters, Bhagat Singh had already done so in his speeches and writings. Yet Fanon is known for this in the West, having argued that decolonization is intrinsically and inescapably a violent process given that the ultimate aim is the complete replacement of one group of people with another. Bhagat Singh is not remembered for this, even though he argued the same forty years earlier. Bhagat Singh was in jail for two years from 8 April 1929 to 23 March 1931, and he is reputed to have written four books during this time, namely *The Idea of Socialism*, *Autobiography*, *History of the Revolutionary Movement in India* and *At the Door of Death*. These books are said to have been smuggled out of prison by Kumar Lajjwati of Jalandhar, the secretary of the Bhagat Singh Defence Committee. She claims to have handed over everything to Bhagat Singh's co-conspirator Bejoy Kumar Sinha in 1938 after he was released from incarceration in the Andaman Prison. Sinha appears to have given them to another unnamed friend, who destroyed them, fearing a police raid. As Chaman Lal observes, '[t]he loss of these invaluable documents must surely rank as one of the greatest tragedies of the period'.[14] What has not been lost, however, is a 'jail notebook' which Bhagat Singh kept. Chaman Lal saw this for the first time in 1984 at the Nehru Memorial Museum and Library, which had acquired it from Bhagat Singh's younger brother Kulbir Singh. Chaman Lal has since published the 'jail notebook', together with Bhagat Singh's statement before the Sessions Court, which makes his justification for the use of force, in that '[f]orce when aggressively applied is "violence" and is therefore morally unjustifiable; but when it is used in the furtherance of a legitimate cause it has its moral justification'.[15] That should have been enough to put Bhagat Singh alongside Fanon; even if his writings were lost, his speeches were not, and nor were his written petitions before the judges.

The reason why this matters is that Bhagat Singh's way of doing politics has not gone away. It is seen in the Black Lives Matter[16] movement, the fight against racism, economic exploitation, and equal rights. It is a counterweight to the West's classic modern thinker, Thomas Hobbes, who in 1651 wrote *The Leviathan* and argued that the brute state of nature, which is characterized by a war of all against all, and where the choice is between Order and Chaos, can only be checked if the state uses strong authoritarian government. Across the world, from Viktor Orban in Hungary to Narendra Modi in India and from Jair Messias Bolsonaro in Brazil to Donald Trump in America, this is what we are seeing. But we are also seeing, as Hobbes saw in his time, the emergence of an extremely unstable and violent world. Mahatma Gandhi found a way to deal with this by recognizing that the concept of a strong authoritarian state was a lie because it was tainted by state-controlled violence, but his way of dealing with it was through non-violent protest. Bhagat Singh, like Fanon after him, argued that if the state itself was the purveyor of violence then the oppressed had to embrace that violence and engage in violent revolution. Today, almost any protest in India or Pakistan sees banners not of Fanon but of Bhagat Singh. Yet he is unknown in the West. With the twenty-first century still in its early years, it is time to recognize that Bhagat Singh's type of politics will be here to stay as the years roll by and instability grows. It is time for the West to learn of Bhagat Singh.

In fact, it is nothing short of remarkable that so little attention has been devoted to the way that Bhagat Singh was tried and executed over a period of nearly two years. How is it possible to overlook this in the light of the fact that the trial proceedings extended all the way from Magistrates' Courts in Lahore to the Privy Council in London? Somehow, nobody in the West has considered it worthy of note that this most high-profile of colonial trials of young socialists, raising the banner of freedom against imperial Britain, was tainted with substantive illegality and procedural irregularities which would be unthinkable in any system governed by the rule of law today. It is one of the mysteries of the twentieth century that this should have been so. It is all the more surprising given that the colonial system of trying those who rebel against the state has become a blueprint for the trial of modern-day terrorism cases, of which the detention centre at Guantanamo Bay in Cuba is today the most striking example. Only in the last decade has there been an attempt to readjust and realign historical accounts among a new breed of young scholars who are referred to in this book.

The trial and execution of Bhagat Singh in 1931 represents the much neglected legal historiography of colonial violence in India. Kim Wagner, a scholar of the history of colonial India and the British Empire, has recently described how 'a growing body of scholarship has explored the role of colonial violence, both epistemic and physical, as an intrinsic aspect of British and European imperialism'. However, Wagner maintains that '[t]he insights provided by such studies have yet to make much of an inroad in conventional historiography of the Empire'. His work thus sets out to examine 'the violence at the heart of British colonial counter-insurgency during the high-point of Empire'[17] instead of merely 'settler violence', on which much has been written. Yet if this shortcoming is true of 'conventional historiography', it is doubly true of the 'legal historiography' of the British Empire in India. The Lahore Conspiracy Case and the trial of Bhagat Singh is a case in point. In fact, the backdrop to Wagner's valuable study is precisely that '[w]ithin the last few years the subject of colonial violence has come to the fore in debates on the legacies of the British Empire, with a range of lawsuits and calls for formal apologies and reparation'.[18] The purpose of this discussion is to demonstrate that the execution of Bhagat Singh falls squarely within this milieu. Indeed, there can scarcely be a more deserving case.

Thus, Wagner has explained how '[B]ritish knowledge and understanding of the people they fought throughout the Empire was invariably shaped by the colonial ideologies and racial hierarchies implicit in the "civilising mission" and central to the imperial experience'.[19] It is worth observing here, however, that what was instrumental in this 'civilising mission' and 'colonial experience' was an elaborate artifice of the law and judicial administration. It is this which, I would suggest here, is the source of the development of law as a form of coercive colonial legalism. He goes on to explain that the '[c]onstruction of the enemy as "un-civilised", "savage", or "fanatic" had severe implications for the conduct of what became known as savage warfare; it dictated and justified techniques of violence that were by the same token considered unacceptable in conflicts between so-called "civilised" nations'. By this standard, a trial process like the Lahore Conspiracy Case, which would have been deemed utterly unacceptable and repugnant in Britain, was considered justifiable in the execution of Bhagat Singh, and was in fact so endorsed by the UK Privy Council in 1931,[20] when no right of appeal lay in India for a man condemned to death by hanging on the gallows.

For this reason, in the words of Durba Ghosh, '[a]mong participants of the underground groups, there were widespread concerns throughout the 1950s and well into the 1960s that the history of revolutionary terrorism would be forgotten',[21] and indeed so it has proved because barely anyone is familiar with the names of these great revolutionaries outside India today, and even within India hardly anyone knows about their contribution to the cause of independence. Ghosh refers to 'participants among the underground groups', but many even in the mainstream are not known. And few even care. Nevertheless, it is a salutary reminder of how freedom is won. In fact, one reason for this is how post-colonial India has extended the narrative. As Ghosh explains, '[b]etween 1947 and 1952, the early years of independent India, as the government of India began a project of national consolidation, it resorted to classifying opposing political movements such as communism, trade union organization, battles for land redistribution as threats to national security'.[22] In this book I argue that the technique the imperial masters used against the revolutionaries was that of *coercive colonial legalism*, and that this is seen most clearly in the way in which the legislative power of 'peace, order and good government' has been misused and deprived of all recognizable meaning. The use of the law as an instrument of colonial brutality enforced through the courts is something which has not hitherto received the required attention from legal scholars at all.

This matters. As a society, we are responsible for our own narratives. If they are broken, we must repair them. If they are erroneous, we must correct them. If they are forgotten, we must strive to remember them. If we do none of these things, we must not complain if the state or our formal colonial masters foist upon us a false national narrative. How many people today know that the stock slogan associated with Bhagat Singh, '*Inquilab Zindabad*' ('Long Live the Revolution'), was first conceived by Maulana Hasrat Mohani? Or that the slogan '*Bharat Choro*' ('Quit India') leading up to Indian independence, associated with Mahatma Gandhi, was created by Yusuf Meher Ali? Or indeed that '*Jai Hind*' ('Victory to India') is attributed to a Hyderabadi by the name of Zain-ul Abideen Hasan? Even the 1857 slogan from the First Indian War of Independence, '*Madare Vatan Bharat Ki Jay*' ('Long Live the Mother Country'), was coined by Azimullah Khan. Perhaps most importantly, the poem 'Sare Jahan se achha Hindostan hamara' was written by Allama Muhammad Iqbal,[23] when he implied before Partition that nowhere was more dear to him on this earth than his own motherland, 'Hindustan'.

What this tells us is that as a people we remain the custodians of our national narratives. While a collective narrative may be instinctively what we want as a distinct people, we should know by now that if the evidence points in the opposite direction then it is only a matter of time before our narratives will be adjusted, modified and reconstructed. Facts are powerful forces. Sooner or later they compel us to face them. The stories we tell about ourselves and about our national essence are immensely powerful. If we ignore the facts, however, our narratives will be challenged. They will not survive forever.

This is why the collective amnesia on Bhagat Singh was bound to end. This is as true of Pakistan as it is of India. Kuldip Nayar, journalist and former High Commissioner of India to the United Kingdom, in the opening remarks to his book on Bhagat Singh in 2000 began with the lamentation, 'There is no arch, no plaque, not even a stone in Pakistan to commemorate the execution of Bhagat Singh and his two comrades, Sukhdev and Rajguru.' Furthermore, he observed that 'Lahore Central Jail, where the three revolutionaries were hanged on 23 March 1931, has been mostly demolished. Their cells have been razed to the ground as if the establishment did not want any sign of their execution to remain.'[24] Yet, the inspiration for his book came to him from his own visit to Pakistan when, attending the World Punjabi Conference in Lahore in the 1980s, his eyes fixed on the only photograph in the hall, and this turned out to be the photograph of none other Bhagat Singh. When he quizzically inquired as to why there was no photograph of the distinguished poet Allama Muhammad Iqbal, 'who visualised the concept of Pakistan', he was promptly informed that 'there was only one Punjabi who sacrificed his life for the country's independence and his name was Bhagat Singh'.[25] Back then, Nayar was soon frustrated in his quest to discover more about Bhagat Singh in Lahore. 'The Archives of Pakistan,' he bemoaned, 'is possibly the best source. But it is not open to Indians. New Delhi and Islamabad have no agreement which allows nationals of one country access to the archives of the other.'[26]

In fact, when Nayar approached the authorities, '[a] lame excuse was offered to deny me access'. What he learnt was that 'they were afraid they might get entangled in the Sikh problem'. As he only too well put it, '[I] could not figure out the connection with the 1931 execution except that Bhagat Singh was a Sikh.'[27] Having trawled through the archives myself, I can confidently say that there is no question of the 'Sikh problem' involved here whatsoever. The obsession with secrecy is a colonial malaise which to this day afflicts the bureaucrats of India[28] no less than those in Pakistan, and due to which the public are denied access to official documentation, no matter what its source, origin or age, without any apparent justification. Both countries would do well to learn from the British Library in London, where scholars and researchers from all the corners of the world are not only welcomed to its doors, but thereafter given every possible assistance in locating the material that they seek. Fortunately, the assistance given to me in Lahore by the Punjab Archives Department and its officials was a model of administrative service and efficiency. Nevertheless, the belief persists that long-suppressed documents on Bhagat Singh languish unloved in the deeper recesses of Lahore's vaults. In 2011, Chaman Lal wrote a well-publicised piece in a leading national daily in which he observed, 'The Punjab Archives in Lahore has 135 files of the Bhagat Singh case. These are not accessible even to Pakistani scholars ... Kuldip Nayar is now trying to get access to them.'[29] The files certainly exist. The record is complete, and maintained to the highest standards. I was fortunate enough to see them.

Given so much of Bhagat Singh's early life and eventual death occurred in Lahore, which is now in Pakistan, writers nevertheless naturally suspected that the richest source of his life and death lay in materials in the archives of Pakistan. Indeed, in Pakistan itself, the researcher and archivist Ahmad Salim found that some records relating to the trial of the Lahore Conspiracy Case were held by the Lahore High Court. He thought that they were still restricted on the basis that the publication 'might affect the integrity of Pakistan'. It has been suggested that this implied 'that the postcolonial state might be forced to accept culpability for executions carried out more than fifteen years before its creation'.[30] This cannot be given any credence, however. Nevertheless, such suspicions did not subside when an Ordinance in Pakistan preventing the gathering of more than five people was used in 2007 to ban celebrations marking the anniversary of the hangings of Bhagat Singh and his two comrades in Lahore. This is despite the remarkable fact that the event had the support of both the provincial authorities and a chief minister of Punjab. The alleged site of the hangings was renamed Bhagat Singh Chowk in 2012, but pressure from Islamist groups, who have sought to 'challenge the official historical narrative' of Pakistan, has led to a reversal of that decision. The matter is currently embroiled in litigation. On a more encouraging note, there are now two organisations in Lahore actively dedicated to the preservation of Bhagat Singh's memory. There is ever-growing support amongst Lahoris themselves to maintain the memory of Bhagat Singh and what he stood for. It is important to be clear, however, that not only are there no files on Bhagat Singh at Lahore High Court yet to be discovered, but that such files as do exist on Bhagat Singh contain no sensitive material regarding Sikhs to justify the authorities in Lahore withholding them from open access.

If Lahoris are fond of Bhagat Singh, there is good reason for this. A free-spirited and defiant people, Lahoris remember the support that Pakistan's founding father, Quaid-e-Azam Muhammad Ali Jinnah, gave to Bhagat Singh at a time when he was bereft of assistance from his own lawyers, who were either not being paid or were having their activities curtailed by the authorities. It was Jinnah, India's highest-paid lawyer, who stepped in. He put up the staunchest of defences on Bhagat Singh's behalf at the time. He did so before legislators intent on depriving the young undertrials of a fair trial. His grounds were that, because they had gone on hunger strike and could not make their way before a judge, their weakened and emaciated bodies should not now be produced in court. The government had planned to pass a Hunger Strike Bill which would allow the accused to be tried in court even if they were not there – a complete betrayal of the principles of elementary criminal justice. Jinnah protested. It was he who made sure that this bill could not be passed. A. G. Noorani writes that '[e]ven by the high standards of parliamentary debate that prevailed in those times, never had its leading members risen to the challenge as nobly as it did on September 12th and 14th, 1929'[31] under Jinnah. However, Jinnah was a veteran at fighting injustices. A strong defender of civil liberties, six months earlier, on 15 February 1929, he had debated the circumstances of the death of Lala Lajpat Rai, with whom he was on very amicable terms – something that is hardly known amongst the people of Pakistan today. Equally, he had earlier pleaded for the release of the Sikh leaders who had been jailed in connection with the Sikh Gurdwara Act in September 1925. He had a solid record in this respect. He had protested against the detention without trial of such notables as Satyendra Chandra (1927), Vallabhai Patel (1930), Sarat Chandra Bose (1935) and Annie Besant (1917). He had done so without discrimination, in just as determined a manner as in his defence of the Ali Brothers (1914) and the detention of Maulana Hasrat Mohani (1924).

Jinnah's stellar defence of Bhagat Singh and his comrades, whilst they lay incapacitated in prison on hunger strike, represents the high water-mark of his assiduous advocacy on behalf of those who most needed protection from a repressive colonial administration. In the Central Assembly on 12 September 1929, he provided a justification for the hunger strike of the undertrials, pointing out that '[t]he man who goes on hunger strike has a soul' and that it is because '[h]e is moved by that soul and he believes in the justice of his cause' that he goes on a hunger strike. A. G. Noorani, in his seminal work on Bhagat Singh, has observed how '[b]y all contemporary accounts, his was a magnificent performance, but it has been completely ignored in all Indian writings on Bhagat Singh and little noticed in Pakistan'.[32] In any case, he stood up for Bhagat Singh in the Central Assembly in a manner and fashion that was not emulated by anyone else. He put a complete stop to the government's machinations, and its insidious designs of installing the trial of defendants *in absentia*. The veteran human rights activist I. A.

Rehman, in his prefatory note to the speech, observes that 'in his coolly logical and convincing manner he played a major role in foiling the attempt to make trial in absentia lawful'. In this way, the government was prevented in its attempt to pass the Hunger Strike Bill. In fact, as *The Tribune* reported at the time,[33]

> Mr Jinnah created a profound impression by the excellent form in which he argued the case. The Government was sacrificing the fundamental principles of jurisprudence and wanted the House to change the law of the land to create a farce. As regards the Lahore accused, they were creatures of the present system. Mr Jinnah was proceeding in this vein winning applause after applause from the spellbound House when the president adjourned the house to Saturday to conclude the debate on the Bill.[34]

The result was that the Indian legislature would not pass a bill that would enable the government to try freedom fighters *in absentia*. This forced the government to find another way to achieve the same end. The legal artifice that it settled upon after this was the use of ministerial *executive* legislation.

This is how the Governor-General's Lahore Ordinance No. III of 1930 was promulgated. The Ordinance would set up a Special Tribunal that would be outside the normal legal system. It would have six months in which to try the twenty-four accused. It would be the master of its own procedure. It could try them as it wished. It could even avoid having to produce them in court. There was one small difficulty, however. Certain statutory obligations first had to be complied with because of the prior existence of Section 72 of the Government of India Act 1919 (which was originally the Act of 1915 by the same name). Under this statutory obligation, the Governor-General could only promulgate an Ordinance 'in cases of emergency', and even then only if this was 'for the peace and good government of British India or any part thereof'. This was the much misused 'POGG (peace, order, and good government) clause'.[35] Moreover, as an emergency measure the Ordinance would be 'for the space of not more than six months from its promulgation'. After that it would lapse. Of all the questions that arose from this condition precedent, the most important was who decided what was an 'emergency' and who decided whether the powers being used were indeed 'for the peace and good government of British India'.

Put another way, was it an objective question which could be determined by an ordinary court of law as an *a priori* question, or was it a subjective question to be decided by the Governor-General? If it was objective, the Governor-General would be acting contrary to the powers given by Section 72 of the Government of India Act 1919 and therefore in a manner that was *ultra vires* (beyond legal authority). If it was subjective, then the Governor-General himself could decide that there was an 'emergency' and deal with the situation as and how he wished. The established view even back in the 1920s was that it was an objective question. The *a priori* question had to be decided to the satisfaction of a court of law. It could not be determined at the mere whim of the Governor-General. Yet, in the Lahore Conspiracy Case of 1930 it was effectively decided that Section 72 of the Government of India Act 1919 could be a matter for determination by the Governor-General alone. What the executive decides cannot be questioned in a court of law. Such thinking was to eventually become the basis by which a military tribunal could be set up to try civilians outside the regular legal system.

The Lahore Conspiracy Case became a blueprint, establishing a precedent which has served governments well in the decades that followed. This has come to be the case not just in the United Kingdom but in other common law countries as well. It has allowed governments to negate the requirements of the rule of law and to dispense a localized form of justice peculiar to their own needs and wishes. It has exposed the mantra of the rule of law to be a hollow shell in hard cases. Governments have been able to obtain convictions on an arbitrary and capricious basis. In fact, as Binda Preet Sahni[36] makes clear, legislation like the Government of India Act 1915 (which by the time of Bhagat Singh's trial was the Act of 1919),[37] the Defence of India Act 1915[38] and the Rowlatt Act 1919[39] have long been used 'to make Crown policy in India more influential' and '[e]ach was directed against local and foreign discontent with British rule'. The way this was done was 'by subordinating the due process of law, as in the Gadar Trials, Amritsar Massacre, and the Bhagat Singh litigation'.[40] However, what is significant about Bhagat Singh's final hearing before the Privy Council in London on 27 February 1931 is that this was 'the last test case by the accused to challenge the flawed emergency Acts',[41] and it was lost – thereby paving the way for modern 'terrorist' trials to be held on the same footing.

- 4. -

<u>THE LAHORE CONSPIRACY CASE.</u>

<u>JULY 10th, 1929.</u>

Accused. 7 turned approvers, 9 are still absconding and the remaining 16 are being actually tried.

<u>The following are the 16 accused:</u>

1. Sukdev: arrested in April (15th) in Lahore Bomb Factory.
2. K. Ratan.
3. Shoo Yarma.
4. Gayaprasad.
5. Jaidev.
6. Jatindra Nath Das. Assistant Secretary of South Calcutta Congress Committee, arrested in Calcutta.
7. Bhagat Singh arrested in Delhi, convicted in Assembly Bomb Case sentenced to transportation for life.
8. K. Nath Trivedi.
9. Butukshwar Dutt convicted in the Assembly Bomb Case. Sentenced to transportation for life.
10. J.N.Sanyal of Allahabad.
11. Agyaram of Sidkot District.
12. Desraj, student, Lahore
13. Prom Dutt of Guyrat,- ex-student, D.A.V. College, Lahore.
14. Surendra Nath Pandey.
15. Mahabir Singh.
16. Ajoy Kumar Ghose.

<u>The Absconders.-</u>

1. B. Charan of Lahore.
2. Yashpal of Dharamsala.
3. Bejoy K. Sinha of Cawnpore.
4. Chandra S. AZAD of Bhilapore, Benares.
5. Raghunath of Benares.
6. Kelash of Jhansi.
7. Satgurday al Ayasathi of Cawnpore, arrested in May, bailed out now absconding.

<u>The following are the Approvers:-</u>

(They have been granted Crown pardon, and their confession recorded by the City Magistrate.)

1. Joygopal, arrested in April (15th) Lahore Bomb Factory.
2. Hansraj Yerah, Lahore.
3. Ramsaran Das of Karpurthala, convicted to transportation in connection with bomb outrage on His Excellency, the Viceroy, Lord Hardingge in 1914.
4. Lalit Mukherji, son of an Allahabad advocate.
5. Brahma Dutt, arrested in Cawnpore.
6. Phanindra Ghose, arrested in Calcutta.
7. Mono Mahan Mukherji of Champaran.

<u>CHARGE SHEET.</u>

Emperor Vs. Sukdev and 24 others commonly known as Saunders Murder and Lahore Conspiracy Cases. The accused along with others have at Lahore and other places in British India and at various others times and occasions commencing from the year 1924 and continuing up to the present time of their arrest, been engaged in conspiracy to wage war against His Majesty, the King Emperor, and to deprive him of the Sovreignty of British India, and to overawe by criminal force or show criminal force, the Governemnt established by law in British India and to collect arms and ammunition and men

for, or otherwise make preparation for the said object and purpose.

They further concealsed the existence of the design to wage against the King Emperor, intending by such concealment to facilitate or knowing that it would be likely that such concealment would facilitate the waging of such war. With these objects, the accused along with others, formed a party known as the "Hindustan Republican Association" and the "Indian Republican Army" and held their meetings at Lahore and other places in British India with a view to overthrow by force the Government established by law in India and to establish a Federated Republican Government in its stead.

A neat description of the Lahore Conspiracy Case, with sixteen undertrials, seven absconders, and seven 'approvers' who from 1924 onwards 'engaged in a conspiracy to wage war against his Majesty, the King Emperor, and to deprive him of the sovereignty of India'. Previously unpublished.

2

The Slipper and the Magistrate

Tum takalluf koh bhi Ikhlās samajhteho'farāz'
Dost hotān Nahin Har Haath Milanevaala

You mistook the overtures of others as expressions of their love, but
Beware! Everyone who stoops to shake your hand is not a friend

Ahmad Faraz

Bhagat Singh's first skirmish with the courts was over the Assembly Bomb Case on 8 April 1929, for which his father, Kishen Singh, enlisted the help of the advocate, Mr Asaf Ali. The trial began on 7 May 1929 before magistrate Mr R. B. Pool, who ambled in at 9.50 a.m. Kishen Singh, Bhagat Singh's grandmother, Jai Kaur, and Ajit Singh's wife, Harnam Kaur, looked on expectantly from where they were seated. The court was full. The trial would last just two months. On 10 July 1929 magistrate Rai Sahib Pandit Sri Kishen would take over. From the beginning, Bhagat Singh demanded to be treated as political prisoner. He was charged under Section 307 of the Indian Penal Code as well as Section 3 of the Explosive Substances Act. Both he and B. K. Dutt were also accused of throwing bombs 'to kill or cause injuries to the King Majesty's subjects'. He knew from the outset, however, that the authorities would deny him the right to be treated as a political prisoner. Knowing this, soon after their arrest on 8 April 1929, when Bhagat Singh was being transferred to Mianwali and B. K. Dutt to Lahore Jail, they had the opportunity to sit together in the train carriage, whereupon Bhagat Singh suggested that the two of them should go on a hunger strike in their respective detention centres. Accordingly, when he faced the public prosecutor, Rai Bahadur Suryanarayan, on 7 May 1929, Bhagat Singh immediately staked his claim to such a status. He declared his wish to make a lengthy statement of his manifesto before the magistrate, F. B. Pool. There were well-established censorship controls, and these applied to manifesto speeches, but Bhagat Singh's statement was designed to circumvent such curbs.

This is how 6 June 1929 was to become the most important day of the trial. It is when Bhagat Singh and B. K. Dutt made their statement (read to the court by Asaf Ali) that Lord Irwin was wrong to refer to the Assembly Bomb as 'an attack directed against no individual but an institution itself' because their purpose was only 'to make the deaf hear' as 'revolution is an inalienable right of mankind' and 'freedom is an imperishable birthright of all'. This explosive statement became instant news. Leading national newspapers competed to publish it. Within a week, on 12 June 1929, a 41-page judgment convicting the two accused was read out by Leonard Middleton, the Delhi Sessions Judge, sentencing them both to transportation for life. An appeal to the Punjab High Court in Lahore landed before Justices Sir Cecil Forde and James Addison, where Bhagat Singh's reliance on the 'importance of motive' was thrown out. This was not without Justice Forde being forced to admit, however, that 'Bhagat Singh is a sincere revolutionary'. Against this background, how well does the legal system come out of this? To answer this question, one only has to look at the conduct of the magistrate of the trial, F. B. Pool.

Pool was acutely aware of Bhagat Singh's intentions, so on 9 June 1929, he ruled that if Bhagat Singh was to make his statement it must have sections of it 'expunged' from the record. He ruled these 'cannot be referred to here, nor, being irrelevant, could they affect the case'. Bhagat Singh could not understand this because the entire purpose of the attack on Parliament by him and by B. K. Dutt was to promote an ideology. As far as he was concerned, the statement was anything but irrelevant to the defence of his case. As it happened, F. B. Pool's censorious action had little effect. By the time of the trial, a truncated version of the written testimony had already been leaked to the press and so was widely available. Bhagat Singh's political intentions were out in public. The testimony was widely distributed in revolutionary circles and ended up being translated into such far-off languages as Bengali and Gujarati.

Nevertheless, as Maclean points out, 'the deletion had a great bearing on the case's progression in the courts because as Bhagat Singh argued unsuccessfully in his appeal before the High Court bench, the removal of the ideological basis of his attack on the Legislative Assembly in Delhi meant that, rather than being seen as political prisoners which they were, he and his two comrades were being wrongly ascribed the status of madmen and fanatics'.[1] The state was determined from the moment the trial started that this should be so. It stuck to this to the end. As Neeti Nair has explained, once the trial was fully underway, the government's tactic was 'labelling these revolutionaries "murderers" and "terrorists" … to dismiss their non-violent demands for rights as "political prisoners"', and this despite the fact that as far as Punjab itself was concerned, 'the quality of anti-colonial nationalism represented by Bhagat Singh was central to the resolution of many of the divisions that racked pre-partition Punjab'.[2] At the end of proceedings before F. B. Pool, the magistrate committed both Bhagat Singh and B. K. Dutt to the Sessions Court, which was initially set to be presided over by Judge Leonard Middleton from the beginning of June 1929, but which from 10 July 1929 was taken over by Judge Rai Sahib Pandit Sri Kishen.

Throughout, the government was determined to quash the revolutionaries' demand to be treated as political prisoners. It viewed the trial in the context of the striking growth of communism in the 1920s, of which it was intensely fearful, and so was determined to curb the activities of left-wing radical groups, which it viewed with increasing alarm given that they were now beginning to take root in Europe and America as well. The accused for their part were no less adamant in their resolve. They were not going to back down from their insistence on being treated as political prisoners. This they did by adopting from the outset the tactic of shouting political slogans. The day would begin with their entering the courtroom with clenched fists thrown into the air amid loud slogans of *'Inquilab Zindabad'* ('Long Live the Revolution'). Bhagat Singh's name became forever synonymous with this slogan. It is heard to this day amongst the student protestors of India and Pakistan. It was cried out in both English and the local language. Little wonder the authorities were worried; they had every reason to be. This was not going to be a normal trial, nor an easy one. In one of the expunged sections of their statement, Bhagat Singh and B. K. Dutt gave a detailed account of their cause. It was not a personal one, but a call for revolution. 'Revolution', they explained, is not a place 'for individual vendetta' and nor is it 'the cult of the bomb and the pistol'. Instead, 'by Revolution we mean that the present order of things which is based on manifest injustice must change', because 'producers or the labourers, in spite of being the most necessary element of society are robbed by the exploiters of the fruits of their labour and deprived of their elementary rights'. No wonder they were popular. Such sentiments appealed to the hearts of the common people in this oppressed country. The feelings they invoke resonate in India and Pakistan to this day.

(True Copy).

To

The Home Member, Government of India,
through the Special Magistrate
Lahore Conspiracy Case 1929,
L a h o r e.

S i r,

We, Bhagat Singh and K.B.KDutt, were sentenced to
life transportation in the Assembly Bomb Case, Delhi, on the
19th April, 1929. As long as we were under-trial prisoners
in Delhi Jail we were accorded a very good treatment and
were given very good diet. But since our transfer from that
Jail to the Mianwali and Lahore Central Jails respectively,
we are being treated as ordinary criminals. On the very
first day we wrote an application to the higher authorities
asking for better diet and a few other facilities, and refused
to take the Jail diet.

Our demands were as follows :-

1. We, as political prisoners, should be given better
diet and the standard of our diet should at least be the same
as that of European prisoners. (It is not the sameness of
dietary that we demand, but the sameness of standard of diet).

2. We shall not be forced to do any hard and undignified
labour at all.

3. All books, other than those proscribed, along with
writing materials should be allowed to us without any
restriction.

4. At least one standard daily paper should be supplied
to every political prisoner.

5. Political prisoners should have a special ward of
their own in every Jail provided with all necessities as
those of the Europeans. And all the political prisoners in
one Jail must be kept together in that ward.

6. Toilet necessities should be supplied to us.

7. Better clothing.

Above and opposite: The demand of Bhagat Singh and B. K. Dutt to be treated as
political prisoners. Previously unpublished.

We have explained above the demands that we made. They are the most reasonable demands. The Jail authorities told us one day that the higher authorities have refused to comply with our demands.

Apart from that they handle us very roughly while feeding us artificially, and Bhagat Singh was lying quite senseless on the 10th June, 1929, for about 15 minutes after the forcible feeding, which we request to be stopped without any further delay.

In addition, we may be permitted to refer to the recommendations made in the U.P. Jail Committee by Pt. Jagat Narain and R.B. Hafiz Hidayat Hussain. They have recommended the political prisoners to be treated as 'Better class prisoners'.

We request you to kindly consider our demands at your earliest convenience.

                              Yours etc.
                              Sd/- Bhagat Singh.
                              Sd/- B. K. Dutt.

N.B. - By "political prisoners" we mean all those people who are convicted for offences against the State, for instance the people who were convicted in the Lahore Conspiracy Cases 1915-17, the Kakori Conspiracy Cases and sedition cases in general.

                              Kishori Lal Rattan
                              19/8/1930

41

The accused spoke for the oppressed multitude, those toiling away for a pittance in this vast land. They were able to touch a raw nerve in doing so. They had drawn attention to 'the peasant who grows corn for all starves with this family; the weaver who supplies the world market with textile fabrics cannot find enough to cover his own and his children's bodies; the masons, smiths and carpenters who rear magnificent palaces, live and perish in slums'. All this was an affront to the nature of colonial governance in India. They were throwing down the gauntlet before their colonial masters. They were taking on the government head-on when they wrote that 'the capitalist exploiters, the parasites of society squander millions on their whims' and questioned '[t]hese terrible inequalities, and forced disparity of chances ... heading towards chaos'. In this way, a group of young men, all too often students, came to pose a threat to the British Raj that seasoned politicians like Gandhi and the Congress Party never could. They were dangerous in a way that Gandhi never was.

In their inimitable style, these young revolutionaries endeared themselves to the ordinary men and women of what are now India, Pakistan and Bangladesh. Indeed, three-quarters of a century after their shrill voices echoed in the Magistrates' room allocated within Lahore Central Jail, they still continue to do so. The more they grew determined to put their political case before the court, the more the authorities were determined to suppress it in that form. This is nowhere more clear than in the treatment meted out to them by the courts. The repressive system with its arcane legal provisions and archaic legal practitioners, the judges robed in antediluvian paraphernalia, participating in implementing the artefact of coercive colonial legalism within the jail system itself to suit the needs of the Raj and to put an end to the impertinent insubordination of Bhagat Singh and his accomplices.

If only these young men had not played the 'political card', they may well have fared better. But their adherence to Marxism was perceived as posing a pernicious threat to the existence of the state. As Maclean explains, 'Marxist ideology was more than seditious; its transitional aspirations made it globally subversive, and the government of India was alert to its growing influence.'[3] In fact, what is even today unknown to the Indian subcontinent is how Bhagat Singh was getting support from the communist movement in Great Britain in the 1930s, precisely because of its global reach. Letters in the British Library demonstrate the risk which the Indian revolutionaries were running by employing Marxism. One letter from the Secretariat of the Communist Party of Great Britain dated 5 March 1931 is addressed to fellow 'Comrades' in Britain and draws attention to the

COPY.

THE COMMUNIST PARTY OF GREAT BRITAIN, 16, King Street,
Covent Garden, London. W.C.2.

5th March, 1931.

Dear Comrades,

Enclosed you will find a statement drawing your attention to the facts in regard to the LAHORE CONSPIRACY TRIAL.

Some of the comrades concerned stand in danger of execution and we are asking that you should organise meetings and demonstrations of protest to demand that Comrade Bhagat Singh should not be executed by the Labour Government.

We believe that the facts that are given you will provide you with the necessary material upon which to wage the campaign.

With Communist Greetings,

Yours fraternally,

THE SECRETARIAT.

A demand on 5 March 1931 by the Communist Party of Great Britain in London, following the handing down of the death sentence on 7 October 1930, 'that Comrade Bhagat Singh should not be executed by the Labour Government' and that to this end 'you should organize meetings and demonstrations of protest' to ensure that this outcome is avoided. Previously unpublished.

Lahore Conspiracy trial, of which its members were clearly aware. It points out that 'some of the comrades stand in danger of execution and we are asking that you should organise meetings and demonstrations of protest to demand that Comrade Bhagat Singh should not be executed by the Labour Government', and asking that they 'wage a campaign' to this effect.

All of this had a marked effect on the way in which the proceedings were conducted thousands of miles away in Lahore, particularly on the way that the evidence was marshalled to convict them. If grievances were raised by the accused they were either given scant regard or summarily dismissed.

The second trial in the Sessions Court actually got going on 10 July 1929. It was subject to the regular law of the land. It had a regular judge. It was a trial like any other. But it was different in one respect: it was taking place within the prison system. Consequently, as Chris Moffat points out, '[d]oubts were raised early … regarding the government's commitment to due process, especially as the enquiry was to convene at a room within the Lahore Central Jail itself'. So much so that on the first day of the hearing, counsel Lala Duni Chand objected to the 'so-called courtroom', which he said 'was surrounded on all sides by the police and was itself a small gaol'.[4] Today this fact has been almost entirely forgotten because the Lahore Central Jail itself has no trace left of it. It was demolished six decades ago. But back then, no less than two dozen bedraggled and dishevelled young men stood before Judge Rai Sahib Pandit Sri Kishen. Bhagat Singh was tried with Bejoy Kumar Sinha, but there were two sets of accused: those like Bhagat and Bejoy, who were detained as adults in Lahore Central Jail; and the juveniles, who were housed in the nearby Borstal Jail. Although he has since been described as 'a first-class magistrate',[5] Judge Rai Sahib Pandit Sri Kishen was soon shown to be out of his depth. He had to deal with many a clever application. These were often cunningly but accurately crafted, and raised timeously by such lawyers who were able to provide representation, such as Amolak Ram Kapoor. Under unrelenting pressure, and with so many defendants in his court, the judge's stock response was a standard and unimaginative refusal to accede to anything. This did little to inspire confidence in him amongst such a large number of accused. Soon he was reduced to being ridiculed. The accused openly laughed at him.

Yet, the proceedings before Judge Rai Sahib Pandit Sri Kishen were an early example of coercive colonial legalism in the Lahore Conspiracy Case. Everyone present knew this was a political trial so coercive colonial legalism was adapted to take two forms. One form was latent; the other patent. The latent form manifested itself in the outright denial of perfectly legitimate legal applications. One such from the accused requested the removal of police officers who even in court accompanied 'approvers' when they were giving evidence for the prosecution. These were perfectly proper applications made by the defence in the interests of natural justice, procedural fairness and due process standards in a criminal case. Yet, they were peremptorily dismissed. The patent form of coercive colonial legalism was even more disturbing. This consisted of open acts of physical violence which occurred in the courtroom itself under the very nose of the magistrate, with the aim of subjugating the accused to the will of the government once they had been charged under Section 307 of the Indian Penal Code and the Explosives Act. This was deemed necessary not least because of their effrontery in shouting out 'Long Live the Revolution' as they entered the courtroom.

If Bhagat Singh and his comrades were being 'political', they had good reason to be. Take for example the evidence of Jai Gopal, who was closely associated with the murder on 17 December 1928. It was he who had mistaken the ill-fated young probationer John Saunders for his superior, Superintendent James Scott, and it was he who had foolishly given Bhagat Singh and Rajguru the green light to fire upon him as he nonchalantly ambled out of the police station. It was a thoroughly ill-devised and ramshackle plan, and it resulted in two unnecessary and pointlessly tragic deaths (policeman Chanan Singh had also been shot dead as he gave chase). No one could forget, however, that it was Jai Gopal who had been the lookout on the day. Yet, here he was on 25 September 1929, brazenly turning up at court to give evidence for the prosecution. He had turned 'approver' for the government against his partners in crime. Nervously, he stepped forward into the witness box, shepherded by a convoy of policemen who stood behind him. But these were the very same four senior police officers who had taken part in the investigation of the case against them all. Here they were in court turning up suddenly to give open support to Jai Gopal as the turncoat. As if this was not enough, the four – Deputy Superintendent of Police K. S. Niaz Ahmed, S. H. Gopal, S. Pratap and Chaudhri Shahab Din – were also rallying behind them other police officers for even more support. Naturally, Amolak Ram Kapoor, the defence counsel for some of the accused, objected to their presence. The evidence from the 'approver' Jai Gopal, he argued, could not be taken in the presence of investigating officers who were now in the courtroom, especially as Jai Gopal had throughout been closely associated with Bhagat Singh. The risk of evidence being given under duress could not be ruled out. At the very least, he had been cowed and brow-beaten into giving his evidence. It was tainted.

Judge Rai Sahib Pandit Sri Kishen's disdain for such an application from Amolak Ram was plain. He rejected it outright. Whatever the high learning in the common law textbooks about the virtues of the rule of law, the judge ruled that all the police officers could remain in the courtroom. At this Bejoy Kumar Sinha and Bhagat Singh objected. They said they could not participate in the trial. Perhaps it had escaped the obtuse magistrate's attention, but these two were undefended by counsel at the time. If it did escape his attention then it ought not to have done – only a day before they had asked to be allowed to meet with Feroz Chand, who was secretary of their defence committee, so that they could reach an agreement with him about their defence. True to form, the magistrate had rejected this request also. In the circumstances, the best they could now do for their defence was to ask the magistrate that he postpone for a day or two the taking down and recording of the statement from the 'approver', Jai Gopal. The magistrate once again point-blank refused. He gave the lame excuse that he had no power to postpone proceedings midstream when the examination of witnesses was already in progress. In fact, he had every power because it is elementary law that natural justice demands that a defendant to criminal proceedings has both notice of what he or she is charged with, and the right to prepare to defend himself against such charges. This includes the right to appointment of counsel.

The bias of Judge Rai Sahib Pandit Sri Kishen against the accused was not lost on Bejoy Kumar Sinha, who was quick to expose the trial for the sham that it was turning out to be:

> You do not want to give us an opportunity to have counsel to cross-examine the approver. Nor have you agreed to exclude the police officers who took part in the investigation of the case from the court during examination of the approver. You have passed an order even before the written application for decision of the police officers was put in. You force us to the conclusion that we should not expect justice from this court.[6]

On this basis, Bejoy Kumar Sinha demanded that the proceedings be adjourned immediately on grounds that the defence wished to avail themselves of the opportunity to file an application before the Lahore High Court requesting that the case be moved to another court. Since the magistrate was not proceeding in an even-handed manner, the proceedings were turning farcical. At this point, the magistrate agreed. He ruled the case be adjourned until 3 October 1929.[7] The accused could make their application to the High Court.

This is when the cash-strapped defence committee of the accused took the opportunity, on the very same day of 25 September 1929, to make an appeal for funds. This is where this case differed so markedly from the Meerut Conspiracy Case, because, as Noorani points out, no legal counsel of nationwide renown were able to get involved in the Lahore Conspiracy Case because the funds were so limited. In fact, as *The Tribune* reported, many lawyers were often not paid at all:

> Now that the Lahore conspiracy case is once again being proceeded with from day-to-day, it seems necessary to call urgent public attention to the defence fund. During the last two months mass collections have been made in most of the important towns of the province, but the total amount collected so far is too inadequate to make fullest arrangements for defence. The defence committee was very fortunate in securing the services of Lala Amar Dass, Advocate of Sialkot, at a remuneration which involved a great monetary sacrifice for him. Knowing the slender resources of the defence committee, Lala Amar Dass accepted no fees for the past two months or so. He has also kindly promised to render occasional aid from time to time whenever necessary, even though he's no longer in charge of the defence.

The extent of the trial irregularities did not end here. For a conspiracy trial, where a large number of defendants were involved, what was required was not one lawyer but a full team:

> Considering the nature of the case and the large number of accused, it can easily be seen it is very difficult for one defence counsel to conduct the case; and, yet, it is not possible to strengthen the defence arrangements further till there is a better response from the public in the shape of money for the defence fund.[8]

Sensing that the proceedings in the Magistrates' Court would fall short for want of the basic tenets of fairness in a criminal case, Amolak Ram Kapoor, on behalf of Bhagat Singh, made an unsuccessful application in the High Court, on 2 October 1929. He argued for the case to be transferred out of the Special Magistrates' Court to the High Court. It was to be in vain. This application too was disallowed – this time by the High Court itself.

When proceedings resumed in Lahore Central Jail on 4 October 1929, the accused marched defiantly into the courtroom to face the magistrate, Rai Sahib Pandit Sri Kishen. As was their usual practice, they each lifted their right hand and loudly raised slogans of '*Inquilab Zindabad*' and 'Down with Imperialism'. This time they even sang a song of revolution based on '*Bharat Na reh sakega hargiz Ghulam Khana*' ('India will never remain house of slaves'). Much of the prosecution evidence they had to hear was mundane and inconsequential. The court happily entertained it nonetheless, even though no such quarter would have been given to the witnesses for the defence. There followed well-timed applications by the defence about the waste of court time in calling for such irrelevant evidence, which began with the prosecution calling evidence about a milk vendor, which was followed by evidence about two proprietors of hotels. There was evidence from Lala Feroz Chand about the existence of a domestic servant.

Feroz Chand, as editor of *Bandematarm*, then described how he met Sukhdev, who had worked as a clerk in the manager's department less than two years ago. When asked how it was that he had come to publish photographs of Bhagat Singh and B. K. Dutt in *Bandematarm* only a few days after the Assembly bomb outrage occurred, he explained that some days after the incident an unnamed man had visited and asked if he would be interested in publishing photographs of Bhagat Singh and B. K. Dutt. This is how they got published. He believed that this man had been sent by Kishen Singh, the father of Bhagat Singh. Given that he was in the business of publishing, he saw no reason why he should not publish them even if they had not already been published anywhere else. Two days later he found two photographs left at his home with no covering note. He did not know who left them there. He proceeded to publish them. It is difficult to see what the relevance of such evidence was to the trial of the accused. It was as pointless as it was trifling. Court time could have been better used by making it available as much as possible to the defence. They were the ones who needed it most.

On this day, however, defence counsel made an application that all 'approvers' in court should be removed from police custody and instead be placed in the custody of the court. The application was immediately slapped down by the magistrate, who blustered that the 'proposition suggested is obviously preposterous'. It clearly was not – it was eminently sensible. Leaving the 'approvers' under the control of the police officers allowed them to be coached by the police. It was clear that this was exactly what was happening in this political trial. Rai Sahib Pandit Sri Kishen also had little hesitation in rejecting another application, namely that the accused should be served with the actual copies of confessional statements made by the 'approvers'. These could have been studied by the accused with a view to working out how the 'approvers' were to be cross-examined in relation to what they were purporting to say. It is an elementary principle of criminal law to know the case against oneself before being required to answer it, and yet this too was perfunctorily rejected by the magistrate.

Despite such tribulations, it was on this day that Bhagat Singh and his colleagues suspended their hunger strike. They did so because the Punjab Jails Inquiry Committee had by the 4 October 1929 submitted its report on what kinds of prisoners were to be treated as political prisoners and in what way. The government had given an assurance that it would consider implementing the jail reforms proposed, and that it would not be penalizing the hunger strikers demanding jail reforms. The decision by Bhagat Singh and his colleagues was, however, contingent on 'the final decision by the government as regards the question of treatment of political prisoners in Indian jails'.[9] This emphasizes the quintessentially political nature of the trial. After all, the proceedings involved hunger strikers appearing in court as defendants who were being prosecuted for murder, conspiracy and waging war against the King. Bhagat Singh and his colleagues felt ceasing the strike was justified as it was 'in obedience to the resolution of the All India Congress Committee':

We are very anxious that all those who are on hunger-strike in sympathy with us should also discontinue it forthwith. We here wish to point out that *as special care was taken by the jail authorities about our health* we have *not suffered much from its evil effects like some of our other friends whose nursing was generally neglected.* Under the circumstances, if for no other reason at least for the sake of such of our sympathisers whose suffering was much more acute than ours, we find it is, indeed, very embarrassing for us to continue the hunger strike further.

The decision having been made to call off the hunger strike, Bhagat Singh and B. K. Dutt now asked Subhas Chandra Bose, who had been asked to preside over the All-Punjab Students' Conference, to read out a message at its second meeting at Bradlaugh Hall in Lahore on 19 October 1929, and which was as follows:

We cannot advise young men to take up bombs and pistols. The students have greater work to do. The Congress is going to declare a grim fight for the country's liberation in the coming Lahore session. At this critical moment of national history, tremendous responsibility will rest on the shoulders of the young community.

All over the world, students have fought till death in the front ranks of the battle for freedom. Will the Indian youths in this hour of trial hesitate to display the same grim determination? The youth have to convey the message of revolution to the farthest corner of the country, to the sweating millions in factories, slums and village huts, a revolution that will bring freedom and would render exploitation of man by man impossible. The Punjab is considered rather politically backward. For that, the responsibility of youth is still greater. Let them prove to the contrary by the unswerving fortitude and firmness in the ensuing struggle following the glorious example of a great martyr Jatinder Nath Das.[10]

As far as the court proceedings themselves were concerned, however, on that same day both Subhas Chandra Bose and Baba Gurdit Singh (of the *Komagata Maru*) were detained for about an hour at the jail gate, despite having permits to enter the courtroom without a search. The paranoia of the authorities knew no bounds. While a phalanx of investigating police officers could accompany an 'approver' such as Jai Gopal into the courtroom, ordinary members of the public were obstructed from doing so, even where they had been granted clearance by the issue of a permit.

When Amolak Ram Kapoor complained to the magistrate about the mistreatment of supporters of the young men who wished to witness the proceedings for themselves, Rai Sahib Pandit Sri Kishen replied asking sarcastically whether they had come to witness the *tamasha* (farce).[11] Eventually, even though both of them did manage to watch the proceedings in the Magistrates' Court for some three hours, Baba Gurdit Singh was not allowed to meet the accused in the courtroom as he wished. The courtroom proceedings were arguably a *tamasha* in any event because as Subhas Chandra Bose and Baba Gurdit Singh entered, the accused rose up in the dock and pluckily exclaimed, 'Long live the revolution', 'Long live the proletariat', and 'Down, down with imperialism'. The treatment of Subhas Chandra Bose and Baba Gurdit Singh was troubling, for if individuals of their political stature were not spared such indignities, others of a lesser status fared even less well. When one accused, Sachindra Nath Sanyal, asked the magistrate why Kiron Chandra Dass (brother of Jatindra Dass, who died while refusing food on hunger strike) was kept waiting outside, the magistrate's reply was that passes had been already issued. When Sanyal asked why those issued with official passes were still rigorously searched before entry, there was no satisfactory reply. Sanyal offered that 'it is an insult to our national self-respect that he should not be allowed to come in without being searched' since the issued passes did not specify the condition of entry being a search. The search of pass holders was clearly illegal. The authorities, however, were not to be outdone.

What happened after Sanyal raised these matters was that the condition of a search upon any pass holder was later added at the instance of the CID. It was clearly an option for the magistrate to rule in open court that those with an official pass would not be searched when entering the courtroom, and Sanyal was understandably indignant when he did not rule in this manner. An exasperated Sanyal asked, 'Will the British Empire fall to pieces if Kiron is allowed in?' He even pointed out how 'in the Kakori case Bhai Parmanand was allowed to sit along with the accused'. Bhagat Singh, noting that the Bengali revolutionary leader Subhas Chandra Bose was now a witness to this drama, took the opportunity to have a good dig at the magistrate: 'This is the impression that Mr Bose will carry of the Punjab to Bengal!' The judge was past being shamed. In response, all the accused decided to collectively admonish the magistrate for his supine and ineffectual subservience to the police authorities in failing to even regulate the orderly attendance of visitors to the courtroom. In this they were once again perfectly correct. His failure to see this meant that he was himself bringing his own court into disrepute, notwithstanding the excoriating words of the accused:

> As we are made to understand at this stage by your honour that your honour has got absolutely no control over the regulation for the admission of visitors in the court *and that the matter rests entirely in the hands of the police authorities*, we request you to kindly inform us as to whom we should apply for the admission of our friends and relatives in court. Kindly be pleased to furnish us with this information immediately and enable us thereby to get permission for K.C Das's admission.

Long before international terrorism became the scourge that it is today, the accused were being subjected to a 'political' trial. The magistrate was imposing restrictions of form and substance that had no place in a system governed by the basic principles of the rule of law. The accused had become acutely aware of this, and they made an application before the court that proceedings must be discontinued until there was positive affirmation of witnesses they regarded as essential to the defence of their cases:

> Further we pray that your honour be pleased to stay the proceedings till the time we are able to get the desired permission for the admission of our friends and relatives *whose presence is indispensable in connection with our defence.*

Bhagat Singh reproached the judge once more. His logic was as unimpeachable as it was searing: 'The magistrate is not expected to be a puppet in the hands of the police. The police is under his authority.' Another accused, Ajoy Kumar Ghosh (who ended up being released due to lack of evidence, but who subsequently went on to become a prominent member of the Communist Party of India in the early 1960s and wrote about the trial of Bhagat Singh) even had the effrontery to berate the magistrate with the words, 'It would be better if police officer sits in the chair of the magistrate.' Bhagat Singh was no less sparing in his withering criticism, blaming the judge for the fact that 'in spite of so many sacrifices made by the Punjabis, the weakness, as shown by the magistrate, is responsible for the backwardness of the Punjab'. These were harsh words but they were surely not misplaced, as he went on to explain:

> Sir, Kiron is coming to the court and not to police station. The order of the magistrate is to be obeyed by the police and not of the police by the magistrate…

If this was a distinction which the magistrate failed to see, then the accused's caustic denunciation of his position was not inapposite. The truth of the matter was that the proceedings before Rai Sahib Pandit Sri Kishen were already taking on the hue of closed court proceedings, with which we are now so familiar in the form of political trials by Western authorities of Afghan, Iraqi and Pakistani detainees.

Soon the magistrate was forced to admit to the fact that executive interference by government officials was taking place concerning the attendance of friends and relatives of the accused, which they deemed to be essential to their defence. This is clear from his abject response that 'searches are being made under the orders of the Executive. I have no hand in the matter.' Such interference extended beyond the searches of those deemed suspect to a denial of requests by the accused to have interviews with their own relatives and friends. An application to do so had to be made properly before the magistrate, and yet when the accused went on to ask for an interview with Subhas Chandra Bose, given that he was present in Lahore having travelled up to the Punjab from almost a thousand miles away, this request was declined on the basis that interviews would only be allowed by the jail superintendent. Bejoy Kumar Sinha remonstrated at how it was that 'it is the local government who control interviews' and asked the magistrate, 'Are you helpless in the matter?' He was met with a disarmingly curt answer from the magistrate: 'My Orders were and are I can't grant interviews in court.' This in itself raised a question: on whose orders was Rai Sahib Pandit Sri Kishen conducting the court proceedings? Bejoy Kumar Sinha sagely reminded the magistrate that 'a great principle is involved in the matter'. It fell on deaf ears. That a magistrate should openly admit in court that he was under 'orders' not to grant interviews is the clearest indication that this was a sham trial ignoring recognised standards of law and justice.

When the magistrate tried to extricate himself from this self-created judicial quagmire with an explanation that 'interviews are regulated according to the Jail Manual', Bhagat Singh had a ready retort, from which the magistrate could not escape: 'This is a court and not a jail. It is your courtroom.' The gravity of the judge's failing in this respect cannot be overstated. It was fundamental. It went to the heart of natural justice and procedural fairness. He who is accused must have the right to prepare his defence. This means seeking advice from legal advisers. It means having the right to confer with those who may be able to provide vital assistance to the accused in their defence. It was precisely because the jail superintendent had set his face against the granting of family interviews to the accused that they were ardently making the application. Given, as Bhagat Singh ruefully reminded the magistrate, 'we will be in the jurisdiction of the jail authorities in the evening', this was all the more reason why the magistrate was wrong to pass an application made in his court during the day to the jail authorities on grounds that the matter of interviews was 'regulated according to the Jail manual'. The exercise of a judicial function is to be performed by the presiding judge, not by the jail authorities. In the event, Rai Sahib Pandit Sri Kishen's refusal to grant the accused the interviews they desired meant that Subhas Chandra Bose left court after the morning session at 2 p.m. and Baba Gurdit Singh left a short while after that on 19 October 1929. Both would doubtless have been able to give invaluable assistance to the accused. Both had little doubt that the fate of the accused was a foregone conclusion.

With the accused increasingly frustrated, on 21 October 1929 there came a turning point in the court of magistrate Rai Sahib Pandit Sri Kishen. One of the accused, a juvenile by the name of Prem Dutt Verma, threw a slipper at 'approver' Jai Gopal whilst he was giving evidence in the witness box. Verma was promptly committed to three months' solitary confinement by the jail superintendent.[12] The gesture was not so feckless as it would appear to a Western mind. The throwing of slippers has a long and illustrious tradition in Eastern countries. One may aptly recount here the Iraqi journalist Muntadhar al-Zaidi throwing his shoes at President George Bush with the words, 'This is a farewell kiss from the Iraqi people, you dog' as Bush made his last visit to the country as President in 2008.

Al-Zaidi wanted Bush to officially apologise to all Iraqis for the ill-conceived American invasion of his country.[13] His gesture was a popular one in Iraqi eyes, and a decade later he even went on to stand in national elections.[14] As was subsequently confirmed to CNN by al-Zaidi's brother many years later, the gesture is an 'incredibly offensive' one. On this occasion it was designed to 'humiliate' the American President, because, as his brother said, '[t]hrowing a shoe on someone means throwing dirt on that person'. In fact, Faegheh Shirazi, Professor of Middle Eastern Studies at the University of Texas, has confirmed that it is offensive 'regardless of the religious practices': 'Throwing a shoe or hitting someone with a shoe or showing the bottom of your shoe when sitting with legs up on a chair and facing another person are all culturally unacceptable and are considered to be a grave insult and belittling to a person.'[15] In India, culturally speaking, the converse of garlanding someone with flowers is to garland them with an array of shoes of different shapes and sizes. The first gesture bestows dignity, respect and honour on that person; the second marks them irredeemably with the taint of dishonour, disdain and discredit.

Prem Dutt Verma's deed was plainly aimed at a fellow co-conspirator who had decided to become a turncoat. It was not aimed at the magistrate. It did not attack officialdom. Nevertheless, the judge dealt with it by consigning Prem Dutt Verma to solitary confinement. One would have thought that this would be the end of the matter, but it was not. What the infuriated magistrate now did was order that all of the accused henceforth be brought into court with both hands in handcuffs. The rest of the accused had nothing whatsoever to do with the actions of the young and immature Prem Dutt Verma. In fact, they had expressed regret at what he had done in order to clearly dissociate themselves from his errant deed. Hitherto, the practice of the jail authorities was to bring the accused directly from Borstal Jail with a handcuff on one hand only. This handcuff was then removed once he had entered the dock. The magistrate's intemperate and precipitous decision saw the existing practice brought to an end in an act of coercive control by the court which was not justified by the facts.

The impact of the ruling was immediately felt. Bhagat Singh and B. K. Dutt, who were already housed in the Central Jail, used to come to the courtroom without any handcuffs at all on either hand. When, therefore, on 22 October 1929, the police tried to handcuff them, they quite understandably protested and refused to go into court in this condition. They saw themselves as political prisoners and not as common criminals to be manacled. The remaining Borstal prisoners also quite understandably refused to go to court fully handcuffed. They could not understand why they were being collectively punished for the actions of a single man, Prem Dutt Verma, who had already been individually and separately punished for his indiscretion anyway. Their recalcitrance meant that they too were subject to coercion under threat of physical harm. They were forced to come to the porch of the Borstal Jail and were handcuffed.

Their coercion did not end there. A number of the accused were brutally thrown onto the back of the transport lorry. When Pandha, Agya Ram, Ajoy Ghosh, Gaya Parsad, Shiv Varma and Kamwal Nath Tiwari arrived, badly bruised, in the back of the lorry, they refused to get out. They were ordered to be taken back. Tiwari, however, told everyone present at the gate of the Central Jail of their degrading and humiliating treatment at the hands of the police authorities. They had injuries to show. They had been mercilessly caned and beaten up. Naturally, the case could not proceed amid all the commotion. There had to be an adjournment of proceedings for the day. The day's events, however, were a watershed in the trial. Hitherto, the atmosphere in the court had been relatively calm. The proceedings were orderly. The business of the day was conducted with tolerable decorum. The precipitous action of the police meant that the stage had now been set for something sinister and altogether uglier. A new tension and rancour arose. The stakes had been raised by the wanton, vicious and gratuitous behaviour of the police. The accused felt that the magistrate had forfeited the trust and dignity that judicial proceedings normally commanded. The next day, after lunchtime, the accused were made to return to the courtroom. The manner of their return did not suggest that the authorities were aiming to lower tensions: they were handcuffed on both hands. They were then physically dragged in and thrown like sacks into the dock. Weakened already by their deprivations, Shiv Varma and Ajoy Ghosh were rendered unconscious. The breathtaking callousness is reminiscent of modern-day terror trials at Guantanamo Bay.

Bhagat Singh and B. K. Dutt were conscious, but they were gulping, choking and panting as they arrived, disordered and bedraggled in their dishevelled and dirt-stained condition.[16] Needless to say, no judicial tribunal acting under due process and the rule of law should proceed with a trial in such appalling circumstances. The accused were by now even more convinced that their trial was a 'political' trial. They could expect no impartial justice. It was easy to see how the atmosphere in the courtroom was irrevocably changed for the worse. The entry of Bhagat Singh and B. K. Dutt saw even louder political chants from the accused. An outraged Bhagat Singh could not contain himself. He pointedly demanded of the magistrate, 'Have you ordered the police to kick us? Can't you control the police?' This gave succour to the other accused in the courtroom, who sneered in derision: 'Shame! Shame!' The daunted magistrate looked up insouciantly from his papers and mildly inquired, 'Who kicked you?' Bhagat Singh jabbed his finger at the police officers, daring to point them all out. He had no qualms at telling the magistrate how 'several persons were sitting on us and kicking on all parts of our body'. For the first time, B. K. Dutt now picked up the courage to speak in court. He confirmed that he had been very badly handled by the police: 'I have received severe blows on my chest,' he complained. By now, others were prepared to speak out. Prem Dutt bitterly described the inhumane treatment to which he and his fellow accused were unnecessarily subjected: 'Yesterday, fingers were thrown in our rectum and kicks were given on our testicles.' Incensed, he wished to know, 'Is it civilisation? You call it civilisation? The time will come when we will turn revolutionaries.'

Seated in court was the government advocate, Carden Noad. He did not denounce on the government's behalf the shocking violence being meted out to the under-trial prisoners. Bhagat Singh accordingly rose to his feet. Angrily, he told the magistrate, 'We were treated in that way by the police, acting under your orders.' He reminded him of his responsibilities. He demanded to know, 'Is this how you are acting in accordance with the High Court ruling to keep at an arm's length from the police and the prosecution?' He asked again why they had been handcuffed, and if it was under the magistrate's orders. The magistrate replied that it was. When Bhagat Singh asked why, the magistrate replied, 'Because there was a danger to everybody here.' However, the sole incident had been the hot-headed Prem Dutt Verma throwing his slipper at the 'approver' Jai Gopal. Bhagat Singh duly asked, 'How many have died?' The magistrate would have none of it. He wished to press on. He gave the matter little more than a banausic consideration. From where he was sitting, it was easy to be dismissive and admonishing: 'Don't discuss the matter with me. I won't argue with you.' But Bhagat Singh was onto him. He was raising a serious issue that went directly to the question of justice. He pressed on. His logic was remorseless and irrefutable. He put it to the magistrate that 'a few days ago you paid tribute to our reasonable attitude. You appreciated it. Why should we have been made to suffer for the mistake of one?' Sanyal added his voice to this. He resentfully reminded the magistrate, 'We dissociated ourselves from that act and expressed regret. It is unjust to order us to be handcuffed in that way.'

The magistrate had no justification for this blatant instance of coercive colonial legal violence against those under his charge. He was running a political trial, and he had a predetermined end in mind. He knew he was veering far off course. He knew also that collective punishment of a dozen defendants for the actions of one errant young man was contrary to law, and against every canon of justice. He knew that his decision in this regard was appealable before the High Court. Bhagat Singh did not hesitate to tell the magistrate that his attitude was 'most absurd', especially as he had even 'refused to record our statement'. 'I want to move the High Court,' he said. 'Will you note that we are going to the High Court?' The magistrate did not reply, but Carden Noad, the government advocate, quipped, 'It is noted.' Bhagat Singh now wanted 'to give a written statement'. He turned to the magistrate and asked, 'Will you please order that one of my handcuffs be removed?' To which the magistrate lamely replied, 'I can't at this time.' Bejoy Kumar Sinha then asked if he could make a statement on behalf of those who were unrepresented. It was to no avail. The magistrate was determined to conduct the trial untroubled by such legal niceties as the conduct of a fair hearing and fair representation.

The magistrate now asked Gopal Lal, prosecuting counsel, to cross-examine the witnesses, whose cases had not been fairly put before the court. On 23 October 1929, the accused indicated that they were prepared to come to court provided that only one of their hands was handcuffed and the other free. The police balked at the idea. Instead, the accused were assured that if they willingly came to court without offering any resistance they would be unshackled. They obliged. Restraining a prisoner appearing before a judge in open court in this manner is unusual in any case. After their arrival at court, Bejoy Kumar Sinha entered the dock. Addressing the magistrate, he made it clear that the accused had not offered any resistance. They had willingly come to court on the basis of the undertakings given to them that in court they would not be manacled. They wished to have the opportunity to explain their situation.

To their great surprise, the government advocate declared that no such assurance was given to the accused that morning. Bejoy Kumar Sinha laboured on that the accused should not be collectively punished for the actions of one defendant who threw a slipper in the heat of the moment. The magistrate's order that they all be punished by being handcuffed on both hands was hasty and ill judged. There had been no inquiries made prior to the passing of the order, which now affected the liberty of every one of the accused as he made the journey from prison cell to courtroom and stood before the magistrate to be tried. The magistrate remained unresponsive.

The accused now refused to participate in their trial. This is when coercive colonial legal violence in a court of law reached its very zenith.

The situation had deteriorated dramatically, and it was now to become menacing. The police decided that the way to bring the prisoners into the courtroom was to bring them out of their prison cells and onto the court precincts, and there to forcibly handcuff them. This was met with stiff resistance from the prisoners, so the police decided that they would first subdue them in custody. This was done by beating the accused in a sustained manner all the way up to the courtroom. The prisoners stoically resisted. The result was a horror scene. In the court compound, witnesses saw several of the accused writhing in agony on the ground as they were overpowered by a bevy of policemen. There was a scuffle in the dirt of the grounds as efforts were made to handcuff the weakened detainees. As the resistance of the prisoners continued, police violence could no longer be confined to the compound of the jail precincts. The prolonged altercation entered the courtroom itself, where the policemen were seen throwing the prisoners into the dock and over the benches. Many suffered lacerations, abrasions and contusions. Some even lost consciousness. The spectacle was entirely unworthy of legal proceedings.

Rarely could a court of law have allowed itself to become so debased and degenerated. Yet, here it was. The indifferent magistrate could only disingenuously say, 'They themselves are responsible for it.' Not for the first time, Bhagat Singh rebuked him sharply: 'I want to congratulate you for this ... This thing is going on under your very nose.' Suddenly, Bhagat Singh noticed that both Shiv Varma and Ajoy Kumar Ghosh had been rendered insensible and comatose. Incensed, he railed at the judge, 'Shiv Varma is lying unconscious, if he dies you are responsible for it.' With this, the situation in the courtroom only worsened. Press censorship was imposed. To the government, restraining police brutality on undertrials seemed less important than preventing the reporting of these ghastly events outside the courtroom. The Senior Superintendent of Police ordered press representatives to 'clear out'. They were compelled to leave, as were the visitors; counsel followed suit just a few minutes later, realizing how helpless they were to do anything further on behalf of the accused. The legally sanctioned violence in the courtroom had made the continuance of the proceedings untenable. As they left, members of the press could hear howls of 'Long live the revolution' and 'Long live the proletariat'. Such was the indomitable spirit of the young revolutionaries in those heady days of the late 1920s that even when they were beaten within an inch of their lives, they remained unbroken in spirit.

3

The Hunger Strike

Zulm Phir Zulm Hai, Badhta Hathon Mein Jatah Hae;
Khoon Phir Khoon Hai;
Tapkga, Toh Jamjaeha

Your repression remains a repression,
though you may call it by another name;
One day it will fail,
For my blood is still red blood;
And one day it will not flow as it spills
But defiantly clot before your eyes

Sahir Ludhianvi

The determined resolve of the revolutionaries was not in vain. The next day, 24 October 1929, when the two sets of accused were to be brought before the court (with Bhagat Singh and B. K. Dutt from within Central Jail and the rest from Borstal Jail), it was agreed that they should be brought with handcuffs on one hand only. The prosecution had its own tawdry reasons for agreeing to this. Dr Robson, the prosecution's explosives expert, had to leave India for London. The High Court ruling and the collapse of the hunger strike meant that he could not be examined in the absence of the accused,[1] so it made sense to let the accused attend handcuffed on one hand as they had long demanded. It was a success for the accused nonetheless. Any notion that they should express gratitude to the court for granting them this boon was quickly dispelled by Bhagat Singh, who rose up to tell the court,

I understand you want us to express regret. There appears to be no necessity for it. After submitting a written application, dissociating ourselves from the act of an individual and expressing regret for it, we thought it would not be necessary in order to calm down the atmosphere, but we are prepared to repeat the expression of regret. But it should not imply that we are in any way responsible for that incident.

The magistrate reminded Bhagat Singh that only the day before he had cried out, 'Shame! Shame!' at him. That being so, it was fitting that he should now give an assurance that he would desist from any such action in the future. Unmoved, Bhagat Singh replied that he had so expressed himself in response to their physical ill-treatment. It was the result of a police thrashing. He was in acute pain. His body ached. He and B. K. Dutt had been seriously mistreated by the police at the gates of the Central Jail. They had then been thrown in the dock, cast off like unwanted luggage. The beatings were not confined to the start of the day, either. Following lunch, they had again been pummelled. In fact, the brutality was deliberate and targeted, he reminded the magistrate. A police officer by the name of 'Roberts' had said, 'This is the man, give him more beating.' There could be little doubt of police interference in the orderly conduct of the trial. They were under orders from the executive to break the will of the accused. Rather than the magistrate having an assurance from him, then, Bhagat Singh wanted an assurance that the police would desist from such a course of action in future, because he had no doubt himself that '[a]part from the question of handcuffing, the police had definite orders to beat us'. His question to the magistrate was simple: 'To whom should we complain? I request this fact may also go on the record.'[2]

In saying this, Bhagat Singh dispelled the popular notion that it was the detainees who were responsible for the slow progress of their trial. The opposite was the case. In the midst of the trial, the court allowed gratuitous repressive, punitive and brutal action to be taken against the accused, many of whom were juveniles. This, as the evidence shows, was executive-backed police mistreatment. What magistrate Rai Sahib Pandit Sri Kishen was presiding over was no longer an ordinary trial subject to ordinary legal procedures but a trial characterized by a form of coercive colonial legalism unrecognised by any legal system governed by the rule of law, and it irrevocably marred and disfigured the proceedings. The accused themselves were at pains to bring this to the attention of the magistrate. They implored him to rectify the malfeasance of state officials in public office before him. He failed to do so. Bejoy Kumar Sinha reminded the magistrate that 'extraordinary events have taken place during the last few days and before this case proceeds, it is essential, in the interests of the accused as well as the court, to get the matters settled so that the case may henceforth proceed in an atmosphere of trust and right and clear understanding'. He pointed out,

> At the outset, I will begin by relating the incident that happened on Monday last. Jai Gopal, approver was brought in and he began his statement. Just after two or three minutes he, *in provoking manner*, uttered: 'I personally feel, *at the instance of the prosecution*, the words '*Janab ye ap ke kiye huye hain, aur sachii haen*' ('These acts having been committed by you and are true'). This utterance was very provoking and one of us, Prem Dutt – *the youngest of all* – got excited and in *the heat of the moment* threw a slipper at the approver. Thereafter the Learned Prosecuting Counsel pointed out that *there was a danger to the lives of those present in court* and that the court should adjourn the proceedings. *Before the Learned Magistrate passed the order* for adjournment, I, Bhagat Singh and others wanted to make a statement regarding the *regrettable incident* as there was much scope for misunderstanding. The Learned Magistrate did not give us an opportunity to get our statement recorded. We, therefore, hastened to file a written statement – the only course left for us – making it clear *that all of us dissociate ourselves from the act* committed by one individual. After that petition was made, I think, *there was no reason why we should be made to suffer for the act of one.*[3]

A number of matters are immediately clear from this supplication to the magistrate. Prem Dutt was a young juvenile. He found Jai Gopal's statement as an 'approver' to be deliberately provocative, and not only for his choice of words. Most importantly, he objected to the fact that the testimony was directed not at the court but the accused themselves, as seen in the words, 'These acts have been committed by you.' Prem Dutt then reacted 'in the heat of the moment' by throwing a slipper at the approver for his treachery. The prosecution asked for an adjournment. The magistrate duly ordered one – even though it is an elementary principle of law that an application by a party before the court must be put to the other side for their response before the court decides upon what order to make.

The accused had moreover collectively made a statement dissociating themselves from young Prem Dutt's actions, and they entreated the magistrate not to punish them collectively for the momentary indiscretion of one young man. But perhaps most noteworthy are the following two matters. First, was it really all that surprising that one of the youths would have such a strong reaction when they came face to face with an 'approver' who only recently had been plotting with them against the government, but who had now switched sides, and now had the effrontery to make an accusation directly into the faces of the accused? Second, does the throwing of a slipper (which, as explained above, has a well-established lineage in the chronicles of cultural profanity, sacrilege and irreverence) really amount to putting in danger the lives of everyone in the courtroom as had been suggested? Neither matter bears serious consideration. For Rai Sahib Pandit Sri Kishen to hastily pass the order that he did was both rash and unjustified.

So ill-considered, unwarranted and unprincipled was the magistrate's ruling in this regard that the following day, 25 October 1929, without any further altercation or cause for concern, the judge ordered that the accused return to court with the handcuffs back on both hands! There was no reason for this change of heart. It was simply another example of colonial legal coercion applied in the courts. When they refused to submit to this treatment, the accused were initially allowed to return to their cells, only to be summoned back to the jail portico, where they were confronted by 300 armed policemen and jail wardens who faced the accused menacingly. The accused still refused. According to Bejoy Kumar Sinha, at this stage, 'Mr. Hardinge ordered the policeman, and Inspectors ordered to get us handcuffed by any means. The constables and Inspectors pounced upon us, and began assaulting us. Each of us was assaulted by at least twenty to twenty-five policemen. The method of assault was most inhuman and unheard of.' Sinha's description of the inhuman and degrading treatment under the jurisdiction of the court of under-trial prisoners was that fingers were put into their rectums and kicks were aimed at their testicles in such a systematic and well-orchestrated fashion that it can only be described as torture. Yet, as he explained,

> All the time we were strictly non-violent because we realised the unequal forces that were at work. We knew all the while that all we could do was to gain a moral victory and in the position in which we stood – 15 against 300 armed police – we could not do otherwise. The struggle continued for more than an hour and the police were able to bring only six of us in the lorry to this court.

How much better it would have been, one may well ponder, if the magistrate had not made such an unnecessary order. All fifteen would have been willing to come. The proceedings would have been conducted with the full cooperation of the accused and in decorum. But one must realise that the order was made for a reason: the magistrate was under executive pressure to humiliate and debase the prisoners in every way possible, and then blame them for slowing down the proceedings so that the government would have an excuse for transferring the trial to a special government-appointed tribunal which would work outside the normal legal system. The longer the case went on, the clearer this became. As Sinha explained, such was the savage cruelty of the actions of the police that

> as a result of the severe injuries, received that day, five of us – myself, Des Raj, Mahabir Singh, Gaya Prasad and Kishori Lal – got fever. All the others had acute pain in different parts of the body. Mahabir Singh and Rajguru had fallen senseless on the spot. During assaults, canes were also freely used. Marks can still be seen on the bodies of some of us – especially Rajguru. I pray the Court may examine him just now.

The court did not examine Rajguru, and the proceedings ran quietly that morning, so later that day the accused did have the handcuffs removed in court. This was when Dr Robson, the explosives expert, returned and gave evidence. He was cross-examined by Amar Dass. Bhagat Singh was still being refused his request to make a statement to the court.

Thus it was that four months after the trial began, the approver, Jai Gopal, now stood in the witness box to give his formal evidence in court. The delay was not attributable to the conduct of the accused in court, as the account above has shown. On the one hand, the judge allowed a trail of irrelevant evidence to be called by the prosecution, such as the testimony of the milk vendor, the two hoteliers and the editor of *Bandemataram*. On the other hand, not only were the accused not given copies of written evidence for the prosecution, or assistance of counsel, but they were also denied any quarter whatsoever. In fact, they were handcuffed in court and beaten up both in court and elsewhere.

In his evidence, Jai Gopal explained the different meetings of members of the revolutionary society. He identified the pistol and revolver exhibited in court as those used by Bhagat Singh and Rajguru in their assassination of John Saunders. He even gave a detailed account of the preparations that preceded the killing. He further explained that there had been a plan, hatched by members of the HSRA, to rob the Punjab

National Bank early in December 1928, only to be abandoned – because none of them could drive!

The longer the proceedings went on, the clearer it became that the magistrate was conducting a political trial. It was not just that the beatings of the accused went unrecorded; any attempt to correct errors in the record was also resisted. Soon the very nature of the 'public trial' itself was under threat as people began to be excluded from court. Such were the nefarious indignities that the accused had to endure as undertrials. On 28 October 1929, Bhagat Singh tried to correct the record of the proceedings of 23 October 1929, pointing out to the magistrate that the accused had not said that 'the magistrate should remember that the days of the revolution are not gone and that the revolutionaries would take revenge' but that 'by such brutalities, inhuman treatment and barbarous torture, you cannot kill our spirit. The government will soon learn that they are dealing with revolutionaries.' This was not allowed.

The record of 23 October 1929 also did not contain a reference to the beatings given to the accused. Bhagat Singh wished to have this corrected. His request was refused. So the record was inaccurate. In fact, on 5 November 1929, Kamwal Nath Tiwari made a formal application, seeking to put on record the beatings on 22 October and 23 October 1929. The judge remained entrenched in his obstinacy. It was not allowed. Bejoy Kumar Sinha then asked the magistrate who would be a fitting recipient for the application because it was clear to all that the magistrate himself was not the right person. He was too servile. When the magistrate responded that he sent the petitions to the District Magistrate, Sinha's sarcastic retort – 'Will you kindly introduce me to the District Magistrate?' – raised peals of laughter which echoed irresistibly in the courtroom. Yet, this was no way to conduct a trial of such a serious nature. It was fast becoming a mockery. The judge was losing respect in his own courtroom. Later, after adopting a more sober tone, Sinha proceeded to ask what had happened to the existing application which had already been lodged. The magistrate's effete reply was revealing: 'I forwarded it to the District Magistrate. There is no reply received yet. I am helpless.' Applications on such serious matters as ill-treatment of the accused not being dealt with expeditiously and effectively but subject to dilatoriness is a sure sign of very flawed and corrupt legal proceedings.

It did not end there. There was also the issue of the trial continuing as a public hearing. It could not be a public hearing if there was a denial of access to other college students, as Bejoy Kumar Sinha made clear when on 7 November 1929 he complained,

We are told of several college students waiting outside the prison gate, and their applications had been torn off by the police. We also understand that in several cases, students have been refused admission on the ground that there is no proof of the Principals of their colleges having permitted them to attend this court. This is scandalous. The proceedings are supposed to be public.

It is not immediately clear why college students would need the permission from the principal of their college in order to attend a public hearing of a trial. Nevertheless, once again, all the magistrate could do was to promise that he would look into the matter. On this basis, admission to the courtroom was subject to heavy police restrictions throughout.[4]

On 26 November 1929, evidence was to be heard from another who had turned approver. This was Hans Raj Vohra. He had managed to save his skin by making a confessional statement to the City Magistrate over a period of two days between 21 May 1929 and 23 May 1929, and had secured for himself a pardon for his own sins against the colonial state. As he began to give his evidence, admission to the courtroom was restricted even more than usual. Indeed, the visitors' gallery was almost empty. Once again there was commotion in the courtroom, and once again it was entirely predictable. The accused now took the opportunity to object to the unfortunate position of the witness box, which allowed for the tampering of witnesses by the Crown, because it was located immediately behind the seats of the prosecution counsel. In order to get a witness to adopt his written account of the evidence, Crown counsel held the witness statements in their hands as the witness read the statement. Crown counsel would then examine or cross-examine a witness from the seats of the prosecution counsel behind the witness box. On the other hand, because the prosecution counsel were so close to the witness box, any question from the defence counsel could be met by a whisper of an answer from the prosecution counsel to the witness box. Of course, prosecution counsel vehemently denied engaging in any such assistance, but it is well established that justice must not only be done but must be seen to be done. The well-crafted common law rules of natural justice are precisely for this purpose. Here they were ignored.

The risk of interference was greatest when a witness turned 'approver' and arrived to give evidence for the Crown, because he could hear the remarks between prosecuting counsel amongst themselves. The witness could even be cajoled into saying what the Crown intended them to say. The objection was not new. The accused had consistently and persistently complained about the situation of the witness box in this way. Their protests had gone unheeded. Nothing was done. Yet, it was easy for the magistrate to give directions which avoided the risk of tampering with witnesses. Any normal witness would have been able to read statements in the hands of counsel whilst they were being examined. They could also hear the remarks made by Crown counsel on the replies given by the witness to questions put to him during cross-examination by the defence counsel. Given that Vohra's evidence was that he had been recruited by Sukhdev, who was his handler, and given that his evidence was on familiar lines to that of Jai Gopal, the accused were bound to have thought that he too had been fed answers from the prosecution side.

Bhagat Singh persisted in asking the magistrate on 26 November 1929 what orders had been passed on the application of Bejoy Kumar Sinha regarding the admission of visitors to the courtroom. The magistrate responded quizzically by asking if he meant admission of students. Bhagat Singh reminded him that he was referring to 'visitors in general'. Bejoy Kumar Sinha fulminated that 'on 24th October, when our handcuffs were removed, you gave us a promise that all facilities would be given to us. Now, in spite of your assurance, we understand that we are to be prosecuted for disobeying the order to come to the court that day.'

Bhagat Singh added that the assurance was given by the magistrate directly to their advocate, Amolak Ram Kapoor. The magistrate's reply was jaw-dropping: 'The order of the application filed on Saturday was, "The general order of this court regarding non-admission of students to the courtroom does not in any way concern the accused or the conduct of the prosecution. Copies of any such orders cannot be granted, not being a part of judicial proceedings."' With impeccable logic, Bhagat Singh countered,

If accused, some of whom are students, are allowed in the dock, why should not the students be allowed in the Visitor's Gallery? Section 352, Criminal Procedure Code, says that the place where any criminal court is held, 'shall be deemed an open court to which the public generally may have access so far as a same can conveniently contain them'. Under that section you cannot stop any particular class of the public from having access to the court-room. Your Order is, therefore, illegal. Moreover, some of the accused are students, and their student friends, who take interest in the case should be allowed admission. I will therefore request you, Sir, to reconsider your order.

It is remarkable that these concerns were raised with such precision. The accused were mostly students and young men themselves. Yet, their legal

Copy of the orders received from the Inspector General of Prisons,Pb, to the Superintendent Central Jail, Lahore, as the orders of His Excellency the Governor of the Punjab.

----

(1) So long as he is on hunger strike, Bhagat Singh will not be allowed to see any of his relations;

(2) He may be permitted to interview a legal adviser, provided he satisfies the Superintendent of the Central Jail that the person with whom the interview is allowed is a bona-fide legal adviser, properly enrolled on the High Court Bar. Such interview must be carried out as provided in para 560 of the Jail Manual;

(3) No interview with the th prisoners in the Borstal Jail can be allowed so long as the prisoner continues on hunger strike.

True copy.

Major O.B.E., I.M.S.,
Superintendent Central Jail, Lahore.

The Governor-General of Punjab himself, Lord Irwin, had decreed that 'so long as he is on hunger-strike, Bhagat Singh will not be allowed to see any of his relations', which resulted in this response from the Superintendent of the Central Jail in Lahore to Bhagat Singh's repeated entreaties that he be allowed interviews with relatives and lawyers. Previously unpublished.

acumen and penetrating insight into the situation unfolding before them is something to marvel at even today. Unsurprisingly, the court wasted little time in summarily dismissing this request.

By the end of the year, far from being in any mood to compromise, the authorities were to adopt an even more hard-line approach. One reason for this was that the revolutionaries themselves were showing no sign of relenting. Events outside the courtroom were also taking a nasty turn, which could not have helped the defendants. The Viceroy's train was attacked by Bhagwati Charan and Yashpal when the latter exploded a mine on 23 December 1929 while the Lahore Conspiracy Case trial was still in progress. The two men had set the mine by rail tracks near the Purana Qila in New Delhi, and detonated it as the Viceroy's train went by. The Viceroy was unhurt, and there was fortunately no loss of life. However, the damage had been done and any sympathy that the authorities may have had for the accused was now fast evaporating.[5] After this the court heard from a third approver, Manmohan Bannerjee, and then a fourth, Phonindra Nath Ghosh. The year was ending badly for the accused. They were now more alone than ever.

In the new year, on 24 January 1930, Lenin Day, the accused entered the courtroom with red scarves around their necks. Upon entry they raised slogans of 'Long live Lenin'. Such was the level of sarcasm, and the manner in which the defendants themselves had internalised their deprivations so as to gain strength from them in order to retaliate in their own way, that Bhagat Singh handed to the magistrate a telegram that he said should be forwarded to the President of the Third International, Moscow. It read,

> On the occasion of the Lenin Day, we express our hearty congratulations on the triumphant and onward march of Comrade Lenin's success for the great experiment carried on in Soviet Russia. *We wish to associate ourselves with the world Revolution movement.* Victory to the workers' regime. Woe to capitalism. Down with imperialism.

The mocking frivolity was not without purpose. It was designed to bring home to the government that the defendants were facing them on equal terms in order to resist their oppression and coercive rule so as to claim back some dignity where little had been in evidence so far. The more the authorities were determined to quash any suggestion of this being a 'political' trial, the more the accused were intent on claiming it as such. In this way, they sought parity with their oppressors in the courtroom. And so the tongue-in-cheek sarcasm continued.

Such was the world of make-believe in the trial of Bhagat Singh that soon the authorities too began to participate in this tongue-in-cheek banter. It was surreal. When the magistrate took in hand the telegram from Bhagat Singh, he proceeded to assure him that he would indeed forward it to the executive authorities so that necessary action could be taken, whereupon Bhagat Singh promptly demanded that the court get him an immediate confirmation of whether the authorities were willing to despatch the telegram or not. This is because if they were not prepared to do so, as he told the magistrate, then the accused were perfectly happy to pay the full charges for the transmission. This demonstrated such remarkable chutzpah on the part of Bhagat Singh that he went on to express the hope that the fate that befell the telegram addressed to the President of the Political Sufferers Conference on Kakori Day should not turn out to be the hapless fate of this telegram as well![6] Such banter aside, Bhagat Singh nevertheless remained very concerned about the prisoners' rights to political privileges. On 20 January 1930, he sent a number of telegrams to the home member. The last one read,

> Suspended hunger-strike on assurance given by the Jail Committee that the question of the treatment of political prisoners was going to be finally settled to our satisfaction within a very short period. Copies AICC Resolutions regarding hunger strike withheld by jail authorities. Authorities refused Congress deputation to meet the prisoners. The conspiracy-case-under-trials were assaulted on 23rd and 24th October 1929 by the *orders of the high police officials.*[7]

One reason why it was impossible for Bhagat Singh to have been in any way satisfied with state of political privileges, even if the hunger strikers had been given an assurance about this question, was that when the matter was considered racial distinctions were openly built into who was, and who was not, a political prisoner. This is clear from the dissent of Chaudhri Afzal Haq, one of the members of the Jail Committee, who was damning of it when he wrote,

> The committee have created a class distinction which is equally, if not more, as that of a racial distinction. The new principle that the criminals may be treated inside the jail, not according to their motive or character of their offence, but in accordance with their mode of life and social status, education or character propounds a novel theory and is absolutely against the accepted principle of jail administration all over the world.[8]

Other irregularities in trial procedure continued apace and Bhagat Singh had to contend with one indignity after another. The lack of legal representation on account of the impecuniosity of the accused has already been mentioned. But even when counsel was willing to provide assistance, in these straitened circumstances, they were hamstrung by the authorities. On 29 January 1930, Lala Duni Chand, a senior member of the Lahore High Court Bar, whilst acting as legal adviser to Bhagat Singh was not allowed to take his seat with defence counsel in court, nor as a member of the Bar. Indeed, he was not even allowed to be present in the press gallery. Such wanton humiliation caused him to storm out of court in protest. All those who were represented by counsel then withdrew their authority and refused to take part in the proceedings. Bhagat Singh had undertaken a short conversation with Lala Duni Chand prior to the commencement of the proceedings, and the latter had informed the court that he was acting as a legal adviser only. When Carden Noad, the government advocate, submitted that he had no *locus standi* to act merely as legal adviser, Lala Duni Chand explained that he also represented all the accused who were represented by Amar Dass. In short, he was not just a legal adviser to Bhagat Singh, but he was also legal counsel to the other accused. Carden Noad persisted with his objections. Bhagat Singh asked the magistrate for a definite ruling on whether Lala Duni Chand could remain in court and watch the proceedings, to which the magistrate passed an order to the effect that there was no such status as that of a 'legal adviser' in law. When a determined Lala Duni Chand then enquired of the court whether, as a member of the High Court Bar, he could sit before a sign plate on the pillar behind him which bore an inscription to the effect of 'For members of the Bar only', the magistrate said that the sign plate was meant only for the defence counsel! This left everyone in court utterly aghast.

Unfazed, the resolute Lala Duni Chand then enquired whether he could sit behind the press reporters' table. The magistrate reprimanded him and told him he could only sit in the visitors' gallery as a visitor. The magistrate must surely have realized what he was asking of Lala Duni Chand. He was effectively being required to relinquish any form of practical support he could render to Bhagat Singh in circumstances where he was not being engaged as a paid-up lawyer on his behalf. Exasperated and now utterly humiliated, Lala Duni Chand could only dejectedly bleat that 'in no part of the world have members of the bar been treated in the manner in which they were treated in this court. I strongly protest against this treatment and I walk out of the court.'

The magistrate had left Lala Duni Chand with no option but to leave the courtroom. Bhagat Singh now told the magistrates that the proceedings were high-handed and that the prosecution, government and court were depriving the defence of an opportunity to engage in proceedings. This was a negation of justice. This only meant one thing: that nothing should stand in the way of the defendants being hanged. However, if this was the desire of the government, Bhagat Singh said that they were prepared for it. For him to have made this observation while the trial was still in the hands of the magistrate in the regular court shows how blatantly obvious it had now become to him that the authorities were committed to putting him to death. Thus, in the words of Bhagat Singh:

> If the country has any spirit, it will see to it. If we are going to be *deprived of all the facilities for defence*, and if we are to be treated in this manner, we don't wish to produce any defence. Whatever is happening in this court is nothing but a farce. Let the British government be proud of this Justice. We have nothing to do with this case. *I declare on behalf of the accused in court that they withdraw their representation.* Let the civilised world know what this government is doing. *We are prepared to be hanged.*[9]

It is clear from this that, with their defence emasculated by the authorities' chicanery, Bhagat Singh knew the fate of the accused was sealed. Participation in this colonial trial, shorn of all the traditional trappings of due process and fairness, was to give legitimacy to a process that was inherently illegitimate and coercive. It was a charade. And Bhagat Singh could see the writing on the wall. It is often said of him and his comrades that he set out in the trial proceedings to actively embrace the prospect of death. The truth of the matter is that he could see which way the wind was blowing. He had little choice. He was aware that the judicial management of the trial had a predetermined end in mind. Having understood this, he calculated that a policy of dedicated, diligent and devoted welcoming of death served to expose the artifice and deceit of the trial as a ruse, little more than an act of judicial murder.

It was at this point that all the accused represented by Lala Amar Dass announced in court that they would withdraw their representation. They made it clear that they would refuse to be defended by counsel any further. This was clearly a boycott of the trial by the defendants. With his instructions withdrawn by the accused, Lala Amar Dass asked the court if he could at least still sit in court. He had been appointed by the defence committee, and its members would want him to watch the proceedings on their behalf. Carden Noad, in no position to complain, stated that he had no objection. No doubt he must have thought this development only made his task of gaining convictions even easier. However, Bhagat Singh, having worked out his strategy, was now intent on pushing it home. He decided to lock horns with Lala Amar Dass. Ever the supreme strategist, he decided that no semblance of validity should be ascribed to this trial. Let it remain as a trial where the accused were prosecuted on capital charges without any legal advice or representation before they were put to death. It was he who insisted that Lala Amar Dass could not sit in court when his own legal advisers were not allowed to be present. The defence committee, he explained, was a third party. Sachindra Nath Sanyal, another of the accused, required the court to be consistent. Faced with this, the magistrate asked Lala Amar Dass whether he had withdrawn representation. He answered that he had not; it was only the accused who had withdrawn their instructions. He was still himself desirous of remaining. He should not be prevented from sitting in the courtroom to watch the proceedings. The magistrate breathed a sigh of relief.

The magistrate duly ruled that Lala Amar Dass could sit in court as he desired. Sanyal, however, would have none of it. Rising with alacrity, he immediately objected. He pointedly asked how there could be rhyme or reason in this when Lala Duni Chand, who wished to do the same on behalf of Bhagat Singh, had not been allowed to sit in court. The absurdity of this must have been plain to the magistrate. Bhagat Singh also was not one to let this pass. He joined in, losing no time in telling the magistrate that the proceedings were becoming a farce. The rulings of the magistrate did not make any sense. The magistrate recognized the glaring anomaly between the two rulings, so he now engaged in a *volte face*. He decided that Lala Duni Chand would also have to go away. An emboldened Bhagat Singh asked him if he would care to read out his order. The embattled magistrate told him to sit down and not fight with him. At this stage, and with deadly effect, Prem Dutt raised loud cries of uproarious laughter when he declared that the magistrate himself had no authority because he too, like all of them, was under the jurisdiction of the jail authorities. Bhagat Singh demanded that the court supply the accused with both its orders and that, moreover, 'let the High Court know of the absurd attitude of this court. This is justice.'

A consultation amongst the accused then took place. The upshot was that Bhagat Singh rose to inform the court that, on behalf of all the accused, he was instructed that they all be sent back to jail and that the proceedings be carried on in their absence. He told the magistrate, 'Let us sit in peace in jail and let the proceedings also go on here in peace.' Lala Amar Dass, still present, also highlighted the futility of their being present in court any longer. 'We are spectators,' he rebuked the magistrate, 'and are watching the proceedings.' In such unedifying circumstances, Bhagat Singh wanted to know what order the court would make. The magistrate replied that the request was unreasonable, which was obviously untrue given how erratic and unprincipled his orders and rulings had been so far. Bhagat Singh said that if that is what the magistrate thought of his request, they would all refuse to come to court from tomorrow. Bejoy Kumar Sinha now also decided to complain to the magistrate that the proceedings in his court had been most unfair because they had been deprived of all the facilities normally accorded to undertrials in similar cases. In his words, 'Everything has been unprecedented in this court. If the court is bent upon not giving us any facilities, then we have no other course left than refuse to take part in the proceedings of the case.' With irrefutable moral force he asserted, 'These facilities are our right and we demand our right. We are helpless for today but from tomorrow we will not come to the court.' The reference to their being 'helpless' based on the denial of 'any facilities', 'unprecedented in this court', starkly demonstrates how the accused were deliberately forced into a situation which made their continued participation in their trial well-nigh impossible.

Having made their protest, Bhagat Singh then asked the magistrate if he planned to allow prosecution counsel to proceed with the examination-in-chief of the 'approver' Phonindra Nath Ghosh, who had been standing in the witness box for a considerable period of time. If he expected the magistrate to show disinclination because of the accused's complaints about the lack of fairness, however, he was mistaken. The trial would continue, the magistrate said. The evidence of the 'approver' would be heard as planned. It was too much for Bhagat Singh. He forthwith informed the magistrate, 'We do not want to waste our time in watching such farcical shows.' This was hardly surprising because here were a group of young men being tried collectively under the full control, not of the court, but of the police and jail authorities. They had been beaten, manacled in court and made to watch 'approvers' giving evidence from a witness box deliberately positioned close to the prosecution counsel bench so as to enable witness tampering and intimidation. They were themselves prevented from giving a statement. They were denied standard legal facilities of legal representation. Finally, their lawyers were banished from the courtroom. All legal assistance to them was either expunged from the outset, annulled or rescinded. Despite all this, the magistrate's stock response was once again to ask the assistant jailer to whisk the accused away to jail, and to adjourn the proceedings. This was not only inept. It was designed to be demonstrably injurious to the interests of the accused in their pursuit of a fair trial which was their birthright.

And so it was hardly surprising when, on 29 January 1930, the accused announced in court that they would not be returning. Indeed, they gave notice in writing to the government that they had no choice but to resume the hunger strike from which they had now desisted for some six months. They referred to their telegram of 20 January 1930 by which they had decided to suspend their hunger strike 'on the assurance that the India Government was considering the Provincial Jail Committee's Reports' whereby the undertaking given by the Punjab Jail Enquiry Committee itself was 'that the question of the treatment of the political prisoners was going to be finally settled to our satisfaction within a very short period'. After the death of Jatindra Nath Dass, 'the matter was taken up in the Legislative Assembly and the same assurance was given publicly by Sir James Crerar'. The hunger strikers had been given to understand that 'there had been a change of heart and the question of the treatment of the political prisoners was receiving the utmost sympathy of the Government'. The result was that 'such political prisoners who were still on hunger-strike in Jails of the different parts of the country then suspended their hunger-strike on the request being made to this effect'. Since then, although 'all the local governments have submitted their reports' and 'a meeting of the I.G. Prisons of different provinces has been held at Lucknow', as well as the fact that the 'deliberations of the All-India Jail Officials' Conference have been concluded at Delhi', nevertheless 'the Government of India has not carried into effect any final recommendations'. With this damning indictment of the government's deliberate intention to stonewall and kick into the long grass any question about the treatment of political prisoners, the hunger strikers called time on the government:

By such dilatory attitude of the Government we no less than the general public have begun to fear that perhaps the question has been shelved. Our apprehension has been strengthened by the vindictive treatment meted out to the hunger-strikers and other political prisoners during the last four months. It is very difficult for us to know the details of the hardships and sufferings to which the political prisoners are being subjected.

It is clear that the hunger strikers feared they had desisted for nothing – that they had been led up the garden path. It looked as if the government in fact had no plans to accede to any of their requests. After all, it is a well-known government ploy to set up an inquiry or appoint a commission, giving the impression to the public that they are serious about acting on its recommendations, and then take no action afterwards while hoping that public anger has meanwhile melted away. On this occasion, such a ploy did not fool those who had been on hunger strike. On the contrary, they were all too aware of the 'vindictive treatment' that hunger strikers 'and other prisoners' continued to be subjected to over 'the last four months'. In fact, the same communication to the government had gone on to say that 'the little information that has trickled out of the four walls of the Jails is sufficient to furnish us with glaring instances'.

The hunger strikers, and indeed the public at large, would not have been oblivious to the way the proceedings had been conducted by the magistrate in the Sessions Court over the last six months, from 10 July 1929 when Rai Sahib Pandit Sri Kishen took over from F. B. Pool. After all, the events were being vividly reported in *The Tribune* and other media outlets. Today we are familiar with Military Commissions of the type that have taken place with the Guantanamo detainees or those at Bagram Base in Afghanistan, of which Bhagat Singh's trial was a forerunner. However, one hundred years ago there was considerable resistance to being treated in this way, especially in one's own country. For this reason, the communication to the government ended with a forlorn hope:

> We still hope that the Government will carry into effect, without further delay, its promise made to us and to the public, so that there may not be another occasion for resuming the hunger-strike. Unless and until we find a definite move on the part of the Government to redeem its promise, in the course of the next 7 days, we shall be forced to resume [*sic*] hunger strike.[10]

With no positive response from the government, the hunger strike was resumed on 4 February 1930. Less than a week later, Bhagat Singh and B. K. Dutt refused to attend court. They explained their reasons in a letter written to the magistrate on 9 February 1930. They pointed out how the majority of the accused came from distant outlying provinces of India, so that even though they were all middle-class people, it was difficult for their relatives to come and help them in their defence. Their repeated requests fell on deaf ears. For example, B. K. Dutt came from the state of

Bengal, a thousand miles away. Kamwal Nath Tiwari's home was only a little closer, in Bihar. Both of them wanted to interview their friends. However, rather than decide the matter for itself as a matter of natural justice, the court bizarrely forwarded all the applications to the jail authorities, who casually rejected them. The hearing of any 'application' is a matter for the court. The practical steps taken thereafter to secure an interview are a matter for the court. It is the court that must give clear directions on what steps should be taken. The decision whether or not to afford interviews cannot be arrogated by the court to the jail authorities. This much is fundamental to any procedure designed to deal with the fair hearing of applications in a judicious manner. The accused found themselves in an invidious position. As they cavilled,

> The underrepresented accused could not afford to engage whole-time counsel to represent them throughout the lengthy trial. They wanted legal advice on certain points during the trial. And, at a certain stage they wanted their legal adviser to watch the proceedings personally *to be in a better position to form his own opinion*. But he was refused even a seat in the body of the court. Counsel are permitted to attend the courts to watch the interests of their clients – who are not present nor even represented by them. *What are the 'special circumstances of this case' that led the Magistrate to adopt such an attitude towards a barrister,* thus discouraging any counsel who might be invited to attend the court to assist the accused?

Finally, as undertrials who had not yet been convicted, the accused were entitled to a supply of newspapers. The refusal of the authorities to accede to this perfectly reasonable request was another of their grievances. They argued that the only justifiable restriction on their access to reading materials was that which was necessary for their safe custody. As they could not be released on bail, they should not be subjected to unnecessary hardships amounting to punishment. Any sufficiently literate undertrial was entitled to at least one standard daily newspaper. Those who could not read English were entitled to a 'vernacular paper'. When a request for a paper in their native language was ignored, the undertrials decided that every day they would reject the English newspaper provided, *The Tribune*, as a protest. In this way, they argued that 'as soon as our grievances will be removed, we will ourselves quite willingly attend the court'.[11]

They need not have held their breath. On 19 February 1930, the government issued a press communiqué on the classification of convicted prisoners and undertrials under the new Jail Rules. It concluded that 'the problems under examination have been found to be difficult and complex and have led to the expression of widely divergent opinions' and that 'the Government of India have endeavoured to give due weight to these'. It suggested that 'convicted prisoners will be divided into three divisions or classes, A, B and C'. Of these, class A represented the most favoured prisoners. What determined the status of this prisoner was, *inter alia*, not only that they 'are non-habitual prisoners of good character' but have 'social status, education and habit of life' and 'have been accustomed to a superior mode of living'. In addition, they of course had to be free of the commission of 'seditious offences' and 'offences relating to possession of explosives, firearms and other dangerous weapons'.[12] The Jail Rules clearly discriminated on the basis of whether or not prisoners were Anglicized or Europeanized. That in itself invited racial bias on the part of the decision maker.

The next favoured category were those prisoners who fell in Class B and these were simply people who 'by social status, education or habit of life have been accustomed to a superior mode of living', and this being so, it was the case that 'Habitual prisoners will not be excluded automatically' although 'the classifying authority will be allowed discretion...' Class C, by contrast, were the most unfortunate and ill-fated. They were not defined as such. One may only assume that this was the case because the new Jail Rules simply ordained that 'Class 'C' will consist of prisoners who are not classified in classes 'A' and 'B'.' On this basis the Jail Rules postulated that 'it should be clearly understood that all prisoners within the 'A' class are eligible for the privileges of that class.' It was emphatically stated that 'no class of prisoner' will be given 'additional privileges on grounds of race.' Whether this was just an aspirational aim is anyone's guess in the febrile atmosphere of the early 1930s.

Nevertheless, it was made clear that 'all privileges now given to special class prisoners will be continued to "A" class prisoners, such as separate accommodation, necessary articles of furniture, reasonable facilities for association and exercises, and suitable sanitary and bathing arrangements'. In addition, 'the diet of classes "A" and "B" will be superior to the ordinary prison diet given to prisoners in class "C"'. Furthermore, 'the existing rules regarding privileges of special class prisoners to wear their own clothing will continue'. In addition to separate accommodation, the government wished 'to emphasise the necessity of a special staff to deal with "A" and "B" class prisoners...' Significantly, it was also recognized 'subject to safeguards' that the government should provide 'for the intellectual requirements of the educated and literate prisoners'.

In the case currently running before Rai Sahib Pandit Sri Kishen, of course, the majority of the under-trial prisoners were literate and educated, being largely from middle-class families. The new Jail Rules provided also that 'literate prisoners may be allowed to read books and magazines from outside subject to the approval of the Jail Superintendent'. They went on to direct that 'newspapers will be allowed to "A" class prisoners' as well as to 'special class prisoners'. In addition, '"A" class prisoners will be allowed to write and receive one letter and have one interview a fortnight, instead of once a month at present.' Broadly the same applied to Class 'C' prisoners. Towards the end, the Jail Rules dealt with the position of 'Under-Trial Prisoners'. Here also there was recognition that 'some differentiation of treatment in the case of under-trial prisoners who, by social status, education or habit of life, have been accustomed to a superior mode of living' will require additional privileges.

However, there were to be 'two classes of under-trial prisoners based on the previous standard of living only'. As for how this would be decided, 'the classifying authority will be the trying court, subject to the approval of the District Magistrate'. Thereafter,

> The diet provided for 'A' and 'B' class convicted prisoners will be given to the former and the diet of 'C' class prisoners to the latter. Under-Trial prisoners in either class, will be allowed to supplement this diet by private purchase through the Jail authorities. Under the existing rules they are allowed to wear their own clothing…
>
> The Government of India are of opinion that the interpretation of the existing rules in a liberal spirit, together with the modifications now proposed and the provision of better cellular accommodation, will effect improvements in the directions which enquiry has indicated as desirable. They, therefore, hope that Local Governments will make every effort to improve the existing accommodation and will at once utilize and adapt their existing resources to the best possible advantage…[13]

In the meantime, for a whole month, from 8 February to 8 March 1930, the case stood adjourned as the accused were on hunger strike. After the trial recommenced, the proceedings ran relatively free of difficulty for the next two months, from 8 March 1930 right up to 3 May 1930. Yet, on 1 May 1930, Governor-General Irwin promulgated an ordinance to extricate the case from the Magistrates' Court and have it installed in a Special Tribunal. This was specifically created to try these troublesome young revolutionaries before what was effectively a three-member national security tribunal. It had no right of appeal and even less regard for the rule of law and procedural niceties. Ajoy Ghosh was one of the accused who was acquitted there in a trial of the twenty-four Lahore Conspirators. More than a decade later, he gave an account in a book, now out of print, that '[a]fter nine months of trial before the magistrate and long before even a small number of prosecution witnesses had been examined, the proceedings were abruptly ended .... "in view of the emergency" that had arisen threatening "peace and tranquillity"'.[14] So 3 May 1930 was to be the last day of hearings before the forlorn Rai Sahib Pandit Sri Kishen. As the case slipped out of his fingers, Bhagat Singh rose to pay tribute to the magistrate, thanking him on behalf of all of the accused, and assuring him of the fact that they bore him no ill will, despite the fact that they had occasionally clashed. In fact, if there was a flaw in his handling of the trial, Bhagat Singh told him, it was that he had been too polite and lenient – a flaw of which the prosecution took repeated advantage!

4

Inquisition by Edict

Ham ko miTā sake ye zamāne meñ dam nahīñ;
Ham se zamāna Khud hai zamāne se ham nahīñ

That this world should remove all of trace of me is no longer feasible;
For I have become part of this world, the world is not apart from me

Jigar Moradabadi

When the British passed the Government of India Act 1919, their alleged purpose was to enhance the involvement of Indians in the governing of their country. To this end, the government adopted by legislation the measures advocated by Edwin Montagu, Secretary of State of India, and Lord Chelmsford, Viceroy of India, in what were known as the Montagu–Chelmsford Reforms. The Act, however, was a temporary measure. It would last for only ten years. It soon became clear to Indians that in truth it was a form of benevolent despotism because it was described as 'a step in the progressive realisation of responsible government in India *as an integral part of empire*', and was never meant to lead to outright Indian independence. Those who wanted full freedom from foreign rule would find no solace in it. Moreover, after ten years of 'progressive realisation', the 1919 Act would be reviewed by the Simon Commission. This was the same Simon Commission which provoked widespread protests in Lahore where Lala Lajpat Rai was mercilessly *lathi*-charged on 30 October 1928 and later died. It was his death that Bhagat Singh and his colleagues set out to avenge in the cack-handed murder of the unfortunate John Saunders, who was so grievously mistaken for the British police superintendent.

The entire edifice of the 1919 Act was therefore patronising to say the least. Annie Besant alluded to it as 'unworthy of England to offer and India to accept' and the Indian National Congress rejected it outright. The Act was complex and far-reaching. It had forty-seven sections and was steeped in legalese. Its most important change was the introduction of diarchy,[1] or 'double government', between a 'governor' and the 'provincial legislature', consisting of eleven provinces, in what was meant to be a federal structure for India. There was to be a 'transferred list' of competences, in areas of agriculture, local government, health and education, which would be allocated to each province. Their government of ministers would be answerable to the Provincial Council. There would also be a 'reserved list' of competences, in areas of defence, military and foreign affairs, and communications, which would remain in the hands of the Viceroy. The Act of 1919 was described by Ambedkar in 1923 as the 'British Constitution of India' in a lecture that he gave to his students. Recent commentary reveals just how deceitful the 1919 Act was. Historian Walter Reid[2] has argued that British perfidy lay in the fact that it had no intention of ever giving up India.[3] Anyone, like Bhagat Singh, who was determined to wrest control of Indian territory from a foreign yoke was bound to be crushed against such a background. And, thus it came to be.

The British government in India did not always run its affairs out of the capital cities. Both Calcutta (capital of British India from 1772 to 1911) and Delhi (where the capital was moved in order to mollify the feelings of Indian nationalists) were too hot for much of the year. British India, therefore, also had an unofficial Indian capital. Remarkably, more work was done out of this obscure and secluded spot than anywhere else. This was Simla (pronounced as 'Shimla' by the Indians). If one place epitomized the romance of India it was the decadent and extravagant Simla, which was to India what 'Happy Valley' was to Kenya, where from the 1920s to the 1940s a group of British and Anglo-Irish aristocrats and adventurers settled into a life of endless pleasure and hedonism. Simla became popular at first because of the need among the British administrative types to escape the baking-hot weather of the valleys below. The temperature in the North Indian River Plain, which extended from Punjab to Assam, would rise in the summer months to 43 degrees. For this reason, the Raj's entire administration would decamp to a town the size of Guildford, the 'summer capital of India'. Here, at the foothills of the highest mountain range in the world, the average temperature was an agreeable 28 degrees. Roughly from April to October every year, this became the residence of the Viceroy and the Commander-in-Chief, the head of the Indian Army, and many government departments. Lots of British soldiers, merchants and civil servants followed suit. At 7,000 feet above sea level, and on a ridge near the Sutlej, the residents of Simla were in sight of the Himalayas. The centre comprised the palatial Viceroy's Lodge, the Christ Church, the Jahjoo Temple, the Ridge and the Mall. British men who had to remain behind on the plains sent their wives and daughters to the cool comfort of Simla.

By the 1830s, the town had a theatre and art exhibitions. The pleasant climate and cultural attractions meant that the population quickly grew. In 1876 the regional government of the Punjab also moved its summer capital from Muree to Simla. The number of bungalows increased. A big bazaar followed. Upper-class families had residential schools built for their children. Soon Simla was famous as the hill station known for brash balls, rowdy parties and screaming festivities. It smacked of Surrey and Switzerland put together. The freelance writer and popular historian Charles Allen, whose parents were born in India, famously said that if British India had an 'upper crust'[4] it was in Simla, which was expensive and had limited accommodation. Simla became a byword for vice, profligacy, adultery and debauchery. It was not just the presence of a disproportionately large number of women. Scores of bachelors and unattached men also thronged the promenade as they absconded from the hot weather of the plains. In Rudyard Kipling's memorable words, it had an unenviable reputation for 'frivolity, gossip and intrigue'.

In late spring, bullock carts would move the entire apparatus of the British Raj from the Indo-Gangetic plains to Simla. Later, a narrow-gauge rail of 2½ feet was added. It would carry the complete paraphernalia of administration, from typewriters to filing cabinets, from embossed imperial paper to rubber stamps and inkpads, in a long and arduous journey up into the hills. From the remote regal trappings of Viceroy's Lodge, the British government managed to rule a vast expanse of millions of different peoples across the Empire. On any view, so astonishing was this feat that it is said that even Adolf Hitler was enthralled and spellbound at how the British managed to govern in this way a territory of tens of thousands of miles, including not just present-day India, Pakistan, Bangladesh, Sri Lanka and Myanmar, but also, even more strikingly, the United Arab Emirates, Yemen and Singapore – all by deploying just a few thousand British soldiers. It was, as is abundantly clear, not for want of ruthless efficiency and a steely, brutal determination to keep control.

It was from here that the Viceroy of India, Lord Irwin, announced that the committal proceedings in the Magistrates' Court, presided over by Rai Sahib Pandit Sri Kishen, which he had been conducting so assiduously since 10 July 1929 for a period of almost ten months, were to be suddenly halted. On 1 May 1930, his savage pen signed off the Lahore Ordinance No. III of 1930 on behalf of both the Viceroy and the Governor-General. At 6 foot 5 inches tall, Irwin was a towering man. His days at Eton had been unhappy, as he disliked games and classics. At Christ Church, Oxford, however, he had excelled, gaining a First in Modern History. With an eye for detail, his route to the position of Governor-General had seen him through various posts, including Under-Secretary for the Colonies. He remains the Governor-General most Indians in living memory are familiar with as he participated in the heady discussions with Gandhi and Jinnah over Partition. Surprisingly, he was known to be more pro-Indian than many Governors-General before him. Having said that, he was not averse to signing the death warrants of troublesome Indians whom he wished to be shot of. In many respects, therefore, he was the ideal man to deal with Bhagat Singh.

Irwin wanted the two dozen accused to be tried by a Special Tribunal, so he created such a tribunal by executive edict to undertake what can only be described as an 'inquisition' into the activities of Bhagat Singh and twenty-three of his fellow accused. Committal proceedings are a form of preliminary hearings. There is a serious charge laid. It is heard by the magistrate, and the decision is then made as to how it should be dealt with. If the trial takes place in the Sessions Court, there is a right of appeal against sentence to the High Court. The procedure is properly regulated, rules of evidence are rigorously observed, and decisions are made by regular judges. Under Lord Irwin's Lahore Ordinance No. III of 1930, the Special Tribunal would consist of three judges appointed by the Chief Justice of the High Court and removable by him 'if, for any reason, any member of the Tribunal is unable to discharge his duties', whereupon 'the Chief Justice shall appoint another judge', without defining what was meant by being 'unable to discharge his duties'. There would be no right of appeal to the High Court in Lahore against a death sentence. Such a right was available to common criminals in Sessions Courts; such criminals also had in the Sessions Court the right to a trial by jury. This was well established as the right of every common criminal. Indeed, the right to trial by jury was not abolished in India until the mid-1950s. But neither the right to a trial before a jury of peers nor the right to appeal against conviction was afforded to those under Lord Irwin's Special Tribunal. This was a case of wide-ranging conspiracy against the Crown. Yet, in one fell swoop, the safeguards of evidence and procedure were gone, and with them the hallowed principles of the independence of judges and the entire pretence of the rule of law being maintained. Ajoy Ghosh, one of those who was eventually acquitted, explained many years later how '[t]here need be no lawyers, no defence witnesses, no accused in the court. Any sentence, including the sentence of death, could be passed by the tribunal ... there was no right of appeal.'[5]

Bhagat Singh, however, was unfazed by this prospect. In the face of such mounting adversity, he refused to be browbeaten. His plucky and fearless attitude, his exemplary courage, was evident just two days later, on 3 May 1930, during his last appearance before the special magistrate. Here he told Rai Sahib Pandit Sri Kishen that Governor-General Irwin's appointment, by executive edict, of a Special Tribunal to try him and his comrades, outside the framework of the regular courts of law and unbound by any stipulated rules of evidence and procedure, was a marked victory for the accused! They had always wanted the government to expose its own inept shenanigans, holding sham trials conducted spuriously, and now they had damned themselves in precisely the manner in which Bhagat Singh and his comrades wanted them to. He could not contain his relish. The rule of law in colonial coercive trials could not be maintained, and it was futile to pretend that it could be. Seasoned observers are today aware that it was not just in India but throughout the Empire, in places as far afield as Kenya, that the same charades were being enacted in the name of law and civilization.

However, Bhagat Singh could not have been remotely prepared for what he would face. Lord Irwin's Ordinance had not been subject to ratification by the Central Legislative Assembly or the Council of State. The reason was simple: it was not an Act of the Indian legislature. An Ordinance is legislation by edict, passed by a single man, the Governor-General, as an act of the executive. It is precisely because of this peculiarity that the imperial parliament in London had made the promulgation of an Ordinance subject to two specific legal restraints. The first was that it had a time limit. Its validity could not extend beyond a period of six months. This meant that if the Governor-General wished to legislate, not through the legislature but by an executive act, he had to be sure that his particular purpose could be achieved within six months. After that, the Ordinance would fall into abeyance. The second restraint was that the Ordinance applied only 'in cases of emergency' where the 'peace and good government of British India or any part thereof' was at stake. If both conditions were not satisfied, the Governor-General could not legislate through an Ordinance. He had to act in the normal way, through established parliamentary procedures, to procure such legislation as was necessary. In fact, even where an 'emergency' existed and 'peace and good government' were needed, it was not inevitable that the Governor-General would make an Ordinance. He had to consider the situation. After that, he 'may' do so. He was under no compulsion. These conditions were set out in Section 72 of the Government of India Act 1919.

Even where an Ordinance was promulgated, it remained open to the British government in London to 'disallow' it on the grounds that the Governor-General had exceeded his authority and acted outside his jurisdiction, in the same way that it could disallow a statute passed by the Indian legislature and assented to by the Governor-General.[6] Significantly, under Section 71, which conferred on 'the local government of any part of British India' the power to propose to the centre 'the draft of any regulation for the peace and good government of the part', there was no reference to 'cases of emergency' being a precondition. Therefore, all that was required under Section 71 was for the Governor-General to assent to the Ordinance, regardless of whether an emergency existed or not.

What all of this meant was that, having escaped the scorching heat of Delhi, the Governor-General had to issue a statement from Simla setting out his reasons for promulgating the Ordinance. His grounds in the preamble declared that 'an emergency has arisen which makes it necessary to provide specially for the trial of the accused in the cases known as the Lahore Conspiracy case' but made no reference to the need to preserve 'peace and good government' in India, even though the Ordinance was purportedly made 'in the exercise of the power conferred by Section 72 of the Government of India Act'. Irwin did issue his reasons: he claimed that the offences were of an 'unusually serious character' because they arose from 'revolutionary activities' and that 'it would be necessary to produce about 600 witnesses'. This was an absurdity which had already been exposed for its humbug by Jinnah in his speech in the Central Legislative Assembly on 12 September 1929. However, Irwin also referred to the 'hunger strike before the commencement of the enquiry' by the magistrate and the adjournments it entailed from 26 July to 24 September 1930. He neglected the fact that this nevertheless still did not amount to an emergency. He went on glibly, pointing out that 'it was then resumed, but there were numerous interruptions owing to defiant and disorderly conduct by some of the accused or demonstrations by members of the public', but which still did not cut it.

This is because the accused were not 'disorderly' and there was no demonstration by members of the public interfering with the committal proceedings before magistrate Rai Sahib Pandit Sri Kishen. Irwin was conjuring a false narrative in order to find support for his ill-conceived Ordinance. Some 230 witnesses had been examined already over the ten months, as he himself recognized, which did not point to evidence of 'numerous interruptions' impeding the work of the magistrate. Yet, he still persisted in the falsehood that the conduct of the accused made it impossible for a regular trial 'to count upon obtaining a conclusion by the normal methods of procedure within any calculable period'. He felt the proceedings should not be allowed 'to drag out to a length which cannot at present be foreseen'. He was determined that the charges should be 'finally adjudicated upon with the least possible delay'. This was dogma, not reality.

A moment's reflection shows that none of these reasons amount to an 'emergency' and none concern the 'regulation of peace and good government in British India'. There was nothing that the Governor-General envisaged in the trial by Ordinance that was not already being done in the proceedings before the magistrate, except that they were subject to regular law before a regular court and under regular procedures. This was despite numerous other irregularities. Now, however, at one stroke of his pen, 'all cases pending in the Court of Rai Sahib Pandit Sri Kishen, Magistrate of the First Class, Lahore, against any or all of the accused named ... shall be tried by the tribunal to be constituted'. [7] The Tribunal would be 'consisting of three persons who at the time of the constitution are Judges'.[8] The evidence before the Tribunal could be marshalled and used in as loose a manner as possible given that 'it shall not be incumbent on the Tribunal to re-call or re-hear any witness who has already given evidence'. In fact, 'it may act on any evidence already recorded by or produced before it'.[9] As for the 'procedure of the Tribunal', once the Special Tribunal was constituted with the result that 'the jurisdiction of the aforesaid Magistrate shall cease',[10] this newly constituted Special Tribunal 'shall, subject to the provisions of the Ordinance, follow the procedure prescribed in Chapter XXI of the Code for the trial of warrant cases by Magistrates'.[11] This unctuously soothing guarantee of procedure, however, was negated by what was said in the next provision, which made it clear what was meant by 'subject to the provisions of the Ordinance':

> for the purpose of applying the said provisions, the proceedings already taken before the aforesaid Magistrate shall be deemed to be proceedings under Chapter XVIII of the Code whereunder the accused persons have been committed to the Tribunal for trial, and the Tribunal shall be deemed to be a Court of Session to whom the accused persons have been duly committed by the aforesaid Magistrate.[12]

So the Special Tribunal was to be a Court of Session, except that it wasn't, and it was now for the 'local government' to 'appoint a person to be prosecutor for the conduct of the prosecution of the said cases'.[13] As for the 'powers of the Tribunal', the position was that '[t]he Tribunal may pass upon any person convicted by it any sentence authorized by law for the punishment of the offence authorized by law' and that 'no order of confirmation shall be necessary in respect of any sentence passed by it'.[14]

But the most controversial provision was that which stipulated the 'special powers of the Tribunal', under which it was decreed:

> the Tribunal shall have powers to take such measures as it may think necessary to secure the orderly conduct of the trial; and *where any accused by his voluntary act has rendered himself incapable of appearing before the Tribunal*, or resists his production before it, or behaves before it in a persistently disorderly manner, or in any way wilfully conducts himself to the serious prejudice of the trial, *the Tribunal may, at any stage of the trial, dispense with the attendance of such accused* for such period as it may think fit and proceed with the trial in his absence.[15]

Where an accused is not present at his trial, however, then the 'dispensing with the attendance of an accused shall not affect his right of being represented by a pleader at any stage of the trial'.[16] Finally, it was declared that 'the judgment of the Tribunal shall be final and conclusive' and that 'there shall be no appeal from any order or sentence of the Court, and the High Court shall not have authority to revise any such order to sentence' and that this was notwithstanding there being 'anything having the force of law'.[17]

In the court of the Special Tribunal,
Lahore Conspiracy Case
Lahore

Most respectfully sheweth:—

1. That the petitioner is an unrepresented accused in this case.

2. That he is not in a position to engage a whole time counsel in this lengthy trial.

3. That he does not want to accept any help from the government.

4. That he wishes to fight his own case with such legal aid as he can afford.

5. That it is prayed that an order be passed to accommodate his legal adviser in the body of the court so that he may be able to get necessary help whenever desired.

Bhagat Singh
Petitioner

7/5/30

Bhagat Singh states that the legal adviser is required to watch the proceedings & to give advise a line of cross examination. He will not cross examine nor address the court. Wants to engage Duni Chand at present.

Mr. Nott O.P. says he has no objection provided seating accommodation is [...]

By the second day of the hearing before the Special Tribunal, Bhagat Singh had made it clear that he did not wish to accept any help from the government. He would fight his own case and take assistance from his 'legal adviser' as and when he saw fit.

What was even more galling than these *avant-garde* provisions of unusual harshness and eccentricity was Governor-General Irwin's 'statement' accompanying the Ordinance. As a matter of law, it had to justify the promulgation of the Ordinance. This justification was contained in five numbered paragraphs. None evinced any basis for declaring an 'emergency' or a need to act for the 'peace and good government' of British India. In the first paragraph, Irwin began by explaining how 'on the 11th July 1929 the enquiry in the proceedings known as the Lahore Conspiracy Case commenced before a Magistrate'. It is then explained that:

1... The offence alleged against the accused are both in their own nature and in their relation to the public security of unusually serious character. They include the murder of Mr Saunders, Assistant Superintendent of Police, and head Constable Chanan Singh in Lahore, on the 17th December 1928, the establishment of bomb factories at Lahore and Saharanpur, the conspiracy leading to the throwing of two bombs in the Legislative Assembly on the 8th April 1929, and various other revolutionary activities. For the purpose of establishing these charges which were concerned with many different places and with events occurring over a considerable period of time, the prosecution considered it would be necessary to produce 600 witnesses.

If one pauses to consider the reasons given in the first paragraph of the 'statement' by Governor-General Irwin, it is clear that nothing here justifies the Ordinance. No law is set out. No break specified. If the activities of the accused occurred in 'many different places' and over 'a considerable period of time', such that some '600 witnesses' had to be called, this still did not make out a case of 'public security of unusually serious character' when it is remembered that Rai Sahib Pandit Sri Kishen had already managed to hear from over a third of them. Had he been allowed to continue, with a right of appeal from his decision to the High Court, he would have doubtless heard the remaining number as well.

The second paragraph of the 'statement' is altogether less convincing:

2. Two of the accused had resorted to hunger strike before the commencement of the enquiry. A number of others followed the same course shortly afterwards with the result that by the 26th July 1929, the case had to be adjourned owing to some of the accused being unfit to attend the Court. The case had to be successively adjourned on the

same ground until the 24th September. It was then resumed, but there were numerous interruptions owing to defiant and disorderly conduct by some of the accused or demonstrations by members of the public. On February 4th, 1930, most of the accused again went on hunger strike, and the case was on this account adjourned from the 8th February till the 8th March.

The passage above is sinister because it clearly appears to suggest Governor-General Irwin's Ordinance was in fact the ultimate trick used by the government to deal with the 'defiant and disorderly' hunger strikers, whom it wished to quell after it had failed to pass the Hunger Strike Bill in Parliament. Jinnah's powerful denunciation of this bill on 12 September 1929, with the stirring words that 'the man who goes on a hunger-strike has a soul', had quashed the bill for good. It left all Members of the House in awe at his eloquence and rendered the passing of this insidious piece of legislation almost impossible. Yet, the passive resistance of a hunger strike, for those who had the 'soul' to embark on it (as Jinnah would have put it), was totally Gandhian in its endeavour. It caused no violence. It attacked no one. It inflicted a severe maltreatment of body and soul only upon oneself. The Governor-General's recognition that 'numerous interruptions' continued to take place because of the determined will of the hunger strikers to carry on refusing to take food had nothing whatsoever to do with the orderly running of the trial itself.

In embarking upon a hunger strike, the accused were making political demands concerning the manner of treatment and conduct of the trials, in which they saw themselves as political prisoners. They were being given assurances that these demands were being looked into and would be settled according to their 'satisfaction'. Once that happened, they would withdraw from the hunger strike. When the assurances were not made good, they determined to return to their ordeal. It was entirely disingenuous for Irwin to lay the adjournment of the trial, for a whole month from February to March 1930, at the door of the hunger strikers. Bhagat Singh in fact wrote to Irwin soon after the Ordinance was promulgated in precisely these terms. What Irwin's Ordinance was designed to do, however, was to ensure that the trial of the conspiracy cases would continue even if the accused were absent from the courtroom on account of their hunger strike, because of the 'special powers of the Tribunal' under Section 9(1). This is why the court proceedings before Rai Sahib Pandit Sri Kishen had to be aborted. It had nothing to do with a 'case of emergency' arising now.

The third paragraph of the 'statement' by Governor-General Irwin is even more devoid of a reasoned basis for the existence of a 'case of emergency' and the need to act for reasons of 'peace and good government'. All it amounted to was a complaint from the Governor-General that the Lahore Conspiracy Trial had taken too long to prosecute. It appears to have escaped Irwin's notice that it was the government's intention to call 600 witnesses, many of whom had been groomed to say what the government wished them to say, that was dragging out proceedings:

> 3. The enquiry has now been in progress for more than 9 months and during that time it has been possible to examine about 230 witnesses, only out of a probable total of 607. The spectacle of these proceedings, obstructed by unprecedented delays, and repeatedly disturbed by disorderly conduct and revolutionary demonstrations, has tended to bring the administration of justice into contempt, and it is impossible to count upon obtaining a conclusion by the normal methods of procedure within calculable period.

The reasons given here are palpably false. A 'contempt of court' is punishable by the court itself. It occurs when a person risks unfairly influencing a court case and gets in the way of a fair trial. This can happen if an accused disobeys a court order, shouts out in court, or refuses to answer the court's questions. Such a person can be imprisoned by the court itself until he or she 'purges' their contempt. It is true that Bhagat Singh and his colleagues shouted slogans of '*Inquilab Zindabad*' in court upon entry. However, these slogans were made before proceedings began and did not delay the trial, and they were in the context of the unfairness of the trial, where they were shackled, beaten in court and even rendered unconscious. But with 230 witnesses of the government already having been heard, it was certainly not the case that 'it is impossible to count upon obtaining a conclusion by the normal methods of procedure within calculable period'. Even if it was, this did not amount to an 'emergency' and it in no way impacted on the 'peace and good government' of the country. The truth of the matter is that the government wished to see a conviction for conspiracy against the King Emperor and a sentence of death passed and carried out as soon as possible, and it had no time for the legal niceties of taking these individuals through committal proceedings and then before the Sessions Court, with the near certainty of an appeal being exercised to the Lahore High Court. Colonial coercive repressiveness prioritized a hasty trial and prompt punishment for the revolutionaries.

The fourth paragraph of the 'statement' can only be described as utterly preposterous:

> 4. After anxious consideration I have come to the conclusion that neither *the ends of justice* nor the *interests of the accused* are served by allowing these proceedings to drag out to a length which cannot at present be forseen. Public policy clearly demands that *the grave charges against the accused should be thoroughly scrutinized and finally adjudicated upon with the least possible delay*, by a tribunal of indubitable impartiality and authority, and that the preliminary proceedings which have already extended over nine months and the end of which is not yet in sight should be terminated. It is also necessary to ensure that obstructions shall not further interrupt the course of justice...

It was not a little risible for the Governor-General to proclaim that 'the ends of justice' and the 'interests of the accused' were being hampered when it was the government's own determination to call 600 witnesses that caused the proceedings to 'drag out to a length'. It was certainly not the case that the end of the proceedings 'cannot at present be forseen'. Even today, with all the facilities of modern trial management, the giving of evidence by an enormous number of witnesses amounting to over 600 would not be completed within a year. The government could hardly argue that it wished to have its evidence called and yet blame the accused for any resultant delay. This is particularly so given that the lawyers on the side of the accused were unable to cross-examine the vast majority of the government witnesses. The Governor-General could not lay this at the door of the accused and then claim that he was acting in the 'interests of the accused'. On any view this was a travesty of justice. Nothing is more revealing of this fact than Governor-General Irwin steering clear of any mention of the legal burden of proof being upon him to show as a matter of law that he was acting 'in cases of emergency' and 'for the peace and good government of British India'. Here he was aborting an existing trial that was in full swing before a magistrate in regular committal proceedings in order to install a Special Tribunal passed in the form of an irregular executive legislative fiat.

It did not take a lawyer to realise how fraudulent the enactment of the Ordinance was. Quite simply, the reasons behind the Ordinance did not stand up to scrutiny. For this reason, within a week the editor of *The Tribune* had little difficulty in declaring,

It would, indeed, be the negation of justice to say that if there is a demonstration by members of the public in connection with the criminal trial, that trial should not be conducted according to the ordinary forms of law ... It has not been alleged that during the last two months there was any interruption in the proceedings or that during the whole of that period the conduct of the accused was not unexceptionable. *It is, however, an open secret that the extraordinarily slow progress of the case during this period was entirely due to the apparent anxiety of the prosecution to produce as few witnesses as possible, because they knew that the ordinance was coming.* During this period, the court seldom sat for the full working hours, and the witnesses were produced and examined in a somewhat leisurely manner. It is no exaggeration to say that evidence which was spread over two months could have been recorded within a fortnight, if the prosecution were at all anxious to expedite the proceedings.[18]

If this is correct, then the use of coercive colonial legalism as a way to provide a veneer of legality to what was, for all intents and purposes, a blatant usurpation of law, is unmistakable. Bhagat Singh himself wasted no time in refuting the hypocrisy and humbug of Governor-General Irwin. In his letter to the office of the Viceroy he wrote,

The entire text of the ordinance for the early disposal of our trial has been read over (to us), whereby a tribunal has been constituted under the jurisdiction of the Punjab High Court. If no reference had been made to the attitude adopted in this case and if we had not been held responsible for that, we would have probably kept our mouths closed. But in the present situation, we consider it necessary to issue a statement.

We have known from the beginning that the government has been deliberately creating misunderstandings about this. After all, it is a war and we very well know that in order to face its enemy, the government would spin a web of misunderstanding as its first stratagem. We have no means of preventing this mean act. But there are certain things in view of which we are forced to say something.

In the ordinance promulgated about the Lahore Conspiracy Case, you have made a mention of our hunger strike and said that two of us had started our hunger strike weeks before the trial investigations started in the Court of the Special Magistrate Pandit Shri Krishna. *Anyone with common sense can understand that the hunger strike had nothing to do with this trial. There were special reasons for starting the hunger strike. When government agreed to solve the problem and appointed the Jail enquiry committee, we called off the hunger strike. We had been given the assurance that the problem would be solved by November. But it was delayed till December.* The month of January also passed, but there was no indication whether the government would really do anything in the matter or not. It appeared to us that the matter had been shelved. Under these circumstances, we again started a hunger strike on 4th February 1930, after giving a full week's notice. It was only after this that the government took some steps to finally settle the matter.

When the government issued a communiqué press in this regard, we called off the hunger strike. We even did not wait to see whether the Government implemented its latest decision or not. Only today, we have realised that the government does not feel shy of taking *recourse to deception even in trivial matters.* In any case, it is not the proper occasion to enter into an argument on this issue, *but we want to emphasise that the hunger strike was not a step against the trial. We did not suffer all the oppression for such a trivial matter.* Jatindra Nath Das did not sacrifice his life for this trivial matter, nor did Rajguru and Sukh Dev endanger their lives for this reason.[19]

Bhagat Singh's protest fell on deaf ears. If Irwin was determined to proceed with the trial at breakneck speed, it was for another reason that was not known to Bhagat Singh. In June 1929, Ramsay MacDonald's Labour government had been returned to power in Britain. Irwin had made a journey to London in the summer of 1929. Returning to India, he made a speech on 31 October 1929 where he alluded to the British government's promise of 'responsible government in India' in 1917: 'I am authorised on behalf of his Majesty's government to state clearly that in their judgment it is implicit in the British Government's declaration of 1917 that the natural issue of India's constitutional progress, as there contemplated, is the attainment of dominion status.' The implication here was that India would acquire the same dominion status as that accorded to Canada and Australia under the 1931 Statute of Westminster, from which India had been expressly excluded, two years after Irwin returned to India from London. The problem was that not everyone on the Indian side was agreed on dominion status anyway. Gandhi was. Jawaharlal Nehru was not, though he supported Gandhi nevertheless. Many wanted full independence from Britain. Subhas Chandra Bose was one of them, and he refused to compromise. He pointed an accusatory finger, trumpeting that 'Jawaharlal has now given up independence at the instance of the Mahatma'.[20]

Those on the left of the Congress were particularly unhappy with dominion status. They had spent years demanding nothing short of complete independence. The Viceroy was aware of this, and he knew that if he set out to foist dominion status on India it would be staunchly resisted by powerful voices on the Congress's left. Irwin had to find a way of breaking the resolve of those who opposed dominion status. A number of them had been put to trial alongside common criminals. This had been done first with the Meerut Conspiracy Case initiated in March 1929, when the British government convicted thirty-three trade union leaders under a false lawsuit, and it was now being done in the Lahore Conspiracy Case. However, the hunger strikers were raising new political demands and the government's attempt at passing the Hunger Strike Bill to deal with them had failed disastrously. The agitators remained unbowed and unbroken. In these circumstances, the Lahore Ordinance No. III of 1930 was an executive attempt at enacting the Hunger Strike Bill. This would be promulgated over the heads of the Central Assembly as this body was unlikely to ever accept it. This was particularly so given that the Bhagat Singh's rising popularity made its passage by specific executive edict even more important.

The Lahore Conspiracy Ordinance No. III of 1930 served the government's interests exactly as it wished. The Chief Justice of the Lahore High Court would appoint a tribunal. This would consist of three High Court judges for the trial of 'all cases pending in the court of Rai Saheb Pandit Sri Kishan'. All twenty-four accused were identified in the schedule to the Ordinance. The judgment of the Tribunal would be 'final and conclusive'. There would be no appeal from any order or sentence given by the Tribunal to the High Court. The High Court had a jurisdiction to issue a writ of habeas corpus. This was an ancient jurisdiction. In England it went back to 1679. Under habeas corpus law, unless lawful grounds are shown for a person's detention, a writ requiring a person under arrest to be brought before a judge or into court would be issued to secure that person's release. Now, at a stroke, that jurisdiction was gone. As if this was not remarkable enough, in the normal course of events any death sentence handed down by a Sessions Court judge was subject to confirmation by the High Court. Not so here. This is exactly what Irwin wanted. The rule of law was torn asunder. What were previously known to be proceedings before the Special Magistrate were now reconstituted as committal proceedings that had already taken place, so that the accused were now to be committed to the Tribunal for trial, instead of the Sessions Court, which would have been the case in any normal circumstances.

The very act of transferring, by way of an Ordinance, proceedings which had already been started before the magistrate and were destined to move onwards to the Sessions Court smacked of retroactive legislation. It is one of the salient hallmarks of the rule of law that a person shall not be subject to a law which was not a law at the time when his offence was allegedly committed.[21] The Governor-General had no problem in absurdly declaring in the Ordinance that 'the Tribunal shall be deemed to be a court of session' even though the Tribunal was not to follow the procedure set down in the Criminal Procedure Code 1898 for trials taking place in the Sessions Court. In any event, the accused were entitled to a trial in the Sessions Court. It is difficult to see how there can be a 'deeming provision' reconstituting a Sessions Court as an executive-made 'tribunal' if what the accused are constitutionally entitled to is a trial by a magistrate in the Sessions Court rather than by three High Court judges in a 'tribunal' created for a period of only six months. Even within its own terms there was a glaring anomaly here. If the Tribunal was 'deemed' to be a 'court of session', one would have expected it to have the procedure of a 'court of session', and this was manifestly not the case.

Ironically, if all Irwin wanted was to hasten the trial of the accused, it is difficult to see why the Sessions Court could not have done so just as well. Already by April 1930, the evidence of four out of the seven approvers had been recorded by Rai Sahib Pandit Sri Kishen. There was therefore enough evidence to warrant a committal. Given that there was no such application made, one can only infer from this that the Governor-General wished to see a hand-picked tribunal of three High Court judges, chosen by the Chief Justice of Lahore, Sir Shadi Lal, to zip through the case and have Bhagat Singh put to death as quickly as possible. This is clear from how the trial by tribunal was subsequently conducted because on 26 August 1930, the prosecutor astonishingly closed the case after 457 of its own witnesses had been examined, but with scant regard to the right of defence counsel to cross-examine these witnesses. This was done abruptly, so as to allow the ordinance to expire on 31 October 1930, after which the Special Tribunal could only give its judgment. Although there existed power in the High Court itself to have the case transferred to it to be tried, no application was made to this effect, and one may wonder exactly why.

Under Section 526(1) of the Criminal Procedure Code 1898, 'where it is made to appear to the High Court division' that it is the case '(a) that a fair and impartial inquiry or trial cannot be had in any Criminal Court subordinate thereto' or that it is the case '(b) that some question of law of unusual difficulty is likely to arise', or that more interestingly it seems '(e) that such an order is expedient for the ends of justice … it may order' in those circumstances '(iii) that any particular case or appeal be transferred to and tried before itself', and in particular '(iv) that an accused person be sent for trial to itself or to a court of session'. Cumulatively, therefore, under Section 526(1)(e) sub-paragraphs iii–iv,[22] it was possible for the High Court in Lahore to deal with every possible scenario presently before the court of Rai Sahib Pandit Sri Kishen. It was possible in order to ensure that the 'ends of justice' were secured, for the High Court to have the case transferred to itself, and to have the accused sent for trial. This was so even if the accused were fond of shouting slogans of '*Inquilab Zindabad*' upon entry into court, or of inflicting grave injurious deprivations upon themselves by their relentless determination to pursue the hunger strike, as an act of protest for not being treated as political prisoners.

The High Court of Lahore may have felt constrained to take the case of the Lahore conspirators from the hands of the magistrate given the backdrop of the promulgation of the Ordinance behind it. A year later, however, in an altogether different case, the highly respected High Court of Bombay took the bull by the horns and showed why it was absolutely necessary to do exactly this. In so doing, the travesty of truth that underlay the Lahore Ordinance No. III of 1930 was laid bare. In *Emperor vs Lakshman Chavji Narangikar*,[23] Justice Madgavkar, in a judgment given on 3 March 1931, explained that although the concept of 'ends of justice', which appeared in the Criminal Procedure Code 1898, was one which 'is a term impossible to define', there were nevertheless well-established principles that were incontrovertible. In lyrical prose, he began by explaining,

> To the particular result in any particular case justice is indifferent. The end of justice is no more conviction than acquittal. It is justice, by the ascertainment of the truth as to the facts on a balance of evidence on each side. If so, do the ends of justice require, or do they not, that the accused person from the moment of his arrest should have reasonable access to his legal advisers…? To this question, the answer is, in my opinion, clear. If the end of justice is justice and the spirit of justice is fairness, then each side should have equal opportunity to prepare its own case and to lay its evidence fully, freely, and fairly, before the Court…[24]

Justice Madgavkar went on: 'Confidence in the Court administering justice on the part of both parties and of the public is also a vital element in the administration of justice, so much so that a reasonable apprehension, tantamount to lack of confidence, has been held by the Courts to render a transfer advisable.' For him, having special judges at a special venue was apt to detract from achieving the 'ends of justice' because '[a] special Judge or a special venue ... is apt or at least is capable of being used to destroy this confidence' so that 'except where the supreme need of justice is clearly such as to override these considerations, the ordinary course of justice is best left untouched'.[25]

This is a resounding indictment of the Lahore Ordinance and its inquisition by edict. The subterfuge of the government was spotted immediately both by the press and by the accused themselves, as is evident in the letter by Bhagat Singh chastising the Viceroy for his actions. The failure of the ordinance to inspire confidence was plain for all to see. In normal legal proceedings, and with a case of such magnitude and significance, the Lahore conspirators would have been entitled to a trial by their peers, whereby twelve upstanding members of their community would have sat as a jury to either convict them or to acquit them of any charges laid against them. Justice Madgavkar accordingly had explained that, 'as to trial by jury, it has always been held by all the Courts'[26] that 'the scheme of the Code shows that in the view of the Legislature it is less advantageous to an accused to be tried with the aid of assessors than by a jury' and that 'in a case of this gravity involving life or death to the accused, it is impossible, in my opinion, for this Court to ignore the consideration that in the present case the accused rightly or wrongly attach appreciable value to this right of trial'.[27]

These basic canons of justice, enshrined in the Criminal Procedure Code 1898 and distilled from the common law, would have been known to all concerned, from the Lahore High Court to the Governor-General who took away the court's jurisdiction to try these cases. Yet, a trial by Ordinance was chosen as a way of dealing with the accused, who were determined to go on hunger strike until such time that their status as political prisoners was recognised, and this the government had difficulty in handling. Its perversity is nowhere better demonstrated than in the fact that no sooner had the Ordinance expired than the government did exactly what it had set its face against doing earlier. Seven months afterwards, in a subsequent Lahore conspiracy case, it proceeded to sponsor legislation that would indeed confer on the accused a right of appeal to the High Court.

In short, the Ordinance was a re-enactment of the Hunger Strike Bill. With no firebrand like Jinnah to oppose it, the government could now have its way. As an act of the executive, it could be even more repressive. This is clear from Section 9 of the Ordinance, which reads,

(1) The Tribunal shall have powers to take such measures as it may think necessary to secure the orderly conduct of the trial; and where any accused *by his voluntary act* has *rendered himself incapable of appearing before the tribunal*, or resists his production before it, or behaves before it in a *persistently disorderly manner*, or in any other way *wilfully conducts himself to the serious prejudice of the trial*, the Tribunal may, at any stage of the trial, *dispense with the attendance of such accused* for such period as it may think fit and *proceed with a trial in his absence*.

(2) where a plea is required in answer to a charge from an accused whose attendance has been dispensed with under subsection (1), Such *accused shall be deemed not to plead guilty*.

(3) an order under subsection (I) Dispensing with the attendance of an accused *shall not affect his right of being represented by a pleader at any stage of the trial*.

The stage was now set for the selection of judges for the Special Tribunal. The Chief Justice of Lahore promptly appointed from the Lahore High Court Bench two English members. These were John Coldstream (its president) and G. C. Hilton. The third appointee was a nondescript Indian barrister from Saharanpur in Uttar Pradesh. His name was Sayyad Agha Haider, and he would go on to distinguish himself in ways that no one could ever have predicted. He was thought by the Chief Justice to be a safe pair of hands, but he proved to be otherwise. Today he is an unsung hero. But first, it is necessary to look at how the Lahore Bar reacted – because that too is a forgotten story.

5

The Lahore Bar Reacts

Jaane kitni uDaan baaqi hai /
Is parinde mein jaan baaqi hai

Wounded I may be,
And limitless may be the Skies,
Who knows the distance yet to be covered;
And, yet there is life still in me to fly.

Rajesh Reddy

The Tribunal commenced its proceedings on 5 May 1930 at Poonch House, located in the leafy Anarkali compound. The Lahore weather was already oppressively hot. Perhaps its scorching heat lay heavy on the members of the Tribunal, because it soon got itself into difficulties. By the end of June it was to change two of its three judges, not once but twice, each time having to reconvene as an entirely reconstituted tribunal. This was Irwin's tribunal to serve 'the ends of justice' and meet 'the interests of the accused'.

One thing one can be sure of is that the blistering heat of Lahore in May would have taken a heavy toll on the prisoners as they struggled wearily into court. The balmy air of the hearing room would have been stifling. Despite this, on the first day of trial they all managed to be present in person. They entered the courtroom in the usual manner. As they did so they broke into revolutionary song, holding their gaze on the Bench all the while. They then joined their hands together, for no less than eight minutes, and chanted a well-rehearsed revolutionary hymn. So much for the Governor-General's lamentations about normal courtroom proceedings being brought into disrepute by their frolics. They were at it again, and this time in front of a specially selected tribunal of High Court judges who were not at all amused. That did not matter to the revolutionaries, who saw the Tribunal as a fake court and immediately challenged its legality, arguing it had no jurisdiction to try them. The Tribunal refused to entertain such a challenge. The trial would go on, they said. So, the accused asked for an adjournment of a fortnight so that they could prepare their case. The Tribunal refused, taking the view that this was an application to delay proceedings. When Rajguru complained that he did not understand the language of the court because he was a Marathi, the Tribunal provided him with an interpreter. The trial pressed on.

The accused still challenged the legality of the Tribunal. A written statement read out by Sachindra Nath Sanyal contained his own objections to the proceedings along with those of Mahabir Singh, B. K. Dutt, Gaya Parshad and Kundan Lal. These four names appeared in the schedule to the Governor-General's Ordinance as accused Nos 9, 10, 12 and 17. The statement damned the Raj. It condemned the Tribunal as nothing more than a 'farcical show'. It rejected its jurisdiction to try them: 'We decline to be a party to the farcical show and henceforth we shall not take any part in the proceedings of this case.' The Tribunal asked them if they wished to be represented by counsel. He would be appointed by the state at no expense to them. Only four agreed. Three of them – Ajoy Ghosh, Kishori Lal and Des Raj – were accordingly represented by a man named Amar Dass. The remaining one, Prem Dutt, was represented by Baljit Singh. The names of these four accused appeared as Nos 13, 3, 4 and 5 in the schedule to the Governor-General's Ordinance. The rest were adamant that they would not be represented.

The evidence presented by the prosecution before the Tribunal was once again formal and ritualistic as it had been before the magistrate. Being the evidence of the 'approvers', it had been rehearsed; the 'approvers' were, after all, engaged in the supreme act of betrayal of colleagues with whom they had only recently stood shoulder to shoulder, and the Tribunal served only to demonstrate how a court of law, used by an oppressive political regime, can become a tool of coercive legalism whose sole aim is to crush the revolutionaries who rise up against it.

The revolutionaries were all too aware of this artifice. They were not for a moment under any illusion that the law was being manipulated to oppress them. This is why, even before the trial started before the Tribunal on 5 May 1930, it was challenged by the Lahore Bar Association on 2 May 1930 through one of the defendants, Des Raj. Once again, it was claimed that the Tribunal was devoid of all constitutional authority. It had no jurisdiction to even hold a hearing. The Lahore Bar Association went on to issue a thorough and detailed report dated 19 June 1930. This was passed by a Resolution of the High Court Bar Association Sub-Committee and signed off by Barkat Ali, Mohammed Iqbal, Gokal Chand Narang and Nanak Chand.[1] In the report they argued (in much the same way as Justice Madgavkar was to do in the judgment the following year in *Emperor v. Lakshman Chavji Narangikar*) that the interests of justice were being sacrificed to government expediency, that the Ordinance was unlawful, and that even if an Ordinance was to create a new tribunal, there was no reason why there could not be an appeal from the Tribunal to the Lahore High Court. Accordingly, in a section headed 'No Justification' they did not mince their words:

> ... the said Ordinance is *ultra vires* of the Governor-General and, therefore, invalid; that, in any case, its promulgation was inexpedient and inadvisable; and that there was no justification whatsoever for depriving the High Court of its power of hearing the appeal from the final order of the Special Tribunal constituted under the Ordinance ... A perusal of Section [72] would show that before the Governor-General can promulgate an Ordinance (a) an emergency must exist, and (b) the Ordinance must be for the peace and good government of India or any part of it.

The report then went on to deal with the 'question of emergency' in a separate section, positing that 'on the question of emergency we are clearly of the opinion that the emergency contemplated in Section 72 of the Government of India Act *does not exist at all*'. This is because the term 'emergency' as defined in *Webster's Dictionary* 'and as generally understood means "an unforeseen occurrence creating a combination of circumstances which call for an immediate action"' and that 'even the statement of reasons and facts issued by His Excellency the Governor-General in justification of the Ordinance promulgated by him does not constitute any case of emergency justifying this extraordinary measure'.

Thereafter the report dealt with the matter of whether this was a 'just decision'. It cited in full the reasons given by the Governor-General and how 'by these means the accused will be assured of a trial before a court of the highest possible authority, and it may be expected that a final and just decision will be reached with no unnecessary delay'. It had little compunction in denouncing them: 'We have sought in vain to find in this statement any facts which would lead to the conclusion that there was an emergency for the promulgation of the Ordinance in question, for none of the facts summarized above constitute an unforeseen occurrence calling for immediate action.' Indeed, as the Sub-Committee of the High

Court Bar Association explained in its resolution, '[t]he only objects of the Ordinance which we have been able to gather from His Excellency's Statement are the prevention of delay' but that 'these objects in relation to the conduct of one individual case do not justify the promulgation of the Ordinance'. To this the Lahore High Court Bar Association could also have added that the idea that a trial before a tribunal was a trial before 'a court of the highest possible authority' was highly contestable. It is the High Court which is the court that deservedly attracts that accolade. It cannot be an *ad hoc* tribunal created at the whim of the Governor-General on entirely spurious grounds, the basis of which he cannot possibly justify. In fact, the Bar Association was conceding too much when it allowed for the ground of 'delay' as being 'the only objects of the Ordinance' which are borne out. The High Court was best placed to deal with cases of delay because under Section 526(1) of the Criminal Procedure Code 1898 it had the power for the purposes of meeting the 'ends of justice' to call up a case before it and have it expedited – and this was so even when the government wished to have all 607 of its witnesses give evidence.

The Lahore High Court Bar Association then expressly dealt with the question of how there was 'no emergency' in this case:

> Coming to the facts of the case itself, we are confirmed in our opinion that no emergency whatsoever has been established.
>
> The case was started on the 11th of July 1929, and a short time after an application was made *on behalf of the Crown* to the High Court asking for an authoritative pronouncement whether a counsel could be appointed to represent an absent accused against his will. This application was decided by the High Court of Judicature at Lahore on the 26th of July 1929 (*vide* 11 Lahore page 220) in which it was held that counsel could not be forced upon an accused against his will.
>
> Again, an application was *made by the Crown* asking for the opinion of the High Court as to whether the evidence originally proposed to be produced against the accused could be curtailed. *The High Court refused to give any direction or advice.*

It is clear from this that it was the two applications by Crown counsel that contributed to the delay. The Crown wanted the recalcitrant accused to be forcibly provided with legal representation against their will to give the trial a semblance of legality. In the first application, made within a week of the trial opening before Rai Sahib Pandit Sri Kishen, the High Court declared this to be impermissible. In the second application, again made by Crown counsel (that it be permitted to limit the number of witnesses it wished to call in order to prove its case against the accused), the High Court gave no order at all, which meant that the issue remained undecided, and the matter of how the witnesses were to be called remained unresolved. In short, the accused could not be blamed for delays in the normal running of the trial. Such applications are commonplace and not unusual.

The Lahore High Court Bar Association went on to explain how proceeding with the trial in the absence of the accused was a matter which had long been entirely within the contemplation of the government. It was not something which had to be provided for in an edict announced by the Governor-General because,

On the 6th of September, Sir James Crear, Home Member of the Government of India, drafted Bill No. 29 of 1929, which was published in the *Punjab Gazette*, dated 20th September 1929. It was proposed in this Bill to amend the Criminal Procedure Code in such a way as to allow the enquiry or trial of an accused to proceed in his absence where the absence was due to the accused's own action. This Bill was, however, withdrawn.

These circumstances show that the Government was fully aware of the delay or the necessity, if any, of the trial being allowed to proceed in the absence of the accused. Nevertheless, no action was taken until the 1st of May [1930] when this Ordinance was promulgated. In addition to the facts mentioned above, it is admitted that some of the accused had started hunger-strike before the commencement of the enquiry before the committing Magistrate, *and it is well-known that the hunger-strike was suspended on an assurance conveyed to them by certain gentlemen who had been appointed by the Government to make an enquiry into the condition of political prisoners* and make recommendations with a view to having certain rules framed *with respect to the treatment of political prisoners.*

In a section headed 'Hunger Strike', the Lahore High Court Bar Association then continued with the explanation:

The accused had definitely intimated to the Government that in case *the grievances of political prisoners* were not satisfactorily settled they would resume the hunger-strike on a certain date and, as a matter of fact, as His Excellency's own statement shows, the hunger-strike was resumed on the 4th day of February 1930, creating the difficulty which this Ordinance seeks to remove.

It is also important to note that when the rules relating to the treatment of political prisoners were published and were considered satisfactory by those accused who had gone on hunger-strike the hunger-strike was abandoned, and from the 8th March to the 1st of May 1930, the case went on in the Magistrates' Court without any interruption or undesirable incident.

It is also clear that the Government itself did not consider that there was any emergency; otherwise it would not have waited so long from the 26th of July 1929, upto 1st May 1930, or in any case from the 20th of September 1929, when the bill for the amendment of the Criminal Procedure referred to above was published, to 1st of May 1930. Even if the alleged defiant and disorderly conduct of the accused could be considered any justification for the promulgation of the Ordinance, it had ceased to exist long before the Ordinance was actually promulgated.

In a section headed 'Good Government', the Lahore High Court Bar Association also commented on the government's objective in setting out to achieve this. In a subsection headed 'Faith in Justice Shaken', it argued exactly how Justice Madgavkar was to argue in his judgment the following year in *Emperor v. Lakshman Chavji Narangikar*:

On the question of peace and good government of India for which alone an ordinance can be promulgated we are of opinion that the Ordinance *instead of promoting peace and good government has jeopardised both*. Far from restoring respect for law this Ordinance, *being most unprecedented* and allowing the trial of a large number of persons accused of the most serious crimes in their absence and *without any right of appeal, has brought not only the administration of law and justice into contempt but has also gone a great way in making the Government unpopular* (emphases added).

We are further of the Opinion that even if it was necessary for the prevention of delay to resort to an Ordinance *there was no justification whatsoever* for depriving the accused to the right of appeal to the High Court, and *depriving the High Court of its powers of super-intendance over the Tribunal*. In our Opinion the taking away of the right of appeal from the highest tribunal of the province *has dealt a most fatal blow to the prestige and dignity of the High Court* and has further considerably *shaken the confidence of the people in the impartiality of the present trial* (emphases added).

Finally, in a section headed 'Appeal in High Court', the Lahore High Court Bar Association rejected as illogical the notion that any action of the accused could cause a delay to the exercise of their right of appeal to the High Court such that it was no longer tenable to preserve the constitutional right of appeal for a convicted person because,

> It will be at once admitted that the question of delay caused by a defiant or obstructive conduct of the accused does not arise at all in relation to an appeal in the High Court. *Once this appeal is filed the course of the appeal is entirely in the hands of the High Court* and cannot possibly be deflected or delayed by any conduct of the accused. *The hearing of the appeal unlike the trial does not require the presence of the appellants at all.*
>
> In our Opinion the Ordinance is not only invalid in view of Section 72 of the Government of India Act but is *a most ill-advised measure*, which goes much beyond the necessities of the case, and is *utterly unjustifiable* so far as it takes away the right of appeal from the High Court (emphases added).

The words of the Lahore High Court Bar Association were prophetic. Each one of them was proven right. It was not long before this 'most ill-advised measure' cast its long and portentous shadow on events. This was a makeshift tribunal. It had no recognizable institutional framework at its core. It was devoid of security of tenure for its members. Yet, it had the power to hand down a sentence of death from which there was no right of appeal. It would therefore have come as little surprise to anyone that within two months of its commencement the Tribunal saw two of its three members sacked. Justice John Coldstream was removed as the presiding judge of the Tribunal for bias against the accused, and then the second most senior judge, Justice Sayyad Agha Haider, was also despatched, this time for bias in favour of the accused. This was an unforgivable solecism – as he was the Indian judge in a trial of insurgent Indians.

It was on 2 July 1930 that the Lahore Bar Association filed a habeas corpus petition on behalf of Des Raj, challenging the Lahore Ordinance No. III of 1930. This was signed by six lawyers.[2] It went before the Lahore High Court, where it was dismissed by Justice A. Broadway. Although he ruled that the existence of an 'emergency' in the Governor-General's opinion was 'final and not liable to consideration by the courts', his brother judge on the Bench, Justice M. V. Bhide, gave a stirring dissent. His judgment, given to the opposite effect, is noteworthy as it was to be proven right in the fullness of time:

The existence of an 'emergency' is *a condition precedent to the exercise of the power* of promulgating Ordinances conferred upon the Governor-General. Similarly, the section [i.e. Section 72] requires the power to be exercised *only for peace and good government* of British India or any part thereof. It follows, therefore, that unless these conditions are fulfilled, no Ordinance promulgated under section 72 will be valid. *If, then a court of law has power to enquire into the validity of an Ordinance, it must necessarily have power to see whether these conditions are fulfilled.* If, for instance, it is found that an ordinance was promulgated in the absence of an emergency whatever or for a purpose wholly unconnected with the peace or good government of the country (a contingency which is, of course, not very likely to arise in practice, but is not inconceivable) can it be maintained that a court of law has no power to declare the Ordinance to be invalid?

A court of law, Justice Bhide had no doubt, should not otherwise interfere with the Governor-General's discretion 'unless it is clear that there were no circumstances which could reasonably be considered to constitute an "emergency"'.[3] In so stating, it is manifestly clear with hindsight that Justice Bhide was not being very radical at all. He was stating the position as it was under the law. All government officials are subject to the law. All of them exercise their power subject to the supervisory jurisdiction of the courts. That power is circumscribed by the statute which confers upon the government official the authority to act in the manner prescribed. It is the duty of the courts to police the exercise of that power so as to ensure that it remains within the four corners of the statutory authority that is conferred. Provided that the official adheres by these limitations, he cannot be criticized for exercising the power that Parliament has bestowed upon him when the occasion demands it. Justice Bhide's view, however, was radical in the context of colonial rule exercised by an imperial power based in London. In this, Justice Bhide had struck a raw nerve. His decision had the propensity to throw the courts into confusion and legal disarray.

This is clear from another case that arose shortly thereafter on 1 September 1930 by the name of *Chanappa Shantirappa And Ors. v. Emperor*. In that case, Justice Blackwell explained:

There has been a difference of judicial opinion upon this question in the Lahore High Court (see *Des Raj v. Emperor*). *I incline strongly to the view that the Court is entitled to enquire into the matter.* Assuming that it is, the Court is not, in my opinion, entitled to enquire into the question whether the facts placed before the Governor-General were accurate or inaccurate. The Governor-General must obviously act promptly, and may sometimes have to make up his mind on information which may afterwards be found to be erroneous. In considering whether there was a case of emergency within the meaning of S. 72, *the Court, in my opinion, is only entitled to require to be satisfied that facts were placed before the Governor-General which, if true, might reasonably lead him to conclude that an emergency existed.*[4]

The case of *Chanappa Shantirappa And Ors. v. Emperor* followed the arrest of Mahatma Gandhi in India on 6 May 1930. On 12 May, the military took charge of the town of Sholapur from the civil authorities and proclaimed martial law. On 18 May 1930, riots broke out in the town. As a result, a shop was wrecked, trees were cut down, and the police fired on a crowd when 'the mob had no arms but only sticks and stones'.[5] When some were wounded, the crowd wreaked revenge by attacking an unarmed police station and murdering an excise inspector and two police constables. In addition, police lorries were obstructed and court buildings were burned.

The court was faced with applications in habeas corpus by the wives and relatives of seventeen persons. They had been convicted and sentenced by the military authorities at Sholapur and were now under detention. The court was tasked to consider the legality of these sentences. Each petitioner was charged and convicted of offences against martial law regulations and sentenced by a military court acting under those regulations.[6] The argument before the court was that any draconian action was uncalled for because 'it was a case of riots which had ceased after the 8th [May], so that tranquillity was restored and could have been preserved and the ordinary laws maintained, at the worst with the help of the military'.[7] One of the three judges of the Bombay High Court was entirely unsympathetic to the plight of the petitioners. Justice Blackwell was quite clear that 'an organized rebellion against established authority, and a determination on the part of those joining in it to reduce the civil administration to impotence' was something which 'in my judgment, amounts to waging war against the State'.[8] Having decided this, he was then able to conclude,

On the materials placed before him, the Governor-General was in my opinion clearly entitled to conclude that an emergency had arisen. I, therefore, think it unnecessary to decide whether the Court is empowered to enquire into the question whether an emergency existed, or whether that is a matter solely for the determination of the Governor-General.

This case, however, was more difficult than *Des Raj v. Emperor* because here 'the Ordinance itself states that it is an Ordinance to provide for the proclamation of Martial Law in the town of Sholapur and its vicinity, and to empower military authorities to make Regulations for administering it'.[9] Nevertheless, the majority judgment of the other two judges was ambivalent and highlighted the tortuously difficult nature of the legal situation before them. These two judges were Chief Justice Beaumont of the Bombay High Court and Justice Madgavkar.

In his decision, the Chief Justice gave rather more credence to Mr Bhide's holding in *Des Raj v. Emperor* that the existence of an emergency is ultimately a question of fact like any other:

> The question whether the determination as to the existence of an emergency is an administrative act to be decided by the Governor-General alone, or whether it is a question of fact which can be inquired into by the Courts has been discussed by the High Court of Lahore in the case of *Des Raj v. Emperor* ...and the learned Judges, who decided that case differed upon the point. *In my opinion the judgment of Bhide, J., is correct, and the question, whether an emergency exists or not is one of fact which the Courts can inquire into*. But inasmuch as the Governor-General is the person who must, in the first instance, decide whether or not there is an emergency upon which he ought to act, and inasmuch as he may frequently have information which in the public interest he may be unwilling to disclose, and which no Court can compel him to disclose, *I think all that the Courts can do is to inquire whether there is evidence upon which the Governor-General may reasonably conclude that an emergency exists*. If that question be answered in the affirmative, there is an end of the matter.[10]

Chief Justice Beaumont stated the principle with admirable clarity. He was, however, rather more circumspect in its practical application. On the facts he was not persuaded that the Governor-General had overreacted by endorsing the use of military law: 'I am not altogether satisfied that it would not have been possible for the civil authorities to have got the situation under control by calling in the military in aid of the civil authority.' This is because '[i]t is the duty of every citizen and not least of those who are in the service of Crown to aid in quelling disorder' and '[n]o doubt, the military authorities, in the interest of military discipline, can stipulate as to the way in which the troops are to be employed and the persons from whom they are to take orders but I should certainly not assume in the absence of definite evidence on the point, that the military authorities had refused to assist the civil authority, except on the terms of Martial Law being declared'. He further explained his reasoning:

> Martial Law is a serious matter not only for the civil population whose rights under the common law are abrogated, but also for the military, who are called upon to perform acts essentially lawless, under the cloak of Martial Law and whose position may be one of embarrassment if the cloak was obtained by any undue pressure.[11]

Having said all this, however, the Chief Justice was then loath to take his argument to its logical conclusion and to hold the Governor-General's adoption of martial law to be unjustified in that 'it is not necessary to determine whether the declaration of Martial Law ... was justified', because the fact was that

> the Governor-General at Simla issued an Ordinance under Section 72 of the Act reciting that an emergency had arisen in Sholapur which made it necessary to provide for the proclamation of Martial Law in the town of Sholapur and its vicinity, to empower military authorities to make Regulations and issue orders...[12]

The habeas corpus petitions would be rejected because 'it seems to me to have been clearly within the competence of the Governor-General to take the view that such a thing would be detrimental to the peace and good government of British India, and, therefore, to provide against it in the Ordinance'.[13] This, therefore, is another example of colonial coercive legalism being preferred by the courts even when justifiable doubt exists as to the grounds for the exercise of power by the Governor-General.

In the same way, although on the particular facts of this case Justice Madgavkar also agreed with the Chief Justice, the question of legal principle was one which he too was reluctant to press against the Governor-General when it came to matters of colonial governance, explaining that,

> Unlike legislation in India, the validity of Statutes of Parliament cannot be questioned in the Courts of British India, Section 72, Government of India Act, empowers the Governor-General to pass such Ordinances in cases of emergency. It is argued for the petitioners that the omission of any word such as 'in the opinion of the Governor-General' after the word 'emergency' suffices to enable us to consider whether there

was such an emergency as to justify the passing of the Ordinance, and further to examine also its provisions to see how far they make 'for the peace and good Government of British India'. Two learned Judges of the Lahore High Court have considered the former question in the case of *Des Raj v. Emperor*... Their difference of opinion seems to me more apparent than real. Section 72, as a whole hardly empowers the Court to consider whether the Governor-General was right or wrong in his conclusion that an emergency existed, much less to examine how far the provisions of the Ordinance tend to the peace and good government of the country. *That responsibility the Statute has laid on the Governor-General and not on the Courts.* Unless the Governor-General thought that there was an emergency, and *he alone under the section is the judge thereof, he would not promulgate the Ordinance to meet that particular emergency.*[14]

Nevertheless, in terms of the legal principles at stake, Justice Madgavkar had no doubt that the courts have to be satisfied that an alleged state of affairs does in fact exist, that its existence cannot be manufactured or created through actions of other government officials, and that where the government has deemed it necessary to act, that 'necessity' is a matter which the court can itself verify as a matter of fact.

He came to this conclusion after having considered three Privy Council cases which supported his decision. These were the 1870 case of *Phillips v. Eyre*[15] (which involved a rebellion in Jamaica and was an action for damages by a planter against the Governor of Jamaica in respect of measures taken for the suppression of that rebellion); the 1902 case of *D. F. Marais*[16] (which arose during the Boer War when military operations extended into Cape Colony, rendering it necessary for the general in command of the lines of communication to take measures against the Boers in Cape Town on the lines of communication, who sympathized with the Boers carrying on the war); and finally the 1907 case of *Tilonko v. Attorney-General of Natal*[17] (which was concerned with a native uprising in Natal). On the basis of these three cases, he concluded,

All the three cases ... leave no doubt on the following points: Firstly, a state of war and armed rebellion or insurrection *must exist* and not merely a state of riot which could be put down with the aid of the military and other citizens. Secondly, neither the military nor citizens can refuse or impose conditions on such aid. Thirdly, the necessity must be proved, not merely of re-course to the military, but also of the impossibility of functioning of the ordinary civil laws and the necessity of their abolition for the time being, *and the Courts have power to go into the question whether such necessity existed*. Fourthly, it is only when the existence of war, whether against foreigners or rebels, and necessity are established, that the jurisdiction of the Courts ceases. Fifthly, the powers exercised by the military commonly but incorrectly known as 'Martial Law' in fact are no law at all and would be, if the fact of necessity for a war is not established, illegal...[18]

All of this emphasised how the Governor-General's powers were statutory powers. They were imposed by the Government of India Act passed by the British Parliament in London. It was for the Governor-General to demonstrate to the court, upon challenge from the petitioners whose rights were at stake, that he had exercised his power within the parameters of the statute. This is because the situation before him may not be so clear-cut. It may be open to doubt. He may even be mistaken. In a worst-case scenario he may even be acting in bad faith:

It may often be a question whether a mere riot, or disturbance neither so serious nor so extensive as really to amount to a war at all, has not been treated with an excessive severity, and whether the intervention of the military force was necessary; but once the fact of actual war is established, there is a universal consensus of opinion that the Civil Courts have no jurisdiction to call in question the propriety of the action of military authorities.[19]

In fact, Madgavkar argued how 'Parliament has by the Government of India Act, 1915 under Section 44 placed a restriction on the power even of the Governor-General in Council to declare war or commence hostilities.'[20] This was an additional reason why Justice Madgavkar had to explain,

... I am quite unable to assent to the proposition that ... when Parliament itself has limited the power of the Governor-General in Council, any executive officer, even the lowest, if his orders are questioned or riots occur, has the right, because of a certain number of evildoers who break the peace, *to declare war against every other person in a large area as a rebel, abolish at one stroke the ordinary laws and tribunals, and place the military in possession free to deal and to punish as they will* and restore tranquillity so called through terror. It was sought indeed to justify this proposition on the not unusual ideal basis of the man on the spot.[21]

Indeed, with a crashing logic, and in language which many a modern judge would be only too happy to emulate in a democracy, he went onto express a truism:

> The law, however, does not invest the man on the spot with superhuman attributes. Being a man, he may be weak or incapable. He may be out of touch with the people. He may be nervous or even vindictive. He may exaggerate a riot with sticks into an armed insurrection, and disobedience of his own orders into a rebellion. Parliament has not, as far as I know, ordained that the existence of the laws and the working of the Courts should cease on the *ipse dixit* and at the will of the man on the spot whether District Magistrate, *mamlatdar* or Police *patil*; or that excesses and breach of peace, arson, or even murder on the part of a small minority of the population should justify the man on the spot into exaggerating disaffection into rebellion, or riot into an armed insurrection and abdicating himself in favour of the military with the abolition of the ordinary law. *Such a state is not the first stage in the suppression of any disorder but the last resort of the civil power.* It is not a sword hanging over the heads of an entire population by reason of disorder or disobedience by a minority to the man on the spot. *It is not a sign of his strength and duty discharged to the end, but rather a confession of helplessness and complete impotence to suppress breaches of the peace and to maintain laws even with the aid of the military.* It is only when practically the entire population of a certain area is so widely and so deeply disaffected and so armed that it is able to enforce its own law, and the King's law and writ do not run, that an armed rebellion or insurrection as distinguished from riot can be said to exist and necessity to arise. *In short, the laws of the State exist and the Courts function through the will of Parliament and subordinate Legislatures within the powers delegated to them by Parliament not at the will or during the pleasure of the executive or any officer high or low.*[22]

One would have thought judging from these words that Justice Madgavkar was inevitably heading towards granting the petitioners the very relief that they craved. It was not to be. As with Chief Justice Beaumont before him, who had also extolled the fine principles of the common law, under which government officials can be held to account, so also with Justice Madgavkar. He too was constrained by the existence of the Governor-General's Ordinance, which had adopted and given validity to the sentences that had been handed down under military law.

In the Court of the Special Tribunal
Lahore Conspiracy Case
Lahore

Crown vs Sukhdev + others
charged under secs 302, 120B + 121A IPC

This humble petition of the accused persons
Bhagat Singh + others most respectfully sheweth

(1) That the petitioners are charged with most serious offences including sec 302 read with secs 120B + 109 I.PC

(2) That the majority of the petitioners have been lo[dged] for the last eight or nine months in jail

(3) That with one exception all the petitioners as th[ey] below belong to distant provinces and as such have relatives here to look after their defence

1. Ajoy Kumar Ghosh — Allahabad U.P
2. Bejoy Kumar Sinha — Cawnpore U.P
3. Prem Dutt — Srinagar, Kashm[ir]
4. Kamal Nath Tewary — Bettiah, Behar
5. Shiv Varma — Hardoi, U.P
6. Jai Dev Kapoor — Hardoi, U.P
7. S. N. Pande — Cawnpore U.P
8. Kishori Lal — Quetta, Baluchist[an]
9. Des Raj {Sialkot, guardian outside India

(4) That five of the petitioners are unrepresente[d] accused defending their case themselves.

(5) That for the reasons stated above in paras [ ] the petitioners can make arrangements for their defe[nce] only through their friends, attorneys + defence comm[ittee] members

(6) That it is therefore prayed that in the interests [of] justice the learned court be pleased to grant the petitioners the following facilities

I Interviews with friends, attorneys, le[gal] advisors + defence committee members o[r] relatives in court during lunch hou[r] or after the rising of the court during the one hours stay of the accused fo[r] their mutual consultation.

II Instructions should be sent to the Supdts of Borstal + Central jails f[or] allowing interviews with the same

Above and opposite: Within a week of the Special Tribunal assuming jurisdiction to conduct the trial of the accused under special procedure, Bhagat Singh, Bejoy Kumar Sinha, Des Raj and others complained about being subjected to unnecessary disadvantages, such that they were unable to have a fair trial. These included the right to have their legal advisers in attendance during proceedings so that they could be advised by them, in circumstances where they were not officially represented. Previously unpublished.

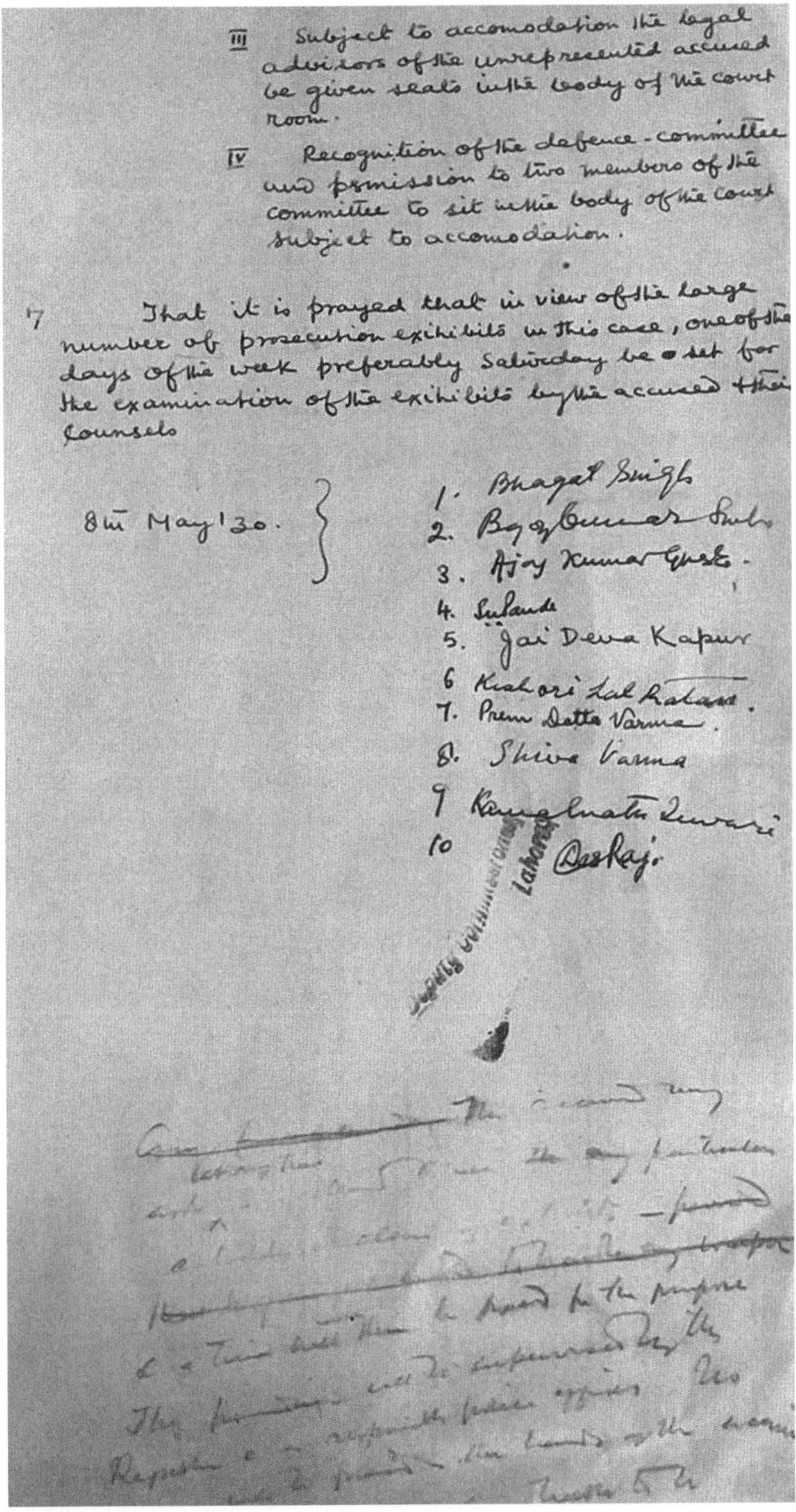

III Subject to accomodation the legal advisors of the unrepresented accused be given seats in the body of the court room.

IV Recognition of the defence-committee and permission to two members of the committee to sit in the body of the court subject to accomodation.

7 That it is prayed that in view of the large number of prosecution exhibits in this case, one of the days of the week preferably Saturday be set for the examination of the exhibits by the accused & their counsels

8th May '30.

1. Bhagat Singh
2. Bejoy Kumar Sinha
3. Ajoy Kumar Ghosh.
4. Sukhdev
5. Jai Deva Kapur
6 Kishori Lal Rattan.
7. Prem Datta Varma.
8. Shiva Varma
9 Kamalnath Tewari
10 Desraj.

The result was that, 'but for the Ordinance we would have had, in my opinion, jurisdiction to examine the legality of these sentences and to order the release of the petitioners, unless the convictions and sentences were proved to be legal'.[23]

However, unlike the Lahore Conspiracy Case, in this case 'the Ordinance is within the power of the Governor-General, and ... it is not open to us to examine its provisions and whether, if at all, they go beyond the necessities of peace and good Government, within the meaning of Section 72, Government of India Act'.[24] The fact that Irwin's Lahore Ordinance No. III of 1930 fell outside Section 72 of the Government of India Act should have made all the difference in the Lahore Conspiracy Case.

The judge who did, however, take the view that the court was entitled to consider whether the Governor-General went beyond the necessities of peace and good government was Justice Bhide in *Des Raj v. Emperor*. The fact that in the case of *Chanappa Shantirappa* all three judges had referred to his decision became a matter of real concern to the Government of India. What if the government had not proceeded on the basis of such a cast-iron piece of legislation after all? What if the legislation did allow, as Justice Bhide thought it did, the possibility of an inquiry by a fact-finding judge into whether there was an 'existence of an emergency'? What if this was a condition precedent to the Governor-General passing an Ordinance even if he was the 'man on the spot' having to deal with an exigency that called for quick action? Surely, they thought, it would mean that the actions of the officials of the executive could be challenged in the courts and be found to be lacking in legal authority.

In his valuable work, A. G. Noorani explains that in the National Archives of India in New Delhi there exists a document entitled 'File N. 250 – Political of 1930' which reveals how Justice Bhide's judgment in *Des Raj v. Emperor* caused utter panic among the officials of the Punjab government. In that case the habeas corpus petition was filed on 2 July 1930, and yet by 29 August 1930 a request had already been made to the central government to have the 'defect' in the law removed through an amendment of Section 72 itself because it was not draconian enough. This came from the Home Secretary, Herbert William Emerson. He had already distinguished himself in his much criticized performance over the Hunger Strike Bill during the debates in the Central Assembly, and he was now seen to be expressing his dismay at Justice Bhide's decision 'that the courts can go into the existence of an emergency', which 'reveals a joint in our armour of which we were previously not aware and which may be the cause of very serious embarrassment'. Accordingly, his minute of 6 August 1930 had already suggested that there should be an urgent amendment to the law, but that 'in the meantime it would appear advisable to "sit tight" until the danger is more serious than at present'. The matter was then swiftly passed over to the Legislative Department of the Law Ministry to consider the appropriate amending legislation so that Section 72 of the Government of India Act could be cleansed of such mischief.

It would appear, however, that wiser counsels prevailed. In the Legislative Department, Sir George Hemming Spence was happily more circumspect and cautious in the advice that he gave. After independence he was to stay on in India to become a legal adviser to the Nizam of Hyderabad from 1949 to 1950. Despite Emerson's evident apprehension, Spence's minute of 13 August 1930 was more measured and level-headed. It would have astounded Emerson because it was a startling admission of the fact that Justice Bhide, far from being wrong, was absolutely right. Spence's view was crystal clear:

> I find it very difficult to refute Mr Justice Bhide's view that as the law now stands, *the courts have jurisdiction in a proceeding challenging the validity of an Ordinance to enquire, to the very limited extent indicated, into the existence of the emergency which must exist before an Ordinance is made.* It was conceded by Mr Justice Broadway, and *is fully established by the previous case law,* that the courts have jurisdiction to examine an Ordinance in order to decide whether it was lawfully made and promulgated. *It is plainly necessary to the lawful making and promulgation of an Ordinance that there should be an emergency,* and *prima facie* the only possible conclusion is that *the courts have jurisdiction to satisfy themselves that an emergency existed.* I find Mr Justice Broadway's reasoning in refutation of this conclusion far from convincing.[25]

Sir George Hemming Spence had no doubt that any other view was logically untenable because 'the existence of an emergency is a necessary condition to the valid exercise of the legislative power conferred thereby and consequently that the admitted jurisdiction of the courts to examine an Ordinance in order to decide whether it was lawfully made necessarily carries with it a jurisdiction to enquire into the existence or otherwise of an emergency'.[26]

Spence went on to forward his file to the joint secretary in the Legislative Department, David George Mitchell, who had no difficulty in agreeing wholeheartedly with Spence. In turn, law member Sir Brojendra Lal Mitter was equally against taking of any 'immediate steps'[27] that would tamper with the existing legislation in Section 72 of the Government of India Act, as is manifest from his own note of 18 August 1930. Yet, despite such staunch opposition from stalwart legal minds, Home Secretary Emerson remained determined to bring about the legislative change he so desired, worried as he was about the future implications of the judgment by Justice Bhide in other cases of a declared 'emergency' by the Governor-General. A week later, Emerson recorded that he had been able to cajole Mitter into seeking an amendment to the law 'when the Act next comes up for revision'. The Governor-General's view would then be final on any question of an action taken on account of an 'emergency' as defined by him. But the uninspiring and colourless Emerson could not have so easily persuaded a man such as Sir Brojendra Lal Mitter, who was later to become the Advocate-General of India from 1935 to 1945 and thereafter the Dewan of Baroda until independence in 1947. It was then that the home member, Sir James Crear, suggested that the Reforms Office, which considers amendments to the Constitution, should be asked about the proposed amendment to the Government of India Act 1919. In the Reforms Office, however, Emerson was thwarted by William Hawthorne Lewis, as is clear from his minute on 27 August 1930, which was to the effect that

> the view taken in this office is that mention in the Reforms Dispatch of the need to amend Section 72 might attract undue, perhaps undesirable, attention to a point of detail. It is suggested that the wishes of the honourable home member may best be met by passing through the amendment simply as a drafting point, when the present act is revised.

What emerges is a tangled web of toing and froing. It arose first between the judges. Justice Bhide stood at one end of the spectrum holding to the view that the existence of an 'emergency' was a condition precedent to the exercise of his power by the Governor-General. Justices Broadway and Blackwell stood at the other end holding fast to the view that it was not. But in between were judges like Justice Madgavkar and Chief Justice Beaumont who agreed with Justice Bhide on the fundamental point of principle but did not agree on whether the Governor-General, having exercised his power, could be held to account in a court of law. Behind the judges acting out a public display of the workings of the law sat the government's own officers of the state, not only versed in the law but possessing detailed knowledge of intrigues and machinations surrounding the politics behind the law.

None of them – not one – had any doubt that Section 72 should be interpreted in exactly the manner that Justice Bhide interpreted it. Spence, Mitchell and Mitter all thought that Justice Bhide was right, and H. W. Emerson was seriously worried that he was. In these circumstances, surely the balance of considerations fell decisively in favour of the view propounded by Justice Bhide on the meaning and intent of Section 72 of the Government of India Act 1919. Surely it was for the Board of the Privy Council in London to give a decision precisely to this effect when it heard the petition of the accused from the Tribunal (which could not be appealed before the Lahore High Court) in the Lahore Conspiracy Case of 1931. The one thing that the Privy Council could not have been seen to do was to have summarily dismissed the arguments made on behalf of the conspirators by their counsel without even so much as asking the government lawyer to respond to a single one of the points raised. That the Privy Council did so is very telling indeed. The express wording of Section 72 was, in the end, misconstrued and misapplied there in a deliberate illustration of how coercive colonial legalism works in the highest courts of the realm.

In the end, it seemed that the muted words of W. H. Lewis in the Reforms Office were correct – that it was better not to 'attract undue, perhaps undesirable, attention to a point of detail' and to let the decision makers themselves do violence to the express language of the statute by allowing the Governor-General to do as he pleased in his colonial territory. It was his great misfortune and bad luck that when a lawyer of the renown of D. N. Pritt KC, who had earlier appeared in the Meerut Conspiracy Case and therefore knew what he was talking about, stood up confidently to plead for the life of Bhagat Singh and his comrades in the Privy Council, that the Board gave him short shrift. The exercise of the Section 72 power on the question of an 'emergency', they told him, was a matter of subjective judgment for the Governor-General. It was not an objective matter to be decided by the court at all. It was to be determinable only by him and as he saw fit. The appeal with these words was thrown out. Bhagat Singh, Sukhdev and Rajguru were to be marched off and hanged on 23 March 1931 without a further thought.

6

'Inquilabi' Justice Agha Haider

Jeenah Mushkil hae keh Ahsaan,
Zara Dekh toh Loh /
Log Lagteh Haen Parishaan,
Zara Dekh toh Loh,

You ask if this life is tolerable or intolerable?
But do not ask the people;
You see them distraught with grief,
And yet do not look into their faces

Javed Akhtar

On 5 May 1930, lawyers for B. K. Dutt and Bhagat Singh wrote to 'The Commissioners' of the Special Tribunal 'at the very commencement of the trial' insisting that they had something to say that was so important that it must 'be retained on the record'.[1] The contents of the letter are so excoriating that they have never before been published. It was signed off by five other undertrials, among them the young wrestler Mahavir Singh. He had been on hunger strike with the rest of his comrades when jail officials tried desperately to break their will, attempting to force-feed them with the assistance of the doctors by inserting a rubber pipe into the nose or mouth. The detainees resisted by coughing in such a way that they could lodge the rubber pipe between their jaws and their teeth. They would then lie on the floor with the pipe held there, making the force-feeding difficult. Even with a team of two doctors, one jail official and ten sturdy prison wardens for each detainee, the authorities were still struggling to force-feed them. The authorities changed tack. It is said that 'those with broad nostrils were fed through thicker pipes' as these could not be held in the mouth by the detainees, and the doctors learnt to insert the pipe with a single jerk as it went into the nostrils. The detainees fought back with all that they had.

This is where Mahavir Singh proved a tough adversary. So strong was this young wrestler that he would block the way of the jail officials as soon as he saw them approaching, resisting them until he was finally overpowered by the prison wardens. Professor Malvinder Jit Singh, who interviewed many of the original figures associated with the trial of Bhagat Singh, recounted that a jail official was once overheard whispering to his colleagues that '[n]ot even a single day during his hunger strike of 63 days it took us anything less than half an hour to force-feed Mahavir'.[2]

In their letter to the commissioners on 5 May 1930, the lawyers representing the five young men wrote, 'We do not propose to take any part in the proceedings of this case because we do not recognize this Govt to be based on justice as established by law.' This was a clear challenge to the jurisdiction of the Tribunal to try the accused. It alleged want of legal authority. It also alleged violation of the rule of law. It went on to say that 'since this Govt is an utter negation of these principles its very existence is not justifiable'. Indeed, it alleged that 'such Govts as are organized to exploit the oppressed nations have no right to exist except by the right of the sword (i.e. brute force) with which they try to curb all the ideas of liberty and freedom and the legitimate aspirations of the people'. Both the government and the law it administered was denounced as a sham:

> We believe all such Govts. and particularly this British Government thrust upon the helpless but unwilling Indian nation to be no better than an organized gang of robbers and a pack of exploiters equipped with all the means of carnage and devastations. In the name of 'law and order' they crush all those who dare to expose or oppose them.

The letter to the commissioners described 'imperialism' as 'nothing but a vast conspiracy organized with predatory motives'. It pointed out how the British government 'by their designs not only commits judicial murders through their law-courts but also organize general crimes like war', thus making it clear why its signatories would not participate in the Tribunal proceedings. The government is such that 'they feel no hesitation in shooting down innocent and unarmed people who refuse to yield to their depredatory [sic] demands or to acquiesce in their ruinous and abominable designs'. It highlighted how 'under the garb of custodians of "law and order" they break peace, create disorder, kill people and commit all conceivable designs'. The right in freedom, the letter claimed, was a basis for a revolt against a government which did not respect the 'inalienable' rights of mankind:

> We believe that freedom is undeniable birthright of all people, that every man has the inalienable right to enjoying the fruits of his labour and that every nation is indisputably the master of his resources. If any Govt. deprives them of those primary rights it is the right of people – nay it is their duty to destroy that Govt.[3] Since the British govt. is a negation of these principles for which we stand it is our firm conviction that every effort made, every method adopted to bring about a Revolution and to destroy this Govt. is morally justified. We stand for a change, a radical change in the existing order of affairs in racial, political and economic spheres and the complete replacement of the existing order by a new era rendering the exploitation of man by man impossible and thus guaranteeing full liberty to all the people in all the spheres. We feel that unless the whole social order is changed and socialistic society is established the whole world is in danger of a disastrous catastrophe.

One question that has always been raised about the tactics of young revolutionaries like Bhagat Singh is whether they endorsed violence. Gandhi himself disapproved of their errant ways. He saw them as a deviation from his own chosen path of 'non-violence', and he refused to wholeheartedly stand by them. Yet, the 5 May letter states their position unequivocally:

> As regards the methods – peaceful or otherwise – to be adopted for the consummation of the revolutionary ideal, let us declaim that the choice rests with those who hold power. *Revolutionaries by virtue of their altruistic principles are lovers of peace – a genuine and permanent peace based on justice and equity*, not the illusory peace resulting from cowardice and maintained at the point of bayonets. *If the revolutionaries take to bombs and pistols it is only as a measure of terrible necessity as a last recourse.*

The letter states that, contrary to the charges levelled against these young men, they were not against 'law and order' because, 'as the supreme juris counsil [*sic*] of Revolutionary France has well expressed', properly conceived and utilized, 'the end of law is not to abolish or restrain but to preserve and enlarge freedom'. What this means is that 'the legitimate power is required to govern by promulgated laws *established for the common good alone* and resting alone *on the consent and the authority of the people, from which law, no one is exempt – not even the legislature'*.

In so stating, the young revolutionaries made it clear that both governors and the governed were subject to law. This enabled them to call into question the very authority under which they were being tried. They maintained that it was not founded on law. They provided a sound and practically coherent basis for why an unjust law cannot provide stability and peace in society. This was a far cry from rejecting the law itself:

> The sanctity of law can be maintained only so long as it is the expression of the will of the people. When it becomes a mere instrument in the hands of an oppressing class it loses sanctity and significance for the fundamental preliminary for the administration of justice is the elimination of every interest.

These words display remarkable foresight and show these young men to have been very much ahead of their time. It took at least half a century after these words were penned for racial minorities to be given recognition that they were deserving of proper protection under the law. These words exhorted the Tribunal to be aware that, 'as soon as the law seizes to correspond to the popular racial needs, it becomes the means for perpetration of injustice and tyranny'. By the 'elimination of every interest' they meant the elimination of 'special' interests in society. It was this which stood in the way of the principle of equal treatment and equality before the law, given that 'the maintaining of such a law is nothing but a hypocritical assertion of a special interest against the common interest'. This is why those under trial were not bound to appear before the Special Tribunal, of three judges appointed under an Ordinance of the Governor-General, for reasons of an 'emergency' which did not exist, and where the presence of the accused could be dispensed with and any judge removed at the drop of a hat. In their crushing statement, they charged that 'the laws of the present Govt. exist for the interest of the alien rulers against the interest of our people, and as such, they have no moral binding whatsoever'.

In short, if the Tribunal had no jurisdiction over the accused, the accused had no duty to appear before it.

> For this reason, we decline to be a party to this farcical show and henceforth we shall not take part in the proceedings of this case.[4]

This boycott of legal proceedings in the Lahore Conspiracy Case on the very first day of the Tribunal proceedings was a shrewd move by its instigators. They would be vindicated in their claims that this was a political trial because these trials always ended badly for those charged since the dice were always loaded against them. They started off with all the appearances of a fair trial, but the emerging reality would foretell a different truth. So it was in the Lahore Conspiracy Case.

Political trials in the interwar years in India were always seen for what they were because the accused made it plain, just as the accused did in the Lahore Conspiracy Case, that the trial was political. The accused would walk stridently into the courtroom. They would engage in histrionics. Many a showy and stagey slogan would be called out. Judges had to get used to this. They knew how to handle such theatrics. It was no different in the Lahore Conspiracy Case – except for the judges, who sat not as judges of a court but judges of a Special Tribunal set up under the executive powers of the Governor-General without the oversight of Parliament.

In the Kakori Conspiracy, nearly a dozen members of the newly formed Hindustan Republican Association took part on 9 August 1925 in a train robbery at Kakori, near Lucknow on the plains of central India. It was organized by Ashfaqullah Khan and Ram Prasad Bismil, both of whom were members of this organization, which later became better known as the Hindustan Socialist Republican Association. They had the express aim of undertaking revolutionary activities against the British Empire in India, which they believed to be the only means of securing Indian independence. In order to accomplish this, weaponry was needed. Their struggle was violent, and their organization was short of money, so they planned a robbery. The Number 8 Down Train was threading slowly from Saharanpur to Lucknow, collecting money from various railway stations along the way, and this money was to be unloaded at Lucknow. The target of the Kakori conspirators was the guard's cabin, where money bags containing 100,000 rupees were held. In the attack, however, one person was accidentally killed. More than two dozen members of the Hindustan Republican Association were arrested within a month of the attack. Twenty-nine of them were put on trial before a special magistrate in Lucknow. An eighteen-month trial ensued. There were ample opportunities during this time for the accused to shout slogans before the special magistrate, and they took delight in availing themselves of the opportunity. Ashfaqullah Khan and Ram Prasad Bismil, together with two others, were hanged at the end of 1927.

More famously, in the Meerut Conspiracy Case, which ran from 1929 to 1933, the British government, fearful of the rise of communist ideas in

India, accused some agitators of a conspiracy to establish a branch of the Comintern, which it castigated as aspiring Bolsheviks. Severe sentences, in some cases transportation for life, were handed down by the Sessions Court in Meerut, notwithstanding the fact that three of the thirty-three convicted trade unionists were Englishmen. The case became a turning point in the rise of anti-imperialist sentiment throughout South Asia, because over the four and a half years of the trial the accused strode into the courtroom defiantly and used the publicity to openly proclaim their cause. They were charged with conspiring 'to deprive the King Emperor of the sovereignty of British India, and for such purpose to use the methods and carry out the programme and plan of campaign outlined and ordained by the Communist International'. Ironically, although the British government brought the case to crush the communist movement in India, the trial led to the rapid spread of communist ideas. Even though not all of the accused were communists (though S. V. Ghate certainly was, becoming the first General Secretary of the Communist Party of India), the prisoners' dock in the courtroom acted as a pulpit from which they could propagate their views. Within a year, the Communist Party of India, which had been formed in 1925, came out with a full manifesto. In 1934, it affiliated itself to the Communist International.

Both the Kakori Conspiracy Case of 1925 and the Meerut Conspiracy Case of 1929 were tried before regular magistrates. Both were prosecuted in the Sessions Court. In both cases what the magistrates had learnt to do was to adopt a series of delicate, diplomatic and discreet strategies which brought no disrepute or opprobrium onto the courts. These ranged from allowing political speeches to be made before the judges entered, to simply ignoring disturbances by the undertrials. Judges would also employ the stratagem of allowing visitors, many of whom were the intended target audience of the accused, but only after the speeches had come to an end.

The Lahore Conspiracy Case, however, saw this carefully honed judicial tactic consigned to the wastepaper bin when, on 12 May 1930, only a week after the Tribunal had taken over conducting the hearing from Rai Sahib Pandit Sri Kishen, Bhagat Singh and his comrades resolutely marched into the courtroom. The three judges were already seated, eager to get on with the hearing. The police began hastily removing the handcuffs from the accused, but they were yet to sing their revolutionary song and raise their cries of '*Inquilab Zindabad*', and so they soon began to sing. The song was a collective endeavour of solidarity in their struggle for freedom. The judges could have allowed them to finish their song; they could then have removed their handcuffs, and the proceedings could quietly have begun afterwards. This, however, was not a normal trial. To the great dismay and consternation of the accused, as soon as the singing started an irate Justice Coldstream ordered that they be shackled in handcuffs and immediately returned to their cells. It was impetuous of him to do so, but the Ordinance gave him the power to proceed with the hearing in the absence of the accused and he now exercised that power. Coercive colonial legalism was at work. The accused were taken aback – Bhagat Singh rose up and told the judge that there was no need to handcuff them and to send them back to their prison cells, as they were entitled to sing their song as they had always done before proceedings began. The song reminded the accused of their political status in what was a political trial. Justice Coldstream, however, would have none of it.

This was despite the fact that ever since their first day before this Special Tribunal eleven days prior, the accused had been allowed to sing their song. This was always done with their handcuffs on because the court was not then in session. Having finished their song, the judges would order the handcuffs to be taken off and the court session would begin. Justice Coldstream's actions on the 12th therefore represented a dramatic break from the practice of the Special Tribunal itself. So Bhagat Singh spoke out. Justice Coldstream, however, took umbrage at his audacity and ordered the police to have the accused removed from court. The signal was clear to the police – they could manhandle the accused. Suddenly, a bevy of 'more than fifteen constables sprang on each accused and handcuffed them one by one, by force'.[5] The accused cried out in pain. In the struggle that ensued, three of them were hurled over the metal barrier into the prisoners' dock and knocked unconscious. The affronted Bhagat Singh railed at the judges, 'You are cowards and mercenaries.' Others amongst the accused called on the Indian judge, Justice Agha Haider, to relinquish his office and immediately resign. An angry Justice Coldstream, however, ordered the hearing to be adjourned.

The next day was even more extraordinary as the Tribunal reconvened. Justice Agha Haider made a statement. Although it was announced on 13 May 1930, it was clearly written on the very day that the fracas took place in court on 12 May 1930, when Justice Agha Haider had refused to sign off the proceedings of the day with his brethren on the Bench. He signalled his complete dissociation from the violence of the courtroom, which was instigated at the behest of the Tribunal's president, Justice Coldstream. His actions must have come as a complete shock to the other judges. It must also have left the Chief Justice of Lahore totally stunned. He had appointed Justice Agha Haider as a safe pair of hands. But the man was no one's fool.

Here was one Westernized Indian grandee not willing to be a stooge. How could the Chief Justice of Lahore have got this so wrong? An Oxford graduate, Agha Haider had been a close friend of Winston Churchill, with whom he had apparently shared a room. Despite that background, his statement made plain his discomfiture with the manner in which the president, Justice Coldstream, was handling his court. Bluntly and in plain English, he gave his order:

ORDER
I was not a party to the order of the removal of the accused from the court to the jail and I was not responsible for it anyway. I disassociate myself from all that took place today in consequence of that order. AGHA HAIDAR. 12th May 1930.[6]

This showed remarkable daring. For a member of the High Court Bench to so completely dissociate himself from the actions of a court involved in a high-profile political trial was quite unprecedented. It must have been plain to the Indian judge that he could not survive long. But Justice Agha Haider came from an illustrious lineage. His father, Meer Sayed Mehdi Hasan Bin Nawab Sayed Sonde Ali Shah, was an exceptionally learned man from Iran, and many of his family members were distinguished lawyers.

Justice Agha Haider was right to object to the beatings on 12 May 1930. Section 9(1) of the Ordinance of 1930, draconian as it was in conferring 'special powers' on the Tribunal, authorized it to deal with an accused who behaves in a 'persistently disorderly manner' such that the judges could 'at any stage of the trial dispense with the attendance of the accused'. However, it did not authorize the beating of the accused in the courtroom. Moreover, the accused were not engaged in 'persistently disorderly conduct'. In fact, previous judicial practice had always carefully ensured that the singing did not take place 'at any stage of the trial', because the trial always started after the singing had come to an end. That is when the prisoners' handcuffs were removed and the visitors were allowed to enter the courtroom and take their seats in the gallery.

Of course, Section 9(1) of the Ordinance of 1930 did start with the conferment of a general power that '[t]he Tribunal shall have powers to take such measures as it may think necessary to secure the orderly conduct of the trial', but it is well established that there is no such thing as absolute power because discretion is an element in all power. The president's exercise of discretion was unlawful in requiring the accused to be handcuffed. It was unlawful in ordering the constables to take physically violent action. It was unlawful in that there were no reasonable grounds to 'think' that it was 'necessary' for him 'to secure the orderly conduct of the trial' when the trial had not yet started. Indeed, the judge's actions were what brought disorder into the courtroom. He did the opposite of what the Ordinance required of him. Furthermore, it was the opposite of what had been intended when judicial proceedings were taken from the hands of a magistrate and entrusted to a Special Tribunal. The proceedings before Rai Sahib Pandit Sri Kishen had become a public spectacle, widely reported upon in the press, which delighted in the magistrate's daily humiliation at the hands of the accused. The chief of the Intelligence Bureau at the time was deeply concerned that members of the public reading newspaper reports of the trial 'could hardly have vestige of respect left either for the Magistrate, the Court he presides over, or to the law he administers'.[7] The same could surely now have been said of the Tribunal of Justice Coldstream after he gave the order to handcuff the accused without any consultation with Justice Agha Haider.

Was this an example of coercive colonial legalism by the Tribunal, a deliberate ploy to banish the accused from the courtroom? It is not beyond the realms of possibility. The Lahore Ordinance No. III of 1930 was in itself a striking example of coercive legalism, allowing a criminal trial to be conducted in the absence of the accused. Amolak Ram Kapoor castigated it as 'subversive of the elementary principles of criminal jurisprudence'.[8] But Justice Coldstream's actions here were even worse. He saw fit to invite police officers to employ wanton physical violence against the accused in his own court. He did so within a week of proceedings commencing, when there was no threat of any disruption from the accused themselves. All they were doing was singing a song just as they had always done, and they were doing it before the start of the day's business in court. In the circumstances, Justice Coldstream must have been aware that the natural consequence of his ill-treatment of the accused, which left three of them unconscious in the courtroom, was that they would no longer attend the proceedings. In that event, the Tribunal could gaily 'dispense with such attendance of the accused' as Section 9(1) of the Ordinance allowed.

After 12 May 1930, the accused indeed boycotted the Tribunal proceedings. The only one of the accused who did attend was Sukhdev on 13 May 1930, and he did not attend after that. Amar Dass was representing four of the accused as counsel and so on 13 May 1930 he asked for permission to interview his clients. He was given permission. When Baljit Singh, another counsel for the accused, expressed his concerns to the Tribunal that many of them now felt they would be subjected to retribution by the authorities, the plucky Justice Agha Haider delighted in assuring them: 'Personally, I think officials will do nothing against the accused.' A short adjournment of two hours then followed. Amar Dass returned after interviewing his clients. He was under instructions, he claimed, to inform the Tribunal that his clients were in no doubt that 'the situation of yesterday was brought about intentionally to proceed with the case in the absence of the accused'. He explained why the accused believed this: 'Without going through this, the trial could not be finished within six months.' Such a view was quite a serious indictment of the Tribunal so soon after it had begun its hearings and indicative of the total collapse of its confidence in the minds of the accused. It also displayed remarkable foresight on their part.

So much was this the case that Amar Dass now told the Tribunal that in the circumstances his instructions had been withdrawn. The accused did not wish to be represented at all before the Tribunal. Upon hearing this, Baljit Singh confirmed that his instructions too had been withdrawn. Justice Agha Haider was the only one to give them solace. bit Justice Coldstream, as the president of the Tribunal, dug in his heels and firmly reminded the lawyers for the accused that 'we will take such legal measures as are open to us, including the removal of the accused, as may be considered necessary for the proper conduct of the proceedings'. However, he made no order dispensing with presence of counsel for the accused, so presumably even he realized that this would be a step too far.

On 14 May 1930, with the accused absent and the lawyers dis-instructed, the Tribunal could now invoke Section 9(1) of the Ordinance. It could dispense with attendance of both counsel and the accused. The Tribunal in fact released all counsel by order, bringing into sharp relief the wisdom of an Ordinance that allowed for the dispensation of the very persons who were being tried – an absurd illustration of a trial *in absentia*. The hearings nevertheless trudged along for the next six weeks. Every day that the Tribunal sat was begun with a futile account from the jailer about why the accused were not present. The jailer reported that 'each of the accused was asked individually to come to court' and each replied, 'I will not come unless I am physically forced.'[9] Given the violence dealt out to the accused a few days before, the idea that the judges were unwilling to force the matter rings hollow so that such theatricality continued to the end of May 1930.

This is when a rift began to arise between the Tribunal members. As the trial stumbled on, news arrived of a botched attempt to rescue

C.W.3/1.
J. Coldstream.
~~Produced by C.W., B. Kala Ram. Place~~
G.C. Hilton.

- -

To

                    The President,

                        Lahore Consp

                            Tribuna

I, Sukhdev, an accused in the Lahore Conspir

hereby declare, that I cannot tolerate the r

arrogant and injudicial attitude of the Presi

the Special Tribunal towards my comrades and

mal-treatment meted out to them on 12th May 1

therefore I also decide not to present myself b

your Court unless and until the grievences of m

comrades are removed to their satisfaction.

Dated 14th May 1930.   Sd/- Sukh Dev.

Produced by C.W., B. Kala Ram. place on the record
            14-5-30.   J. Coldstream

Sukhdev, who came to be known as the brains behind the Lahore Conspiracy Case, as he was the one who recruited most of the young men involved, refused two days after the assaults of 12 May 1930 to attend court in protest at what had happened. Previously unpublished.

Bhagat Singh. It had been planned by the HSRA and had tragically backfired. Bhagwati Charan Vohra was the propaganda secretary of the HSRA when it was formed in 1926. Together with Bhagat Singh, he had drafted the manifesto of *Naujwan Bharat Sabha*, which exhorted India's young to adopt the tripartite slogan of 'service, suffering and sacrifice'. It was Bhagwati Charan Vohra who had in 1929 rented room No. 69 of Kashmir Building in Lahore to use as a bomb factory. It was he who made the failed assassination attempt on the Viceroy, Lord Irwin, by exploding a bomb under his train whilst he was travelling on the Delhi–Agra line on 23 December 1929, and faced the wrath of Mahatma Gandhi's condemnation in a strongly worded article, 'The Cult of the Bomb'. On that occasion, Vorha had responded in kind with an equally emphatic article, 'The Philosophy of the Bomb', in which he rebuked Gandhi:

> There is no crime that Britain has not committed in India. Deliberate misrule has reduced us to paupers, has 'bled us white'. As a race and a people we stand dishonoured and outraged. Do people still expect us to forget and to forgive?

Had Bhagwati Charan Vohra lived he would have played a pivotal role in post-independence India. It was not to be because he had now planned to have a bomb thrown at the police party near the main gate of the central jail at precisely the moment when Bhagat Singh was being brought to court and to free his comrade in the confusion. Before he could carry out the plan, the bomb had to be tested. An attempt was made to do this on 28 May 1930 on the banks of the River Ravi outside Lahore. Unfortunately for Vohra, those engaged to help him were less than careful. The bomb exploded during testing, and Bhagwati Charan Vohra was killed instantly. He left behind his devoted wife, Durgawati Devi, more popularly known as 'Durga Devi', the woman who had helped Bhagat Singh make his miraculous escape from Lahore on the night of the killing of John Saunders on 17 December 1928, and one of those rare revolutionary women who actually took up arms against the British. She lived on until 1999 and is survived today by their son, Sachindra Vohra.

Although news of this event tightened the resolve of the Tribunal against the accused, the fact remained that for days on end now the trial was being conducted in the absence of not only the accused but their counsel as well. As a result, Crown witnesses could not be cross-examined by the Defence. This was too much for Justice Agha Haider. Here were key witnesses for the prosecution. They had been co-conspirators with the accused and had turned 'approver' to save their own skins. Their evidence was central to the Crown's case. No judge worth his salt was going to sit there and just accept such evidence at face value. And so it proved for Justice Agha Haider. He began asking questions of the 'approvers' himself. This is not uncommon for a judge to do when a party is unrepresented. It would not have been remiss of the other two European judges to do so as well – predictably, however, they did not.

Justice Agha Haider's questioning was thorough, as befitted the forensic skills of a man of his stature. He challenged the prosecution witnesses, picking holes in their evidence as they stood before him. After Jai Gopal had given his evidence, Haider whipped through Phonindra Nath Ghosh and Manmohan Banerjee, the second and third witnesses, before setting upon Hans Raj Vohra, because ultimately it was the latter's evidence which was most damaging to Bhagat Singh. This led to a parting between Justice Agha Haider and the other two judges, Justice Coldstream and Justice Hilton. It also led to a perception that the other two judges were not concerned with the fairness of proceedings, which were already lopsided. Justice Agha Haider further distanced himself from his two English brethren at this time, dissatisfied with their approach, and continued to take some of the prosecution witnesses to task. His fellow judges disapproved of him in turn. A sense of alienation set in.

Justice Agha Haider was particularly unyielding with the 'approver' Hans Raj Vohra when he was summoned to give evidence. Like Jai Gopal before him, Vohra had been recruited by Sukhdev. He was an eloquent twenty-one-year-old student, and spoke directly in English without an interpreter. Vohra began by explaining how he had passed the matriculation examination from the Central Model School in Lahore, with a particular interest in history. He turned against the British in 1921 or 1922 after witnessing a European headmaster inflicting corporal punishment on some students who had been picketing at the school gates. He formed the view that the severity of the punishment was due to the fact that these students held nationalist beliefs. In 1925, after he had matriculated, he joined the Forman Christian College in Lahore, where he became interested in politics. Despite such a background, the measure of his treachery must have become abundantly plain now to Justice Agha Haider when he recounted how Sukhdev was actually the brother of his uncle's wife. In fact, Sukhdev used to visit Vohra's father's house. They did not talk about politics in the house because his father disapproved of it. Vohra insisted that he wanted to serve his country through journalism, but Sukhdev steered him in the direction of joining the HSRA. If that was right, then turning 'approver' in the Lahore Conspiracy Case served Vohra well because after the trial he went on to work as journalist in the 1950s in California with more than a little helping hand from the British government.

Justice Agha Haider was not so easily swayed by evidence from an 'approver' who had not been tested by cross-examination in court, so he challenged Vohra when he oozed loquaciously about how he had incorrectly entered not just his own name but also that of his father in the visitor's register at the Rawalpindi branch of the Arya Samaj offices. He was asked in no uncertain terms, 'Did you feel any compunction in putting these deliberate lies in the register?' Vohra's asinine reply was, 'Inasmuch as I was keeping alive for a higher purpose, I did not feel any compunction.' He might have had a little more credibility if he had simply said with a straight face that he had no qualms whatsoever. In the same way, when he testified to seeing Bhagat Singh's handwriting on posters taking credit for the murder of Saunders, it was only Justice Agha Haider who cross-examined him as to the details. Vohra confirmed that he had seen Bhagat Singh on 17 December 1928, when Saunders was shot and killed, copying the posters. Justice Agha Haider forced Vohra to concede that he had not taken care to scrutinize the handwriting of Bhagat Singh at any stage. However, Justice Agha Haider was still not finished. He asked Vohra whether 'after joining the party' he had been 'frank with members of the party in relation to affairs of the party', to which Vohra gave an entirely evasive answer, explaining that 'as a general rule the leaders of the party did not give any information to the subordinate members', which did not quite answer Justice Agha Haider's question, and which seemed implausible given his evidence that 'the subordinate members were expected to give every information and not keep any secret from the leaders'.

On the subject of giving all information up to leaders, Justice Agha Haider asked Vohra, 'Did you act to this principle?' Vohra was confident that his conduct had been beyond reproach, declaring, 'As far as it was possible for me I acted up to this principle ... I could speak frankly about any matter with Bhagat Singh or Sukhdev, but not with Jai Gopal or Kishori Lal or Rajguru ... I was frank with the leaders and kept nothing from them.' He then astonishingly described how he 'told them that, after my return from Rawalpindi, I was shadowed by the police' but that 'in spite of that they decided to take me to the bank raid'. For an organization as secretive as the HSRA, which even Vohra conceded was subject to such an iron rule that he was not even allowed to 'speak frankly' with 'ordinary members', this stretched credulity. When it is remembered that most of the twenty-four names in the schedule to the Lahore Ordinance No. III of 1930 worked under aliases to escape detection, it seems unlikely that the leadership would risk bringing Vohra along with them to rob a bank in full knowledge of the fact that he was being shadowed by the CID.

By now prosecution counsel had sensed that Vohra was on the ropes and so decided to follow up on Justice Agha Haider's question by re-examining Vohra and asking him what precautions he was taking in order to avoid being followed by the CID. Justice Agha Haider abruptly cut the prosecution short. He did so for the best of reasons – in the absence of legal representation on behalf of the accused, he had taken it upon himself to ensure that the ends of justice were not sacrificed. He accordingly informed the prosecution counsel,

> In my judgment the answers given to my question by the witness were perfectly clear and did not require any further elucidation. The questions which I put to the witness *were in the interests of justice* and in order *to get at the truth as far as possible.* I do not think it is necessary at all in the interests of justice … to grant permission to the public prosecutor to put cross-questions arising out of the answers given to the questions put by me to the witness. It shall be open to the Learned President and my brother Hilton to put such questions as they might consider desirable.

In so stating, Justice Agha Haider goaded his brother judges to say something to Hans Raj Vohra. Justice Hilton decided to speak, as lawyers often do, in grandiose tones: 'As the questions were actually put and the answers recorded after a statement made by the prosecutor that intended to put such questions, I think the answer as already given and recorded should remain on the record, and the permission, if necessary, to put those questions should be taken as having been granted.' This must have been immediately understood by Justice Coldstream, for he promptly agreed. It demonstrated to the other two judges that Justice Agha Haider had acted entirely properly in the way that he had just asked these questions of Vohra.

Shortly thereafter, on 30 May 1930, another approver, Ram Saran Das, stepped into the witness box to give evidence. The need for Justice Agha Haider to take it upon himself to question government witnesses 'in the interests of justice', as he put it, became even more plain in his case, when he arrived following the evidence of Lalit Kumar Mukerji, yet another 'approver'.

When Das arrived, twenty-four days had passed since the Tribunal began its hearing on 5 May 1930, and the authorities must have thought things were going rather well. To their great shock, however, as soon as Ram Saran Das entered the witness box he began to retract his statement on the grounds that it had been made at the insistence of the police. If this was true of Ram Saran Das, one must wonder why it cannot also have been true of the evidence of Hans Raj Vohra and the others.

In these circumstances, Justice Agha Haider 's questioning of such witnesses was only to ensure the ends of justice were met. Indeed, such was the extent of witness tampering that the statement of Ram Saran Das, made before the magistrate on 11 June 1929, had already been altered once and the police had then forced him to sign off on it. But now, in a damning impeachment of the trial, he told the Tribunal,

> I wish to put in a document which *shows how approvers are tutored.* I hand in the document. I do not wish to remain in the custody of the police. This *document was given to me* by a police officer *who told me to learn it by heart.* This was shown to me off and on by the officer who was with me. It passed on from officer to officer as they changed. I hand in the document.

Faced with this, a confounded Justice Coldstream could now only admonish the police with the order, 'Let this witness be sent to the judicial lock-up and not kept in custody of the police. He should be produced in court at 11 a.m. tomorrow. He should not be allowed to converse with the accused persons in the case.'[10] This was surreal given that it is what all the accused had always demanded – that the 'approvers' should not be kept in police custody, where their evidence would be at serious risk of interference, but in judicial custody. The brazen audacity with which Ram Saran Das referred to such interference surely suggested that all 'approvers', even at this late stage, should have been transferred by Justice Coldstream from police custody to judicial custody. They were not. Nor was it the case that Justice Coldstream saw fit to recall the evidence of the other 'approvers', whose evidence must now have been rendered questionable. It was almost as if he knew that the evidence of the 'approvers' could only be made good if it could be doctored by the police in police custody.

When the public prosecutor, Gopal Lal, insisted on examining-in-chief his witness to test his knowledge of the principal conspirators, Ram Saran

Das made it quite clear that he had never met Bhagat Singh or Sukhdev at Agra, where it was being alleged that the conspirators were making bombs. When Gopal Lal asked Ram Saran Das what his object was in going to Calcutta in that case, Justice Agha Haider interrupted to say that such a question was more in the nature of cross-examination. Eventually, against this background, Ram Saran Das did turn into a 'hostile' witness; this happened when he began to explain how, after he was arrested in Kapurthala and brought to Lahore on 6 June 1929, he made a statement before the additional district magistrate on 13 June 1929. This was then altered because, as he was told by Police Inspector Atta Ullah Shah, it included a reference to Ram Saran Das going to Agra and there meeting both Bhagat Singh and Sukhdev. When the police inspector had brought the statement to him to sign, Ram Saran Das did not protest, explaining that approvers were in no position to protest. Having added his signature to the altered statement, on 25 June 1929 he was taken to the additional district magistrate, E. S. Lewis, and a pardon was issued to him. So, here was a clear example of how the police operated in getting 'approvers' to come forward. It was nothing short of a cloak-and-dagger operation.

When Gopal Lal applied to have his own witness, Ram Saran Das, declared 'hostile' on the grounds that he was now denying facts which he had previously accepted before the additional district magistrate, permission to expressly cross-examine him as a 'hostile' witness was given by Justice Coldstream. Emboldened by this, Gopal Lal asked Ram Saran Das whether or not he had previously met Bhagat Singh and Sukhdev and whether he had stated before the magistrate that they had formed a secret society with the same object as the Ghadar Party (to overthrow British rule in India). Ram Saran Das exclaimed that he had done so, but that he 'made this false statement at the request of the Police'. When he was asked to confirm that he had also made it clear that the object of this society was to uproot the British government by all possible means, he replied that this too was 'a false statement'.

Always acting with scrupulous fairness, Justice Agha Haider wished to know what he meant by 'a false statement'. Ram Saran Das replied, 'I made this statement at the instance of the police.' When asked by Justice Hilton to identify the officers involved, he identified Police Inspector Atta Ullah Shah and the Kapurthala Superintendent of Police, whom he said was a Sikh gentleman but whose name he could not recall. Despite persistent questioning from Justice Hilton, Ram Saran Das held firm to his statement that everything he had previously said had been directed by the police. In the end, the prosecution announced that as the witness had turned 'hostile' they did not wish to proceed with his evidence. At this stage, something quite extraordinary transpired: Ram Saran Das asked the court to be granted permission to explain *why* he made the false statement. Revealingly, but astonishingly, the Tribunal told him he could not do so. Once again, the Tribunal passed over an opportunity to probe into the source of the evidence as well as its nature and quality. With the evidence of Ram Saran Das totally discredited, the prosecution withdrew its request for the production of Bhagat Singh and Sukhdev so that they could be identified by Ram Saran Das.[11] It was a truly grotesque spectacle.

Justice Agha Haider may have acted with complete honour and integrity, but he had also sealed his fate in doing so, perhaps as early as 12 May when he had distanced himself from Justice Coldstream's objection to the accused singing their revolutionary song. Thereafter he had been punctilious in his painstaking questioning of the evidence provided by the witnesses, who had been marched in one by one to give evidence that was not subject to any official cross-examination from defence counsel. After Justice Agha Haider was done with them, six of the seven eye-witnesses' testimonies collapsed! The one who remained, Abdullah, was said to have been 'a chance witness who contradicted himself'.[12] Taking this into account, it looked likely that Justice Agha Haider was not going to convict the accused. If he did not, and the verdict was split, the Tribunal would not be able to pass a sentence of death. That prospect must have led many in officialdom to throw up their hands in despair. Justice Agha Haider could not be allowed to continue his work on the Tribunal. He had to be removed.

The last day on which the Tribunal sat as originally constituted was 20 June 1930. There was no official announcement until 4 July, although the Lahore Chief Justice had already decided to reconstitute the Tribunal on 20 June. People could only speculate about the rift. It could have been an impasse created by the accused demanding that Justice Coldstream apologise and that the two English judges step down. It could have been Justice Agha Haider's failure to toe the line with the two English judges.[13] Whatever the case, on Sunday 22 June 1930, *The Tribune* reported,

> The Special Tribunal for the Trial of the Lahore Conspiracy Case has been reconstituted and that with effect from Saturday it will be presided over by Mr. Justice Hilton and the other two members of the Tribunal will be Mr. Justice Tapp and Justice Abdul Qadir.

How Lahore's *The Tribune*, which had been so consistently critical of the trial, should have known this is anyone's guess. It is not unlikely that the information was leaked for them to report in the absence of an official announcement because an official announcement was not made until 4 July. Bhagat Singh's insistence on a change of judges likely played a role, but so had arguments from officialdom demanding the ejection of Justice Agha Haider, whose relations with the other two judges had completely broken down.

Section 5(1) of the Lahore Ordinance, however, did not grant anybody power to summarily sack a sitting member of the Tribunal – it only allowed for the chief justice 'to appoint another judge' in circumstances where 'for any reason, any member of the Tribunal is unable to discharge his duties'. It was remarkable that on 20 June 1930, the Chief Justice of Lahore decided to dispense with both Justice Coldstream and Justice Agha Haider 'for reasons of health' when none had shown any signs of ill health at all. Arguably, even in cases where the requisite terms were met, the chief justice was only entitled 'to appoint another judge, additional judge, or officiating Judge of the High Court to be a member of the Tribunal'. In such a case, additional judges would be asked to sit with a judge who was 'unable to discharge' his duties. It does not appear that the Viceroy envisaged the possibility of someone rendering himself *unfit* to discharge his duties, only *unable* to do so. This is consistent with the general position at common law, which makes the removal of a judge an extremely rare event. The fact that there was no official announcement suggests that, even within the draconian terms of the ordinance, those who were exercising the power to remove two judges knew that they were exceeding their jurisdiction in doing so and were acting unlawfully.

It is said that S. M. A. Kazmi, the Dehra Dun correspondent of the *Indian Express*, was told by relatives of Justice Agha Haider that the Governor of the Punjab received a complaint from Justice Coldstream about his colleague's 'non-cooperative' attitude. The government advocate, Carden Noad, was then sent to Justice Haider's home 'to pacify him, but the latter turned him out, saying, "I am a judge, not a butcher."'[14] It is said that Justice Agha Haider was then removed from the Tribunal.[15] It would, of course, have been highly inappropriate for prosecution counsel to visit a sitting judge in the privacy of his home on the matter of a trial that he was presently conducting. It would have been still less appropriate if he visited him to ask him restrain himself in the conduct of his judicial duties. If he did, Carden Noad should not have been surprised to receive a severe reprimand of exactly this sort.

On the other hand, if Justice Agha Haider was to go, then Justice Coldstream had to go as well. If the former had lost the confidence

Judicial.
The 4th July, 1930.

The Hon'ble Mr.Justice Coldstream and the
Hon'ble Mr. Justice Agha Haidar having, for reasons
of health, become unable to discharge their duties
as members of the Tribunal constituted under sectio
4 of Ordinance No.III of 1930 by my order, dated
2nd May, 1930; I, the Chief Justice of the High
Court of Judicature at Lahore, in exercise of the
powers conferred by section 5, sub-section (1), of
the said Ordinance do hereby appoint the Hon'ble
Mr. Justice Abdul Qadir and the Hon'ble Mr. Justice
Tapp to be members of the Tribunal.

I appoint the Hon'ble Mr.Justice Hilton to
be the President of the Tribunal.

SHADI LAL, Kt.,

ChiefJustice,

High Court of Judicature at
Lahore.

Lahore,
Dated June the 20th, 1930.

TRUE COPY.

Registrar,
The Lahore Conspiracy Case Tribunal,
Lahore.

An order dated 4 July 1930 announcing the removal of Justices Coldstream and Agha Haider 'for reasons of health'. Previously unpublished.

of his colleagues on the Bench, the latter had lost the confidence of the accused, and likely of the Chief Justice of Lahore as well. The scenes that had unfolded under his watch, and on account of his direct order that the accused be manacled, were of unimaginable horror and shock in a court of law. Accordingly, on 21 June 1930, both judges were sacked from the Special Tribunal. The reason given for their removal was officially that they were no longer able to perform their judicial functions for health reasons. One judge recusing himself for health reasons is one thing; two judges out of three on a tribunal doing so (and on the same day) is hardly credible.

The accused now agreed to return to the courtroom. When they did so, on 23 June 1930, they found the Tribunal presided over by Justice Hilton. Given that he too had been a party to the order of 12 May 1930, the accused demanded that if the trial was to proceed he too must apologise and dissociate himself from the order. Within a few days, Bhagat Singh had complained in writing to the commissioner of the Tribunal to this effect:

To
The Commissioner,
The Special Tribunal,
Lahore Conspiracy Case,
Lahore
SIR,
Whereas two judges of the Tribunal have withdrawn or have been made to withdraw themselves from the Tribunal and two new judges have been appointed in their place, we feel that a statement is very necessary on our part to explain our position clearly so that no misunderstanding may be possible.

It was on 12th May, 1930, that an order was passed by Mr. Justice Coldstream, the then President, to handcuff us. In asking the court to inform us as to the cause of this sudden and extraordinary order was not thought worth consideration. The police handcuffed us forcibly and removed us back to jail. One of the three judges, Mr. Agha Haider, on the following day, dissociated himself with that order of the President. Since that day we have not been attending court.

Our condition on which we were prepared to attend court was laid before the Tribunal on the next day, namely that either the President should apologize or he should be replaced; *by this we never meant that a judge who was a party to that order should take the place of the President.*

For more than five weeks no heed was paid to the grievances of the accused.

According to the present formation of the Tribunal, both the President and the other judge who had dissociated himself from the order of the President, have been replaced by two new judges. Thus the judge who was a party to that order – as the President gave the order on behalf of the majority – has now been appointed the President of the Tribunal. In these circumstances we want to emphasize one thing that we had absolutely no grudge against the person of Mr. Justice Coldstream. We had protested against the order passed by the President on behalf of the majority and the subsequent maltreatment meted out to us. We have every respect for Mr. Justice Coldstream and Mr. Justice Hilton that should be expected from man to man. And as our protest was against a certain order we wanted the President to apologize, which meant apology by the President on behalf of the Tribunal who was responsible for that order. *By the removal of the President the position is not changed because Mr. Justice Hilton, who was a party to the order, is presiding in place position has added an insult to injury.*

Yours, etc.
Bhagat Singh, B.K. Dutt
25th June, 1930

In the end, of the judges only Justice Agha Haider comes out of this sordid saga with any credit. His principled disagreement with the other two judges calls to mind the dissenting attitude of another Indian judge many years later, in another trial which also called for a principled approach based on the rule of law. This was Justice Radhabinod Pal, who sat less than two decades later as one of the judges on the International Military Tribunal for the Far East (IMTFE) to try the Japanese leadership for abuses committed at Japanese-run prisoner of war camps during the Second World War. General Douglas MacArthur had convened the Tribunal and it led to the IMTFE issuing sentences in November 1948, convicting twenty-five defendants. Justice Pal, however, vigorously dissented from the other judges at great length, declaring that he would have acquitted each defendant. Atrocities, he said, had undoubtedly been committed by all sides in the Pacific Rim, but a principle edifice of the rule of law was that one cannot punish individuals retroactively for offences which were not offences in international law at the time of their commission. Moreover, some of the charges lacked clear individuated evidence against the accused. International law could not, he claimed, sanction the Japanese leadership for having mimicked the colonial imperialism of the West.

Unlike Justice Agha Haider, however, for whom no memorial exists today anywhere in either India or Pakistan, Justice Pal's well-studied defence has not been overlooked by the people of Japan, who honoured him after his death in 1976 with a memorial that sits between the Yasukuni Shrine and the Yushukan war museum dedicated to the Japanese military. There is another memorial to him in Kyoto. Four lines · drawn directly from Justice Pal's 250,000-word dissent are ceremoniously showcased on the face of the memorial. They were originally written in 1888 by the slaver Jefferson Davis, the first and only president of the failed Confederate States of America, in the immediate aftermath of its crushing defeat in the US Civil War. Despite this inauspicious origin, Justice Pal felt that the words were a fitting riposte to the majority decision of the IMTFE, which he saw as victors' justice. Engraved vividly on a silver plaque, they are written in English and they strikingly invoke the mood of the moment as follows:

When Time shall have softened passion and prejudice
when Reason shall have stripped the mask from misrepresentation
then Justice, holding evenly her scales, will require
much of past censure and praise to change places.[16]

One wonders what a memorial to Justice Agha Haider would look like today – what it would depict of him, and how it would demonstrate the differing balance of considerations between himself and his brother judges, which eventually led to his removal – and the hanging of Bhagat Singh, Sukhdev and Rajguru.

7

Trial without the Accused

Sutoo – e – daar par rakhte chalo,
saron ke chirag Jahaan Talak,
Yeh Sitam Ki Siyaah Raat Chale

Like burning lamps which alight the darkness of night,
Forget not to shine in the hangman's noose,
Even as the dark night of the oppression continues.

Majrooh Sultanpuri

With Justice Coldstream and Justice Agha Haider removed, the remaining judge, Justice G. C. Hilton, became the new president of the Tribunal. He was now joined on the Bench by a new English judge, Justice J. K. M. Tapp, and Justice Agha Haider was replaced by another Indian judge, Justice Abdul Qadir. One can be sure that Qadir was going to be altogether less troublesome to his two English judges then Justice Agha Haider ever was. In fact, he ought not to have been appointed at all – Sir Abdul Qadir was not just a barrister and a man of letters but, more worryingly, a former government minister. For two years, and as recently 1927, he had been a Minister for Education in the Punjab government itself. Worse still, upon completion of his ministerial tenure he was appointed to the Governor-General's Executive Council. So an Ordinance promulgated by the Governor-General had a judge sitting on it, appointed from the Governor-General's Executive Council – hardly 'a tribunal of indubitable impartiality and authority', to use the words of the Governor-General in his statement attached to the Ordinance.[1] Thus, the entire apparatus of trial under the Tribunal now had very much the appearance of a covert under-the-table intrigue in which to convict the accused.

With the appointment of a new Tribunal, six weeks into the hearing of a conspiracy case against two dozen absent defendants, most of the accused now decided to turn up. But Agya Ram (alias 'Masterji'), the second named in the Viceroy's schedule to the Lahore Ordinance, still stubbornly refused. Noorani writes that the other accused could also have refused to attend given that the one judge who was predisposed towards doing justice to them had been removed 'as if it was a private affair between the Viceroy and the Judges'.[2] On 23 June 1930, seventeen of the accused once again brazenly stomped into the courtroom with fists clenched and arms raised, shouting the slogan of '*Inquilab Zindabad*' and singing their usual song, before deciding to settle down. The judges then took their turn to enter the courtroom – a clear demonstration of how Justice Coldstream should have conducted himself on 12 March 1930, as indeed the Tribunal had done on the first day of the hearing on 1 March 1930. Once again, Bejoy Kumar Sinha asked that they be released from the handcuffs. Holding a defendant in handcuffs is a negation of a free and fair trial – but this, of course, was no ordinary trial.

Justice Hilton began by asking the police officer in charge if he had any objection to the handcuffs being removed. The officer said he had none, so the judge ordered the handcuffs to be taken off. From the beginning, the Tribunal judges had deferred to the police. They had given them absolute physical control over the accused. When Bakshi Lal Chand, assistant jailer at Borstal Jail, informed the Tribunal that Agya Ram had refused to attend court, the defendants wished to ask him why. The first to rise was the lawyer Shiv Varma, but Justice Hilton told him not to bother as only Agya Ram and his counsel were entitled to ask questions on this point. Bhagat Singh interrupted to say that since Agya Ram was their co-accused they had a right to ask the assistant jailer the reasons for his non-attendance. It was only at this stage that Justice Hilton allowed a question to be asked.

Clearly, the newly inaugurated chairman, Justice Hilton, was no more favourably inclined towards the accused than Justice Coldstream. Bhagat Singh took his chance and asked Bakshi Lal Chand why Agya Ram was not in attendance. The assistant replied that Agya Ram 'does not recognise this tribunal as a court'. Plainly, therefore, the existence of jurisdiction still remained a question for many of the accused. The removal of Justice Agha Haider had alienated them. It did not end there, either. Sinha wished to read a statement explaining why the accused had stopped attending after the incident of 12 May 1930, when they had been beaten up in court, but Justice Hilton stopped him: 'You can put it at the time of the defence,' he growled. When Sinha tried to explain that the statement was an explanation by the accused on the first day of the hearing after a month-and-a-half of non-attendance at their trial, and that 'it has nothing to do with our defence', Justice Hilton again slapped him down with the words, 'If it has nothing to do with your defence, it has nothing to do with the trial.' This was hardly a way to conduct a fair and proper trial. Sinha protested that they wished to clear their position, but Justice Hilton admonished him coldly: 'You give it in writing.' It was clear that if Coldstream had little tolerance for the accused in his courtroom, Hilton had even less.

Such an attitude could hardly have inspired confidence in the Tribunal. This was disturbing given that the new Tribunal was supposed to start with a clean slate, free from bias and accusations of heavy-handedness. Any other Tribunal would have considered an opening explanation from the accused to be a matter of courtesy. After all, the accused had been absent from the hearings for six weeks. A statement explaining their absence was entirely in order. Why would the presiding judge of a tribunal object to it? It would have cleared the air. Justice Hilton's refusal to allow it ruined the chance for a fresh start. The bad blood was set to continue.

In fact, when Bejoy Kumar Sinha followed up on Justice Hilton's recommendation and handed over a written statement, he was then brusquely told that it could not go on the record at this stage but must be included in the accused statements at the end of the trial.

There were other applications before the Tribunal on that first day. Ajoy Ghosh wanted to be represented by Lala Amar Dass. Kishori Lal wanted Amolak Ram Kapoor as counsel, whereas Ram Dutt asked if he could be defended by Baljit Singh. Des Raj, on the other hand, continued with his wilful stance of non-cooperation with the Tribunal. He had no intention whatsoever of disclosing to the Tribunal who, if anyone, would represent him.[3] Plainly, the defendants' strategy of calculated and purposeful obstruction was one which had been planned well in advance by the seventeen who attended court that day. It was purposeful in that it was intended to make it clear to the Tribunal judges that if the accused were to participate in the trial proceedings, there had to be an end to the brutal mistreatment such as they had received at the hands of the police right under the judges' noses on 12 May 1930. In the meantime, they would insist on legal representation.

The new Tribunal's open antipathy to the accused was not lost on the prosecution, which sought to emasculate their evidence even further. When on the next day, 24 June 1930, the nefarious approver Jai Gopal

To

The Commissioners
The Special Tribunal
Lahore Conspiracy Case
Lahore.

5-7

Sirs
    Whereas two judges of the Special
Tribunal have been made to withdraw or
have withdrawn themselves from the tribunal
and two new judges have been appointed, we
feel that a statement is very necessary on
our part to explain our position clearly
so that no misunderstanding may be possible
We have come here today to make this
statement.
    It was on the 12th May 1930 that an
order was passed by Mr Justice Coldstream –
the then President to handcuff us in the
court and he also directed the police to use
force. Our request asking the court to inform
us as to the cause of that sudden and extra
ordinary order was not even thought worth
consideration. Then the police handcuffed
us forcibly and removed us back to the
jail. One of the commissioners Mr Justice
Agha Hayder on the following day dissociated himself from that order of the President
    Since that day we have not been
attending the court. The condition on which
we were prepared to do so was laid down
before the Tribunal the next day, namely
that either the President should apologise
or should be replaced, by which we never
meant that a judge who was a party to
that order should take the place of the
President.
    According to the present constitution
of the Tribunal both the President and the
other judge who had dissociated himself
from that order of the President have been
replaced by two new judges. The third judge
who was a party to that order has now
been appointed the president of the Tribunal.

146

2.

In these circumstances we want to emphasise one thing that we had absolutely no
grudge against Mr Justice Coldstream
personally. We had protested against the order
passed by the President on behalf of the majority
and the subsequent maltreatment meted out
to us. We have every respect for Mr Justice
Coldstream & Mr Justice Hilton that should
be expected from man to man. As our protest
was against a certain order we wanted the
President to apologise which meant an apology
by the President on behalf of the Tribunal
By the removal of the President the
position is not changed because Mr Justice
Hilton who was a party to that order is
presiding in place of Mr Justice Coldstream
All we can see is that the present position
has added insult to injury.

In conclusion we wish to point out
that in case Mr Justice Hilton dissociates
himself from the order referred to above
and gives us an assurance for future or is
replaced by some other judge we are prepared
to continue coming to this court. Otherwise
we shall have to refuse to come to the court
from tomorrow.

Yours etc.
Shiva Barma
and others.
Shiva Varma

D{ 23rd June '30 {

P.S. We wanted to make this statement
on the very first day of our coming to
court this time but could not do so earlier
owing to lack of opportunity.

Above and opposite: The request from the accused for an 'apology' for Justice Coldstream's conduct and for Justice Hilton to 'dissociate himself from the Order' of the court. Previously unpublished.

was called to give evidence before the Tribunal, Carden Noad, the government advocate, took the specious stance that since he had been examined-in-chief in the Magistrates' Court in the presence of the accused already, he would not be called to give evidence now – therefore, it would on that basis be unnecessary to tender him for cross-examination! If that was the case, his evidence should be taken as having been unchallenged. However, this was procedurally incorrect. Skulduggery may have been afoot, but it was for the Tribunal to hold it in check. Jai Gopal should still have been subject to fresh examination-in-chief in this Tribunal by the prosecution. It was Carden Noad's duty to do so. Lawyers present on behalf of the accused should still have been given the opportunity to cross-examine him. Trial by tribunal under an executive Ordinance may have been ordered, but this did not alter the basics of how the evidence should be produced and tested before a judge. The Code of Criminal Procedure 1898 still applied. Carden Noad, however, knew full well what he was doing. He was riding roughshod over legal standards and deliberately short-circuiting the procedure because he well knew he was racing against time to complete the government's evidence. The Tribunal only had a lifespan of six months, after which, whether the evidence was complete or not, it would vanish. With Jai Gopal not being called by the prosecution, Amolak Ram and Baljit Singh, as counsel, asked for copies of the record of the case – they needed time to study the evidence. In response, the Tribunal quietly adjourned the case for the day.

In fact, on 25 June 1930, orders were passed by the Tribunal to dispense with the accused's attendance altogether. The dock stood eerily empty before the presiding judges. The accused continued with their own tactics, handing a petition to the assistant jailer for the attention of the Tribunal. They would not attend the trial, they said, unless they first had a response to their earlier petition that 'Mr Justice Hilton dissociates himself from that order' which was passed by Justice Coldstream 'and give us an assurance for future or is replaced by some other Judge'. The folly of the provision in the Ordinance for the dispensation of the accused was being exposed spectacularly at this point. Defence counsel before the Tribunal found themselves in a situation entirely of the judges' making. It saw Sir Abdul Qadir (who had replaced the redoubtable Justice Agha Haider) absurdly suggesting to defence counsel that, whilst he appreciated that they were without instructions from their clients in court, they could still proceed with the cross-examination of the Crown witnesses, and interview their clients the next day and take instructions then. How defence counsel were to be informed by their clients about precisely what questions to ask, at what point, and of which Crown witness, was not explained to them by the suave Sir Abdul Qadir. The obvious retort from the defence lawyers was that they wished to interview their clients not the next day but at once. With that they stormed off to Borstal Jail to see them. Upon their return they made it clear to the Tribunal that, if the accused were not in attendance before the court as was their right, then they were now under strict instructions not to represent them. The situation had left Amolak Ram, Baljit Singh, and Amar Dass floundering as defence counsel.

The prosecution now had a clean sweep. All it had to do was call its witnesses to tell their story; they would not be questioned by defence counsel lawyers who were not even in court. A preposterous criminal trial if ever there was one! If the proper identification of the accused was vital, then the witnesses for the prosecution could only correctly identify someone who they could see in court, and if that identification was faulty it had to be subject to cross-examination by the defence counsel. It hardly made any sense for this exercise to be undertaken. Yet, with all the advantages at its feet, the prosecution still failed to cover itself in glory. W. J. G. Fearn was a traffic inspector in Lahore on 17 December 1928. On 8 July 1930, he was called upon to give his evidence-in-chief by the prosecution. He was the one living person who had been present at the scene of John Saunders' murder throughout. He was there from the beginning, when Saunders shuffled out of the gate with his motorbike, and he was there right to the very end, when policeman Chanan Singh was shot dead as he chased Saunders' attackers. Yet, astonishingly, Fearn was unable to identify either Bhagat Singh or Rajguru in any of the 'several' identification parades he attended. With a disarming nonchalance, all he could say was, 'I attended several identification parades but failed to pick up the two assailants of Mr Saunders.' This was despite the fact that one of them actually fired directly at Fearn as he too gave chase.

All Fearn could muster was a description of the man who took a shot at him: 'When we had gone up Court Street a little distance, he turned and aimed at me. As he fired, I ducked so he missed me. I continued running after him.' Try as he might, Fearn was unable to pinpoint who the shooter was. In the chaos Fearn had slipped in a small drain at the side of the road. All he could now manage was some self-pity as he lamented, 'I came down very heavily ... while I was on the ground, the man whom I was pursuing aimed at me again, but his shot misfired.' The second shot was fired three minutes after the first, and there was no doubt that Fearn had seen two assailants during that time. One of them was slightly built, and stood at roughly five feet six inches, but the other was taller, and all Fearn could say of him was, 'To the best of my knowledge this man did not fire at me.' He ended calamitously: 'I was not certain which of the two men had actually fired at me.'[4]

But then, even Fearn's suggestion that it was the shorter of the two men who had shot at him was directly contradicted by two other witnesses. First, there was Fakir Syed Wahiduddin, a pillar of Lahori society whose forefathers served with distinction in the government of Maharajah Ranjit Singh a hundred years before. He claimed he was calmly attending to the call of nature, relieving himself opposite Government College, when he heard a revolver being fired. He spun around immediately and saw that a police officer had fallen off his motorbike and two men armed with revolvers were standing over him. Wahiduddin then saw a car coming to a halt near the Government College hostel. Three or four people emerged and went to check on Saunders. Unlike Fearn, at one identification parade Wahiduddin had been able to identify Bhagat Singh as the taller of the two gun-toting assailants. But Fearn had been sure that the taller of the two assailants did not fire at him. Subsequently, and at another identification parade, Wahiduddin was able to identify Rajguru as the other assailant. There was also a bicycle shop owner, Ata Muhammad, who testified that on the day of Saunders' murder somebody snatched a bicycle from his shop and made off with it. This person he singled out at an identification parade as none other than Bhagat Singh, insisting, 'I had no doubts about his identity.' A defence counsel cross-examining these witnesses would have made mincemeat out of them given the disparities in their testimony, and yet neither the accused nor their counsel was in attendance to engage in such forensics.[5]

On 10 July 1930, copies of the charge sheets were served by the Tribunal on fifteen of the accused in prison as they had chosen not to attend court. Their pleas would be recorded the next day. On 11 July 1930, however, their pleas were dispensed with. The court invoked the Ordinance and ruled that the accused were either refusing to attend or were medically unfit to do so. The fact that the Ordinance could be invoked for reasons of ill health shows it for what it was – a draconian piece of coercive legal control with scant regard for the elementary principles of criminal justice. In the meantime, prolonged incarceration was taking its toll on the inmates. Kamwal Nath Tiwari had literally gone mad after a month in solitary confinement in the parched heat of Lahore Jail.[6] How could the Tribunal possibly justify invoking the Ordinance against a person in such a situation? The three or four people Wahiduddin described emerging from the car gave evidence on 16 July 1930, and this also went untested by cross-examination. Chaudhri Habibullah explained that he was a passenger in the car, driven by a man referred to as Abdullah, along with his nephew Kamal Din. He saw Saunders being shot and claimed that during the identification parades he had been able to identify Bhagat Singh and Rajguru as the two assailants. His evidence went unquestioned.

By now, with its evidence unchallenged by the defence counsel, the prosecution was on a roll. One by one came a steady stream of witnesses, rapidly confirming the events of 17 December 1928 from the certainty of a witness box that might as well have been a pulpit. The prosecution could hardly conceal its delight. The witnesses ranged from cultivated, self-assured students such as Som Nath, Abnash Chand and Aftab Ahmad, who were residing in the hostel at the college, to the humble plebeian Ajmer Singh, who was about to be relieved of his bicycle by the accused when he bravely fought them off as they hurriedly made their escape following the shooting. All went unchallenged as witnesses. All gave their evidence in the conspicuous absence of the accused. It mattered not that some were medically unfit or were on hunger strike in prison. The prosecution merrily pressed ahead with its troupe of witnesses, and the Tribunal just as merrily with its parody of a trial.

Amolak Ram Kapoor now saw his chance. In a petition dated 21 August 1930, he complained about the entire flawed process from beginning to end. He argued that 'the Tribunal has no jurisdiction to try and determine this case'.[7] As special counsel to the accused, he had made assiduous efforts to cross-examine the 457 prosecution witnesses, but he was firmly refused all permission. Of the five approvers, he was only allowed to cross-examine one. He was not allowed to present evidence himself as the accused had been dismissed. Given that this was the very negation of the trial system itself, on behalf of Kishori Lal Rattan, who was confined as an undertrial at Borstal Jail, Amolak Ram Kapoor now challenged the jurisdiction of Lahore Ordinance No. III of 1930 'to try the Lahore Conspiracy Case' in a petition directly addressed to the Special Tribunal. The thrust of his argument was that (i) the trial had been progressing well before Special Magistrate Rai Sahib Pandit Sri Kishen, even though there was 'unnecessary hardships and improper treatment' of the detainees such as being given bad food and being confined 'in solitary cells'; (ii) that although there were some adjournments, in itself 'the case went on quite smoothly'; (iii) even when their grievances went unaddressed, 'nor any reply' given to them; so that (iv) they went on hunger strike on 4 February 1930; (v) which hunger strike they in fact abandoned on

20 February 1930 as soon as they learnt that the government would adopt the recommendations of the Punjab Jails Inquiry Committee; (vi) and yet, despite this, from 8 March 1930 the prosecution itself proceeded very slowly with the case because they were 'in [the] know' of the fact that an Ordinance was about to be promulgated by the Governor-General which would try them under a Special Procedure with no right of appeal; (vi) and which was in fact done on 1 May 1930.

So convinced was Amolak Ram Kapoor that the Tribunal lacked all jurisdiction to try anyone that he openly challenged it, arguing that the Ordinance was quite simply void for lack of legality because:

1) They are tried in their absence by the Special Tribunal under Section 302 and Section 109 after they were originally before Special Magistrate Rai Sahib Pandit Sri Kishen on 10 July 1929.
2) The accused are subjected to unnecessary hardships; improper treatment, in solitary cells, not allowed the necessary interviews with counsel, with friends, or with relatives, remanded to police custody by illegal orders, given bad food, and refused necessary facilities.
3) Some adjournments were given, and the case went on smoothly from November/December 1929 until January 1930, even though the accused had grievances.
4) On 4 February 1930 the accused went on hunger strike. When the main recommendations of the Punjab Jails Inquiry Committee were adopted by the government on 19 February 1930 or 20 February 1930, they gave up their hunger strike, and they attended court on 8 March 1930.
5) But from 8 March 1930 to 1 May 1930 (the latter being the date when the Ordinance was issued by Viceroy Irwin), 'the case went on without any interruption although the prosecution proceeded very slowly with the case, being in the know of the information that an Ordinance was going to be promulgated'.
6) On 1 May 1930 the Viceroy promulgated Ordinance No. III of 1930, creating a Special Procedure and 'depriving the Petitioner of the valuable right of appeal'.
7) On 4 May 1930, when the accused came for trial (three days after the Ordinance was issued) there was a challenge to jurisdiction on the basis that the Special Tribunal 'had no jurisdiction to try the case' and this 'was raised at an early stage of the case' but has not been decided so far:

8) This is because:-

i) There is no emergency contemplated by Section 72 of the Government of India Act 1919, on which the Ordinance is based.

ii) The reasons appended to the Ordinance by the Governor-General are not such as to constitute an emergency.

iii) The provisions of the Ordinance are not calculated to 'promote peace and good government of British India, or any part thereof', as required by Section 72 of the Government of India Act.

iv) The Ordinance goes beyond Section 72, 'as it seeks to make provision for matters wholly lacking the essentials of an emergency in so far as it deprives the accused of the right of appeal, to the High Court, and the High Court of its powers of confirmation, revision, and superintendence'.

v) The Ordinance is against 'the fundamental principles of the Constitution of the UK and Gt. Britain and Ireland *whereon depends in a large degree the allegiance of His Majesty's Subjects to the Crown'.*

vi) The Governor-General has not gone into the question of Emergency on a proper consideration of the case of both parties, 'the defence never having been asked to or given opportunity of rebutting any of the representations made by the prosecution ... *regarding the expediency or emergency of providing an Ordinance of such an extraordinary nature'.*

vii) No facts shown or warrant establishing a Special Tribunal 'or extraordinary procedure'.

viii) That in any case 'there is no emergency warranting the establishment of a Special Tribunal or the extraordinary procedure prescribed in the Ordinance'.

It took the Tribunal a week to reject the Kapoor's petition on 26 August 1930. The Tribunal's reasons were that they could not go into the question; they could not even record any finding. If they were to record a finding that they were properly constituted under a valid ordinance, the application that their status was without legitimacy was bound to fail! On the other hand,

if we recorded a finding that our proceedings are invalid, we could then pass no valid order either releasing the accused persons or remanding them to custody or in any way directing ourselves or the case or directing the accused persons to be tried by any other court. To record

In the Court of the Special Tribunal,
Lahore Conspiracy Case, Lahore

Crown Vs Sukhdev & Others.

Charged under Sections 121, 121A, 302 + 120B etc

Most respectfully sheweth :—

1. That the petitioner has today on 22nd Aug. '30 been supplied with the copies of the orders of the learned court bearing the dates 11th August and ~~22nd August~~. 22nd August '30.

2. That inspite of the order of 11th August, no interview has so far been allowed to him.

3. That it is impossible for the petitioner to represent his case personally before the Court on 25th August due to the weakness caused by hunger-strike.

4. That unless and until he is allowed to see his relatives he is not in a position to engage any counsel.

5. That unless and until he is allowed to consult his coaccused he can not decide about other matters concerning the defence.

6. That it is for the Court to see that their orders are carried into effect properly.

7. That it is prayed that the court be pleased to issue immediate orders to the jail-authorities to allow these interviews without any further delay.

22nd Aug '30

Bhagat Singh
Central Jail,
Lahore

Bhagat Singh's complaint here mentions numerous issues: he has not been granted an interview with his father; finds it 'impossible' to defend himself 'due to weakness caused by hunger strike'; is 'not in a position to engage any counsel'; has not been allowed to even consult his co-accused so that 'he cannot decide about other matters concerning the defence'; that 'court orders are not carried into effect properly'; and that the court should 'issue immediate orders to the jail authorities to allow these interviews without any further delay'. Previously unpublished.

such a finding would be infructuous. We are of opinion that the finding to the effect that the proceedings of this tribunal are not valid and issuing of an order consequent upon such finding, regarding the stay of the proceedings, and regarding the disposal of the accused persons, could only come from a court authority other than ourselves.

With this derisory explanation, the Tribunal then considered whether or not the accused could be questioned 'generally on the case' given that under Section 342 of the Criminal Procedure Code such an examination is not to cross-examine the person but to enable him 'personally to explain any circumstances appearing in the evidence against him'. Yet, rather than avail itself of this provision, the Tribunal casually declared, 'We do not consider it necessary to take any further steps towards examining the accused persons under Section 342, Criminal Procedure Code, inasmuch as the order passed under Section 9 of the Ordinance dispensing with their attendance today precludes such examination.' But this did not follow at all. The 'special powers of the Tribunal' under Section 9(1) of the Ordinance were specifically in order 'to secure the orderly conduct of the trial'. At a time when the Tribunal was beset by many of the accused either being on hunger strike and therefore unable to attend trial or not attending because they felt it lacked legitimacy, these provisions applied where 'any accused by his voluntary act rendered himself incapable of appearing before the Tribunal'. Indeed, they also applied to where such a person 'resists his production before it, or behaves before it in a persistently disorderly manner'.

In short, the provisions applied to prevent 'serious prejudice of the trial'. There was simply nothing in these provisions that prevented the taking of steps by the Tribunal towards examining the accused in any other way. In fact, if Section 9(3) of the Ordinance was to the effect that 'an Order under sub-section (1) dispensing with the attendance of an accused shall *not* affect his right of being represented by a pleader at any stage of the Trial' then such a pleader could have the evidence of an accused who was not in attendance brought before the Tribunal in another way. By its actions, however, the Tribunal was not only ejecting the accused physically from the hearing but also ejecting all consideration of his evidence, which may otherwise have been made available. The proceedings were therefore conducted in such a manner as to avoid not only dealing with the accused in the courtroom but having to deal with their evidence at all. Put simply, as far as the Tribunal were concerned, if the accused were out of sight then they were also to be put out of mind. But if the import of Section 9 of the Ordinance was to prevent 'serious prejudice of the trial' then it was difficult to see how the Tribunal was not violating it on its own terms by acting as it did.

That was not all. On 26 August 1930, the same day that the Tribunal rejected a challenge to its jurisdiction, Carden Noad suddenly and without warning made the dramatic announcement that he was closing the case for the prosecution. He had examined 457 prosecution witnesses at breakneck speed and he still had a further 256 to go. Astonishingly, he declared that those still remaining in the list were to be abandoned. What a grubby way to try a case involving a conspiracy against the Crown this was turning out to be! His fatuous reason was that the 256 had been abandoned because some were only there in the list for the purposes of corroborating the evidence of the approvers, whilst some had given their statements on points that had already been covered by the others, and this made them redundant! This was as shambolic an approach to the conduct of a criminal trial, where conviction would lead to a sentence of death, as it was legally squalid. The truth of the matter was that the prosecution was racing against time and the trial had to be concluded before the Tribunal reached its six-month limit. It was living on borrowed time. Soon, all trace of it would vanish.

The seasoned lawyer A. G. Noorani has said that this 'was a charade that was being played out',[8] in which the authorities didn't even try to show fairness to the accused. They knew they could exclude the accused under the Ordinance, so they made no attempt to secure their attendance. The absurdity can be highlighted by the words of Lord Justice Flaux in a 2020 British case that '[i]t is one thing for an appeal to proceed without the participation of the appellant' when this is 'an appellant who chooses not to participate', but that '[i]t is quite another to proceed with an appeal without the participation of the appellant because the appellant is unable to participate meaningfully and effectively'. Indeed, 'far from remedying the unfairness, this would seem to compound it' and that indeed, 'it is difficult to conceive of any case where a court or tribunal has said we cannot hold a fair trial, but we are going to go on anyway'.[9] Yet, this is what the Special Tribunal under the Lahore Ordinance was getting up to when it excluded all participation of the accused. No steps were taken to explore any possibility of taking their evidence, despite the fact that most of them wished to attend but felt unable to do so in the circumstances. The Tribunal shrugged of all responsibility, content to proceed in a manner that was intrinsically unfair to the accused. Lest there be any doubt, on 1 September 1930, less than a week after Carden Noad announced an end to the calling of his evidence, there was an application by Amolak Ram Kapoor on behalf of Bejoy Kumar Sinha and Ajoy Ghosh. They asked that

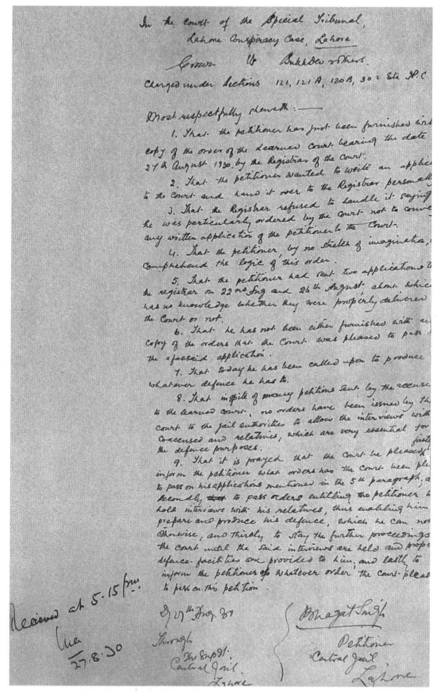

Bhagat Singh drawing attention to a string of irregularities in the proceedings to date, one day after the prosecution closed its evidence, and asking that the matter now be stayed. Previously unpublished.

they have the right to cross-examine *all* of the prosecution witnesses, after first having the opportunity to consider the evidence arraigned against them in consultation with their defence counsel.

Their petition made it clear to the Tribunal that '(1) they think it was necessary to cross examine all the prosecution witnesses without which they cannot effectively place their case before the tribunal'. In order to do so, they naturally needed a short break in the proceedings because '(2) it was not possible to start cross examination forthwith without some respite enabling the accused and their Counsel to go through the evidence and examine the exhibits, the paper books having been applied for on the evening of 30 August, 1930', so that 'at least a week's adjournment was necessary for the purpose'. All this was necessary as 'they never anticipated that the Approvers would be produced today without previous notice for cross examination'. They also complained that '(3) the printed paper books cover about 1000 pages and more than 400 witnesses have been examined' and this made it 'necessary that the accused must be informed of the Order in which the prosecution witnesses were produced', so that 'in any case one day's notice was necessary before any witness was brought in the witness box for cross examination'. Elementary principles of justice were at stake in that '(4) each of the applicants should be afforded with the help of a Counsel on Government expenses', but if the Tribunal could not accede to this request then 'the accused think that no useful purpose can be served by their taking part in the proceedings'.

Amolak Ram Kapoor must have known that his request faced an uphill struggle. He was making his application just a month before the Tribunal would cease to exist, for it was to become *functus* on 31 October 1930. Kapoor had no instructions from the accused, languishing in prison. Although he had gone to meet them there, he had returned two hours later with no instructions from them at all. Nevertheless, having made his application, Kapoor promptly withdrew from the court, claiming that he had only been instructed to make the application. He did not wait for the Tribunal's decision; for all the eloquence of his petition, he knew he was only making a desperate attempt to postpone the evil day of the accused's conviction. He knew no adjournment would be granted to him. So it came to pass. The Tribunal rejected the application on three grounds. First, that the accused had sufficient opportunity to cross-examine the prosecution witnesses but had not availed themselves of it; second, that they were specifically told to furnish a list of witnesses that they wanted to summon through the court but failed to do so; third, that the 'approvers' had been present in court but they were not cross-examined by the accused or their counsel. The Tribunal concluded that in these circumstances the adjournment request for a week would cause unnecessary further delays to the proceedings. Carden Noad then made his closing speech on 10 September 1930. It was all over for the accused. The hangman's noose swayed over the head of Bhagat Singh.

Knowing this, on 20 September 1930, Bhagat Singh's father, Kishen Singh, made a frantic and panic-stricken attempt to have his son saved from the gallows. In a draft that was obviously written by a lawyer, he petitioned the Tribunal from Bradlaugh Hall in Lahore, and raised an issue of considerable significance. He claimed that the identification was tainted, because the accused had been shown to the witnesses even before the identification parade took place. In this way, Bhagat Singh's guilt had already been prejudged. The distraught father even alleged that his son could not have been guilty of John Saunders' murder as he was a thousand miles away in Calcutta, which was not true. 'I still humbly pray that Bhagat Singh may be given an opportunity to produce his defence,' he pleaded.[10] Even though the forlorn anguish of a grief-stricken father was evident to all, Bhagat Singh rebuked his father: 'I don't think you were at all entitled to make such a move on my behalf without even consulting me.'[11]

On 7 October 1930, the Special Tribunal gave its judgment. Of the fifteen arraigned before it, twelve were convicted. Ajoy Kumar Ghosh, Sachindra Nath Sanyal and Des Raj were acquitted. Prem Dutt was sentenced to five years of rigorous imprisonment, and Kundan Lal received seven years. Seven were sentenced to transportation for life: Kishori Lal, Mahabir Singh, Bejoy Kumar Sinha, Shiv Varma, Gaya Prasad, Jai Dev and Kamwal Nath Tiwari. Bhagat Singh, Sukhdev and Rajguru were sentenced to death.

Within a week, on 12 October 1930, Jawaharlal Nehru had angrily denounced the judgment in a speech in Allahabad. His excoriating criticism was not reserved for the Tribunal alone but extended also to Lord Irwin, Viceroy and Governor-General of India, who was shortly to retire during the most turbulent and tempestuous period in Indian politics. It was not just that these years had seen the failure of three Round Table Conferences between the British government and the Indian National Congress to discuss constitutional reform in India – it was the raising of stakes in India's struggle for independence. In 1928 alone, India saw the visit of the Simon Commission to Lahore, the death of Lala Rajpat Rai at the hands of the police, the avenging of his death in the murder of John Saunders by Bhagat Singh, and the Hindustan

RAM KAPUR,
B.A. (Hons)., LL.B,
ADVOCATE HIGH COURT,

CUTCHERY ROAD,
LAHORE.

July 2nd, 1930.

To,

Malik Fateh Khan, M.A., P.C.S.,
    REGISTRAR,
    Lahore Conspiracy Case Tribunal,
    L A H O R E.

Sir,

I beg to enclose herewith my bill for fees for two days viz: the 24th and the 25th of June, 1930. I attended the Court in compliance with your No. 86 dated 23rd June, 1930. The appointment was made by the Tribunal on the 24th June, 1930, when I took up the representation of Kishori Lal accused. It terminated at 2.30 P.M. on the 25th June, 1930 when the Court cancelled the appointment on account of the refusal of the said accused person to be represented by counsel in his absence from court.

I shall be obliged if you will get the enclosed bill duly sanctioned by the Tribunal at your earliest convenience and return the same to me for presentation to the office of the Legal Remembrancer. In case it is not necessary to present it to the Legal Remembrancer, please let me know if any special procedure has been laid down by the authorities for the final approval of such bills.

I have the honour to remain,
S i r,
Your obedient servant,

Amolak Ram Kapur

Encl:- One bill for
    Rs. 100/-/-.

Report if the applicant attended the court for the days he submits his bill.

P.T.o.

Amolak Ram Kapoor tendering his bill two months after the trial commenced before the Special Tribunal, for his defence of Kishori Lal, until his retainer was terminated 'on account of the refusal of the said accused person to be represented by counsel in his absence from court'. Previously unpublished.

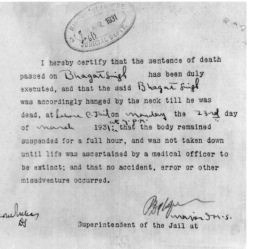

Above: Specimen handwriting of Bhagat Singh dated 19 April 1929, before the Delhi Bomb Case started on 7 May 1929.

Above right: The Jail Superintendent confirming the execution of Bhagat Singh in April 1931.

Right: Crowds marching at the death of Bhagat Singh.

Below right: Portrait of Lala Lajpat Rai.

Below: D. N. Pritt as a barrister in London.

Jawaharlal Nehru at the Amritsar Congress, 1919.

The Tomb of Anarkali amid the beautifully manicured gardens diligently attended to by the numerous gardeners.

The main hall of the Tomb of Anarkali as one enters. Directly ahead is a huge painting depicting Maharajah Ranjit Singh in a gathering at Sheesh Mahal in Lahore Fort after the conquest of Kashmir.

Above: Church paraphernalia in the Tomb of Anarkali, including a number of rough-hewn planks of a pew fastened together with nails.

Right: The alleged grave of Jahangir's wife, Saheb Jamal, inside the Tomb of Anarkali.

The residence of General Jean Baptiste Ventura, of Maharajah Ranjit Singh's army, now a functional government department.

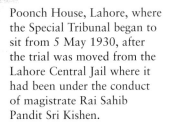

Poonch House, Lahore, where the Special Tribunal began to sit from 5 May 1930, after the trial was moved from the Lahore Central Jail where it had been under the conduct of magistrate Rai Sahib Pandit Sri Kishen.

Top left: The author with Mr Syed Fakir S. Aijazuddin, the direct linear descendant of Fakir Nuruddin (to his right), and Mr Abbas Chugtai (to his left), the Director of the Punjab Archives, in the latter's office.

Middle left: The author working in the offices of Syeda Shamim Asghar Jafri, the Research Officer, in the Punjab Lahore Archives.

Bottom left: A nationalist publication from Lahore identifying Bhagat Singh and B. K. Dutt as the perpetrators of the Delhi Assembly bombing on 8 April 1929.

Below: The revolutionaries were acutely aware of the forces of communalism, often encouraged by the government, which threatened to rip their country apart, and were determined to fight them.

Opposite, top: The members of the Meerut Conspiracy case. The Englishmen are in the back row standing.

Bandematram, Lahore.

P.T. Jubal

Live and Constitutional Bombs in Assembly.
Latest Photo of Sardar Bhagat Singh and Bhut Keshwar Datt.

Who threw bombs in the Assembly Chamber on the 8th April 1929, voluntarily surrendered themselves to the police. They explain their motives by saying that it needs a loud voice to make the deaf hear.

Bhut Keshwar Dutt.

Bhagat Singh.

COMMUNAL HARMONY, OUR HERITAGE
COMPOSITE CULTURE

کیا انہیں مذہب کی بنیاد پر تقسیم کیا جا سکتا ہے؟

CAN YOU DIVIDE THEM IN RELIGIONS!
INDSCRIBE   NO

Sardar Bhagat Singh   Chandrashekhar Azad   Ashfaqullah Khan

www.anindianmuslim.com
क्या इनको मज़हब में बांटा जा सकता है ?

Below: The leading protagonists of the Second Lahore Conspiracy Case. Only Bhagat Singh, Sukhdev and Rajguru were hanged. Jatin Dass died on hunger strike in jail. Mahavir, Shiv Verma, Jaidev Kapoor and Vijay Kumar Sinha were sentenced to transportation for life. Kundan Lal and Prem Dutt were given seven and five years respectively. Des Raj, Jatinder Nath Sanyal, and Ajoy Ghosh were the only three released.

DAILY MILAP, LAHORE. OM 9TH OCTOBER 1930.
LAHORE CONSPIRACY CASE JUDGEMENT.

Sardar Bhagat Singh.
Sentenced to hanging.

Shri Jatenderanath Dass
Died in Jail.

Mr. B. K. Dutt.
Case withdrawn.

Shriman Raj guru.
Sentenced to hanging.

M. Sukh Dev.
Sentenced to hanging.

M. Kishori Lal.
Transportation for life.

M. Jai Dev Kapur.
Transportation for life.

Shiv Verma.
Transportation for life.

Gaya Parshad.
Transportation for life.

Kanwal Nath Tiwari.
Transportation for life.

Mahabir Singh.
Transportation for life.

Vijey Kumar Sinz.
Transportation for life.

Kundan Lal
Seven years.

Prem Dutts.
Five years

L. Des Raj.
Acquitted.

Ajey Kumar Ghose.
Acquitted.

Mr. Sanyal
Acquitted.

A particular feature of the Lahore Conspiracy Case was the difficulty that the accused had in procuring adequate representation throughout the proceedings as the anxiety exhibited in this early letter by the journalist Bejoy Kumar Sinha shows.

A letter from Shiv Verma in borstal asking for legal defence. The Special Tribunal throughout remained oblivious of the fact that it was dealing with juveniles who needed immediate access to their family members and lawyers. Indeed, many of them were all alone in a Lahore jail a long way from home. Previously unpublished.

Uncle & Nephew.

S. AJIT SINGH JI

ਸ੍ਰ. ਅਜੀਤ ਸਿੰਘ ਜੀ
ਖਟਕੜ ਕਲਾਂ (ਜਲੰਧਰ)

ਭਾਈ ਭਗਤ ਸਿੰਘ

ਜੋਹੜੇ ਅਜ ਕਲ ਅਸੰਬਲੀ ਦੇ ਬੰਬ ਕੇਸ ਵਿਚ ਗ੍ਰਿਫ਼ਤਾਰ ਹਨ।

ਇਹ ਤਸਵੀਰ ੧੯੦੭ ਦੇ ਜ਼ਮਾਨੇ ਦੀ ਹੈ।
Whose whereabouts is not known.

ਇਹ ਤਸਵੀਰ ਭਾ: ਭਗਤ ਸਿੰਘ, (ਸ੍ਰ: ਅਜੀਤ ਸਿੰਘ ਦੇ ਭਤੀਜੇ ਤੇ ਸ੍ਰ: ਕਿਸ਼ਨ ਸਿੰਘ ਖਟਕੜ ਕਲਾਂ (ਜਲੰਧਰ) ਦੇ ਸਪੁੱਤ੍ਰ) ਦੀ ਹੈ।

BHAGAT SINGH
s/o Sr. Kishan Singh & Nephew of Sr. Ajit Singh who it is alleged created a sensation in the Assembly by throwing a

Above left: Ajit Singh, uncle of Bhagat Singh, as a revolutionary freedom fighter.

Above right: Ajit Singh compared with Bhagat Singh in a poster of the time. The photo of Bhagat Singh on the right is one of only a handful of genuine photos of him known to exist.

Right: The family tree of Bhagat Singh. His mother, Mata Vidyawati, lived well into her 90s and was able to impart valuable information about him to Prof. Malvinderjit Singh Warraich in detailed interviews.

Below right: Bhagat Singh at his first arrest, wrongfully made in 1927, on suspicion of being involved in bombing a crowd in Lahore during the Dussehra celebrations, of which he was entirely innocent, but of which the police accused him on the basis that he was testing a bomb which he would later use to free HRA members who stood accused in the Kakori Conspiracy Case.

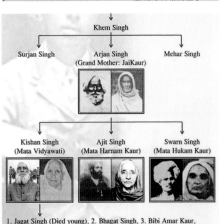

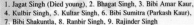

1. Jagat Singh (Died young), 2. Bhagat Singh, 3. Bibi Amar Kaur,
4. Kulbir Singh, 5. Kultar Singh, 6. Bibi Sumitra (Parkash Kaur),
7. Bibi Shakuntla, 8. Ranbir Singh, 9. Rajinder Singh

Above: Bhagat Singh during his student days (fourth from right) in one of the few genuine photos of him.

Left: Quaid-e-Azam Mohammed Ali Jinnah as a young lawyer, immaculately dressed as always.

Below left: Jinnah in Jullunder, 1940.

Below: An exhibit from the Registrar of D.A.V. College Lahore, through which Bhagat Singh and his fellow assailants made their escape, which confirms Des Raj as having been a student there. Des Raj was one of the three in the Lahore Conspiracy Case who was acquitted. The petition raised by the Lahore Bar Association was in his name challenging Lahore Ordinance No. III of 1930.

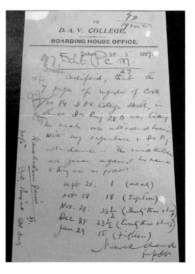

Above right: Rai Sahib Pandit Sri Kishen, Special Magistrate in the Sessions Court, recording on the very first day of the proceedings before him on 10 July 1929 how Bhagat Singh and B. K. Dutt 'repeatedly shouted' the slogan of 'Long Live Revolution' and 'Down with Imperialism' despite being reprimanded.

Right: Edward Wood, Lord Irwin, Viceroy of India and Governor-General from 1925 to 1931.

Below: As soon as the trial before the Special Tribunal began on 5 May 1930, Bhagat Singh petitioned to have an interview with his father, which was denied to him.

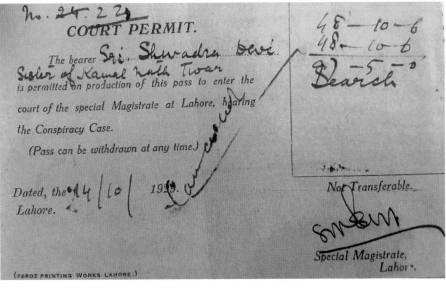

Above left: Mr Justice Agha Haider in his prime.

Above right: The father of Mr Justice Agha Haider.

A group photo marking the retirement of Chief Justice Shadi Lal of Lahore (front row, centre) with Justice Coldstream (on his immediate right) and Justice Agha Haider (third to his right).

Above left: Syed Zahid Hassan, one of Justice Agha Haider's nephews, who became a prominent lawyer in his day.

Above right: Syed Hamid Hassan, another of Justice Agha Haider's nephews, who also went on to become a leading lawyer. Both he and Syed Zahid Hassan were born of Syeda Masooma Khatoon, sister of Justice Agha Haider and the daughter of Meer Ahsan Ali.

Right: The door to the ancestral family home of Justice Agha Haider in Saharanpur, India.

Amolak Ram Kapoor was a dedicated and determined lawyer in Lahore who rose from humble beginnings to become one of the giants of the Lahore Bar. Nonetheless, he remained humble and humane in his dealings with people throughout his life. (Courtesy of Ms Sunaina Suneda)

the river side. I could not attend the funeral because I had to attend the college. In these days the infant mortality in Lahore has been very enormous. The future of the Hindu nation in physical health is precarious. May God give us intellect and high principles of ideals so that we should reform all the evils existing in us as individuals and as members of our society. The greatest reason that accounts for all this is that India is becoming poorer and poorer day by day. Its wealth and energy is drained into wider bellies, and faster mouths. The aliens have sucked off all the blood and vitality that was ever to be found among the brave Hindus of the Hindustan. May our fellow brethren get the true knowledge of all that is happening and that what is contrived by the subtlest heads of the foreigners to annihilate the very seed of the native inhabitants by constantly sweet persecution. I cannot find time in

A page from the diary of Amolak Ram Kapoor when he was just a teenager at college. (Courtesy of Ms Sunaina Suneda)

Above left: The author with Begum Nafisa Khalid in her home in Gujranwala, Pakistan.

Above right: Lord Thankerton, one of the judges on the Board of the Privy Council that heard D. N. Pritt's appeal on behalf of Bhagat Singh. He was known for his habit of knitting while hearing cases.

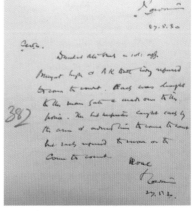

Above left: The gallows at the Lahore Central Jail. They were eventually taken down in the 1960s.

Above right: Handwritten notes of Mr Justice Coldstream during the hearing confirming how Bhagat Singh and B. K. Dutt refused to return to court.

علامہ اقبال علیگڑھ مسلم یونیورسٹی رائیڈنگ اسکول کی ٹیم کے ساتھ

A rare photo showing the distinguished poet Allama Iqbal, who was in practice at the Lahore Bar at the time of the conviction of Bhagat Singh, and who was a signatory to the petition against the sentence of death before the Privy Council on 27 February 1931.

Left: D. N. Pritt in his later years.

Below left: The file of Justice Hilton, the only Tribunal judge to have served throughout, given the removal/resignations of Justice Coldstream and Justice Agha Haider, both at the same time, 'for reasons of health'.

Below right: Bhagat Singh was an avid reader, and remained so even in prison, as is demonstrated by his request to the Delhi District Magistrate dated 25 April 1929, for 'the use of daily newspapers and books', of which he was routinely denied.

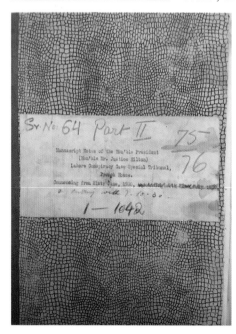

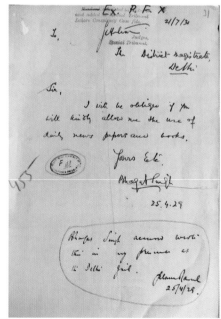

Right: The most famous iconic photo of Bhagat Singh, which led to his being compared with another revolutionary, Che Guevara, an Argentine Marxist who was a major figure in the Cuban Revolution.

Below right: The photograph of Bhagat Singh at his youngest.

Below left: Bhagat Singh's uncle, Ajit Singh, from whom the young Bhagat Singh took so much of his inspiration in his struggle for a fair and equal society, free from colonial rule, where everyone could live free of fear and injustice.

Above: Protests in Bangalore with placards bearing the image of Bhagat Singh in December 2019.

Left: Protesters from the 'Progressive Students Collective' in Lahore proudly bearing a banner in the name of Bhagat Singh in 2019.

Below left: A telling Republic Day poster in 2020 from India demonstrating how even today, in the eyes of many, Bhagat Singh stands tallest among all independence fighters.

Republican Association becoming the Hindustan Socialist Republican Association under Chandrasekhar Azad and Bhagat Singh. In 1929 there was the throwing of the smoke bombs in Delhi Legislative Assembly Hall by Bhagat Singh and B. K. Dutt. Next to this, Mahatma Gandhi's Civil Disobedience Movement was altogether more tame an affair when in 1930 he undertook his defiant 'salt march' to the sea in protest at the British monopoly of salt. There was hardly a comparison.

All this was to climax violently in 1931 when Bhagat Singh, Sukhdev and Rajguru were secretly executed ahead of their allocated time in Lahore Central Jail. The authorities were increasingly afraid of the backlash that they knew would inevitably follow the hangings after a sham trial. Now came Nehru's furious inquiry:

> If England were invaded by Germany or Russia, would Lord Irwin go about advising the people to refrain from violence against invader? ... Let him ask his own heart what he would have felt if Bhagat Singh had been an Englishman and acted for England.[12]

So much for the thoughts of a politician like Nehru. But what of the lawyers? All too often, Partition has seen the lawyers who took on the cases of revolutionaries – at great risk to themselves – lost to the collective memory of the independence movement on both sides. Amolak Ram Kapoor is one person who can be brought to life today. This is largely because of how his descendants in India have continued to remember him. By all accounts he was a precocious young man, acutely sensitive to the travails of his countrymen under the British Raj. By 1918, he was writing about their impoverishment. This is most revealingly shown in a personal diary that he kept as a schoolboy. When Amolak Ram Kapoor was still very young, his mother died and his father remarried. His home life thereafter was unhappy. He joined D.A.V. College in Lahore at the tender age of fourteen in 1914, and this is when he began writing a diary. That year, the First World War engulfed Europe. Its tremors were felt across the British Indian Empire. On 17 September 1914, Kapoor records, 'I bought ... books for 15/4 though the real price was not more than 13/-. IT IS BECAUSE OF THE EUROPEAN WAR.'

Kapoor's diary offers glimpses of his sorrow when his father, whom he describes affectionately as 'my simple and gentle father', also died, leaving the orphaned Amolak Ram Kapoor and his two younger sisters to face a life of struggle and hardship. As if such a calamity was not enough, their stepmother had upped sticks and abandoned the three children, leaving the family home and taking her own son with her. Nevertheless, Kapoor's generosity of spirit shines through and he is seen referring to his half-brother in the diary with affection, and even to be yearning for this child, because he is the missing link in the family, without whom the family is incomplete. Kapoor's uncle in Lahore soon assumed care and custody of the three orphaned children, raising them in a house that was built by Kapoor's father. There the three orphaned children lived with their uncle, aunt and two cousins, but life did not get better. It was as if they were being buffeted from pillar to post, because all three orphaned children were severely mistreated by their aunt, although their uncle was not free from blame. In his diary, Kapoor makes it clear that he holds his uncle responsible as he was in a position to stop the abuse but chose not to do so. The young Kapoor records the day-to-day tribulations the three children had to face, which ranged from being made to go hungry to the regular verbal abuse that they had to endure, as well as money for books and school fees being withheld. Small wonder, then, that when Kapoor did eventually buy some books he considered it worthy of note in his diary.

The diary is Kapoor's trusty companion and his lodestar as he lives out his lonely life denuded of the love and care of his parents. Each page is prefaced with a phrase, such as 'A true foe is better than a false friend' or 'Do not speak a lie'. Indeed, in his diary he exhorts himself to be a better person because he has no parents of his own to guide him. He confesses to procrastination. He appeals to God, asking Him to help him tread a righteous path. In one of his earliest diary entries, on 18 September 1914, he reflectively muses, 'I have not spoken a lie today as yet and hope I would do the same for the rest of the day. I have not begun to perform *Sandhya* [prayers] but I hoped would try to do it soon.' He is conscious of living a life free from sin, taking care to avoid harming even insects: 'I have not committed any sin today except unknown faults as the trampling of any insect under one's feet.' He ruminates over the real-life consequences of not undertaking *Sandhya*, speculating, 'My not performing *Sandhya* may be called a sin or may not be called a sin.' However, he reasons with himself that not doing so does not mean he can find no redemption for himself on this day: 'I threw some bits of bread to crows today as it was rainy season and they could not easily get their food and were all drenched under rain. This is one kind deed of today.'

In the same way, the diary entry for 19 September 1914 is that 'since last 24 hours I have not spoken a lie and am obliged to God for the supernatural help in this. I have committed one "heavy sin"; and pray to God to help in future not to commit such a sin.' Reading through the diary, it is clear that instead of worrying about prayer he is more concerned with carrying out good deeds that have real benefits for the people around him. In this way, the seed of his future as a lawyer fighting for unpopular causes, and running the gauntlet of claims against the government, becomes unmistakably clear. Kapoor was not averse to religion; he made a point of visiting the Arya Samaj Mandir every Sunday, either at Wacchhowali or Anarkali in Lahore. However, what mattered most to him was the performance of good deeds over empty rituals.

During his days at D.A.V. College Kapoor even penned a work, 'Notes on King Arthur', and sold its copyright for 40 rupees to one Lala Hukam Chand BA, who proceeded to publish it under his own name. Amolak Ram Kapoor, determined not to be deprived of what was his due, urged readers to remember that it was he who wrote it! There is also a reference in his diary to writing 'Two Hundred Model Q & A on the History of India'. After noting that 'the work is yet in its infancy', he later indicates that he has added some further questions to the exercise.

Kapoor took history, English, Sanskrit, mathematics and economics at D.A.V. College, and it is clear that he was meticulous about what he studied, because shortly after commencing the year, on Friday 20 November 1914, he applied to change from history to philosophy. Principal Lala Saini Dass rejected his application, saying it was too late. This was a blessing in disguise, for Kapoor went on to finish top of his history class, as he records in his entry of 18 March 1917. The following year, in June 1918, he scored a handsome 265 marks, and he gaily records, 'My position in our college is 6th and in the Panjab University it is 39th. The first gets 337 marks.' Kapoor had every reason to feel pride in what he had achieved. His had not been a gilded life. No silver spoon had ever been put in his mouth. Every day of his life had been lived under the boot of grinding poverty. Yet, he had persisted in the pursuit of his goal, slowly but surely taking his family to heights that would have been unimaginable for most.

This was a man who early in his life had studied under the light of a kerosene lamp, and even that could not be taken for granted for there were times when he did not even have enough money to buy kerosene. Then there was the matter of books. His daughter, who lives in Delhi, recalls how one of his friends, Shiv Dass, had given him a rupee to buy an essential book, without which he could not have continued his education. She recalls how Kapoor to his dying day remembered the kindness of his friend in giving him that one rupee. Later in life, when he was a successful lawyer and a father, he made sure that the priceless debt was never forgotten. He made it a point to remind his three sons, 'We are what we are today because of that one rupee.' Yet a man of such honour could not let matters rest there. He took steps to ensure that the family of Shiv Dass was never left in want for anything, so much so that he made his sons promise to assist them after his death.[13] His may have been a rags-to-riches story, but Kapoor never forgot his humble origins as he blazed a trail to the heights of the legal profession.

By his second year at D.A.V. College, as an adolescent teetering on adulthood, Kapoor demonstrated a developed sense of patriotism. In his diary entry for 27 January 1916, he writes that British imperialism is making India poorer by the day, that it aims 'to annihilate the very seed of the native inhabitants', and that Indians must show 'intellect and high principles' if they are to survive:

> In these days the infant mortality in Lahore has been very enormous. The future of the Hindu nation in physical health is precarious. May God give us intellect and high principles of ideals so that we should reform all the evils existing in us as individuals and as members of one society. The greatest reason that accounts for all this is that India is becoming poorer and poorer day by day. Its wealth and energy is rained into wider bellies, and vaster mouths. The aliens have sucked off all the blood and vitality that was ever to be found among the brave Hindus of the Hindustan. May our fellow brethren get the true knowledge of all that is happening and that what is contrived by the subtlest heads of the foreigners to annihilate the very seed of the native inhabitants by constantly sweet persecution.

After that, an entry in his diary in 1917 states how during a school session 'I read out an essay on "Patriotism – Indian Standpoint" to the Association meeting of 3rd Year Class.' Thereafter, his diary ends abruptly in September 1918.

Amolak Ram Kapoor suffered many hardships in his defence of Bhagat Singh, not least of which was having to worry about being paid by the government for his legal services. He was not alone in this. Other lawyers for the defence fared just as badly. Kapoor, however, was a gifted student. While still studying law in Lahore, a reputed criminal law barrister by the name of Nand Lal (who had incidentally been called to Lincoln's Inn on the same day in 1906 as one by the name of Allama Muhammad Iqbal!) had sent his *munshiji* (secretary) with instructions to find him the ablest young law student in the city. The *munshiji* returned with the name of the orphaned Amolak Ram Kapoor – whereupon Nand Lal promptly arranged to have his eldest daughter married to the talented young Kapoor!

Amolak Ram Kapoor never forgot the difficult years of his childhood. Nor did he forget the generosity of those who had a hand in changing the delicate course of his fraught life. The result was the flowering of his generosity and his munificence towards others. He kept an open house in Lahore, where he was secretary of the Bar Association. People came and went. Those with political gripes and difficulties were especially visible at the house. When after Partition he moved to Delhi and found himself living in Civil Lines, his house remained just as crowded, now by members of his extended family who looked to him for food and shelter. His practice was no different after he shifted to Simla. He did not spare his transgressing stepmother with his generosity. She, who had disclaimed and disowned all responsibility for him and his two sisters, was magnanimously helped, as was his half-brother. In the early days of his career he had even welcomed his offending uncle and aunt back into the fold, putting aside the dreadful cruelty that they inflicted on him and his siblings. It is not known whether they survived the horror of Partition, for they have not been traced after independence.

Mr Khurshid Mahmud Kasuri was a noted Pakistani politician and writer. After his education at Government College Lahore and Cambridge University, he served as the Minister of Foreign Affairs. He was also the chairman of Pakistan Tehreek-e-Insaaf's taskforce on Kashmir. He is best known for his book *Neither a Hawk Nor a Dove*. In it he explains that when his family migrated from India after independence they took over the house of Amolak Ram Kapoor in Lahore. This was situated along the fine tree-lined row of houses a stone's throw from the Lahore High Court. As he explains,

Our residence, 4-Fane Road, Lahore, belonged to one of Pakistan's most successful lawyers before Partition, Amolak Ram Kapoor and after Partition, it became our home and acquired quite a reputation in Lahore among the media, the political circles and the legal fraternity. It was the centre of major political activity.

Indeed, in a section headed 'Fane Road Residence: An Open House', Kasuri writes that 'the atmosphere at our Fane Road house greatly influenced my formative years' because 'almost anyone who had been in the opposition at one time or another, or was on the other side of the government of the day, found my father welcoming them'.[14] In so stating, Kasuri was keeping alive the esteemed traditions of 4 Fane Road. Whilst Partition broke the continuities of the Indian subcontinent, they appear not to have done so at 4 Fane Road. In fact, upon assuming occupation of the house, his father had the wherewithal to despatch to Amolak Ram Kapoor his entire library. The two families, on both sides of the border, continue to this day to retain amicable relations. In 2015, Mr Khurshid Mahmud Kasuri visited Amolak Ram Kapoor's daughter, now living in Delhi, and in turn her own daughter went to Lahore on the occasion of his book launch. Indeed, at the invitation of Kasuri's younger brother, she had even earlier managed to stay at 4 Fane Road, her grandfather's illustrious former home – such is humanity at its very best.

Amolak Ram Kapoor never spoke to his family about the Bhagat Singh case. The Special Tribunal had made life difficult for him, and it was no different for many other defence counsel who appeared for the accused. None spoke of the case. This is not surprising. The lawyer who represented Bhagat Singh before the Privy Council in London, D. N. Pritt, did not mention the Bhagat Singh case anywhere at all in his autobiography.[15] So must it also have been with Amolak Ram. So humiliated were these lawyers by the farce of trial proceedings that, just like the Partition Indians who came across the border after witnessing the carnage there, they never spoke of it again. Yet, in their conscience they must have wrestled with the events of those days to the very end of their lives.

Heresies of the Raj

Ab hum bhi sochte hain ke bazar garm hai;
Apni zameer bech ke duniya khareed lein

Together with Others I too have convinced
myself to sell my Soul for worldly possessions

Iqbal Azim

One striking feature of the Lahore Conspiracy Case of 1930 was its almost entire dependence on the evidence of 'approvers'. Without them there would have been no convictions. Yet, the 'approvers' had been bribed into becoming 'turncoats'. They were induced to snitch on colleagues with whom they had exchanged vows, rubbed shoulders and stood side by side. To be effective their evidence needed independent corroboration. It needed testing under cross-examination. Neither was possible in the trial before the Tribunal. Two of the approvers openly alleged pressure from the police and retracted their statements. There was no jury to assess the credibility and demeanour of the witnesses. Only the judges could do this. They alone could ensure that standards of fairness and justice were upheld. They failed spectacularly in both.

The Special Tribunal began sitting on 5 May 1930 in the stately splendour of Poonch House in the Anarkali precincts. Within days, two of its three judges had been replaced. One, an English judge, made his position untenable by allowing the police to beat up the defendants in the courtroom before his very eyes. The other, an Indian judge, did so by distancing himself from the above action and therefore being deemed too partial to the accused. Then there were the 'approvers'. Only the Indian judge, Justice Agha Haider, bothered to probe their evidence in any way.

One is bound to ask how this could have been a competent tribunal of fact, or how it could properly have determined the guilt or innocence of the accused. At the end of the day, those arraigned before the court were facing capital charges which if proven could see them sentenced to death by hanging. More than a decade later, Ajoy Ghosh, one of those who was eventually acquitted, succinctly summed up his position: 'Due to the tremendous popular enthusiasm that the case had evoked, a number of key witnesses had turned hostile, more were likely to follow suit, and two of the approvers had retracted their confessions.' Indeed, 'the whole case was in danger of ending in fiasco', which would not have occurred 'if ordinary legal procedure was followed and ordinary legal facilities allowed us'.[1]

It is important to note that the flaws in the trial procedure did not start when the Lahore Conspiracy Case shifted to Poonch House. They can be traced right to the beginning of the committal proceedings before Rai Sahib Pandit Sri Kishen in the Magistrates' Court, when the accused were not produced in court whilst held on remand. Instead, it was the magistrate who was taken to selected places where the accused were incarcerated without access to their families or legal advice. There, too, the 'approvers' were left throughout the proceedings in police custody, where they could be groomed by the police as to how their evidence should be given. This was despite repeated pleas from the accused that the 'approvers' be transferred to judicial custody. Their application fell on deaf ears, being rejected time and time again. For this reason, the accused avoided participating in the hearings at this time as well. The judicial tone was hostile throughout. The court did not care that the accused were being denied natural justice. When, for example, on 4 October 1929 the magistrate rejected an application for the removal of the 'approvers' to judicial custody, he spoke to the accused scathingly:

The Learned defence counsel does not hold a brief on behalf of the Approvers to be in a position to plead for them quite uninvited and the proper time for him to elicit details of the nature alluded to by him in his application would be when the Approvers would come into the witness box, and the accused shall have a right to cross examine them. In short, *there's no jurisdiction of the accused to dictate to the court* as *to how and where the Approvers should be kept* and to enquire as to their whereabouts at this stage and I, therefore, reject the application.[2]

This is completely incorrect. It is entirely within the remit of a defence counsel to raise a question of procedural fairness that goes to the very jurisdiction of the Tribunal, where the approvers are kept in police custody, and where they can be tutored in their evidence by the police. Moreover, defence counsel were not assuming 'jurisdiction' so as 'to dictate to the court'. This is a fundamental misunderstanding by a judge of the word 'jurisdiction', which is something only he exercises in a court of law. All that counsel for the accused was doing was making an application to the court that the 'approvers' should not be kept under the control of the police. He was entitled to that. The very implication which the judges would have wished to avoid – that the 'approvers' were not being interfered with – actually manifested itself in the way that the judge responded. The reason why this matters is as follows.

First, the evidence of approvers after they had been kept in police custody for months on end was plainly tainted. That taint was not removed by a magistrate using flagrant language in order to reject an application that asked for the 'approvers' to be kept in judicial custody away from the police. Second, this only helps confirm Jinnah's interpretation of the government position as expressed in his speech in the Central Assembly in 1928: 'We will pursue every possible course, every possible method, but we will see that you are set either to the gallows or transported for life; and in the meantime we would not treat you as decent men.' Third, the only eyewitness of any value was 'Abdullah' (P.W. 34), but as A. G. Noorani explained pithily in 2018, when writing in Pakistan's leading English-language publication, 'Six of the seven eye-witnesses' testimonies collapsed. The survivor, Abdullah, was a chance witness who contradicted himself.'[3] The other witnesses crumbled, and they did so either because they could not identify the persons they were meant to identify, or because they simply lacked credibility given the inordinate delay that had occurred between their appearance in court and their original statement to the police. Fearn was the only one who chased the accused, and remarkably he was the one who failed to identify Bhagat Singh. He claimed that the tall one did not shoot at him, whereas the other witnesses said it was the tall one, Bhagat Singh, who did the shooting. Given the huge disparities in evidence given by Fearn and Abdullah, one would have thought that they would be subject to a thorough and detailed questioning, and yet Abdullah's evidence was not subject to any cross-examination at all by the accused. Fourth, even the identification parades made next to no sense, because Bhagat Singh's photographs had already been widely circulated in the newspapers. On top of that, some of the accused, in particular Bejoy Kumar Sinha, found that the police had themselves pointed out the accused to the witnesses, who then proceeded to finger the accused in court when they were giving evidence for the prosecution.

In the Special Tribunal itself, Justice Hilton alone served throughout. Yet, he hardly intervened to uphold the requirements of justice even though he alone had heard all the evidence. He alone knew that key witnesses for the prosecution had retracted their statements when the other judges had not heard all the evidence. Carden Noad led the government case in the Tribunal just as he had done in the Magistrates' Court. Although now accompanied by public prosecutor Khan Saheb Kalandar Ali Khan and L. Gopal Lal, his performance was derisory when compared to that of Bhagat Singh, who had chosen to represent himself. The Record of Proceedings discloses only that he had 'put in an application stating that he wanted *a legal adviser* to watch the proceedings of the Tribunal and *to give him advice on lines of cross examination*'. This adviser was to be Mr Duni Chand, who would neither cross-examine the government witnesses nor address the court. Carden Noad could hardly have disagreed with this as it was better than Bhagat Singh insisting on having representation by counsel. He happily consented so long as seating accommodation was available in court and 'the tribunal sanctioned the arrangement proposed'.[4] But when Carden Noad opened the case for the prosecution, his first witness was G. T. Hamilton, the Senior Superintendent of Police, who could not have been a worse witness. He simply rattled out what he had said before the Special Magistrate at the beginning of the case on 10 July 1929, in a statement that was astonishing in its candour: 'I do not know the facts of the case nor did I make the statements made in the complaint. I am acting only as a formal complainant *under the instructions of the government.*' It was then that Carden Noad began to rely on his 'approvers', without whom he had no case. It was the 'approvers' whose evidence convicted the accused in the Lahore Conspiracy Case of 1930. It was ultimately a case won through the mouths of turncoats.

In addition to this, the judges of the Special Tribunal remained singularly unable to appreciate that the accused were all young men in their twenties, and that if only they had not been subjected to police brutality on 22 October 1929, on 23 October 1929 and on

12 May 1930, there would have been no reason for them not to have attended court. Even after the abuse they suffered, they might have been persuaded to participate if some compromise had been offered. It is worth recalling from the last chapter that Bhagat Singh handed a statement to the Tribunal relating to the incident on 12 May 1930 which emphasised how they had 'not been attending the court', and would only do so on condition 'that either the president should apologise or should be replaced'.

It is clear from this that if the grievance of the accused was that they had been mistreated on 12 May, then retaining Justice Hilton as chair of the Tribunal was only going to rub salt in the wound. Not only did the accused have no faith in Justice Hilton, they considered him to be biased against them: 'According to the present constitution of the Tribunal, both the president and the other judge who had dissociated himself from that order of the president had been replaced by two new judges. The third judge was a party to that order and has now been appointed to the president of the tribunal.' It will be recalled how the statement went on:

> The removal of the President and the position is not change, because Mr Justice Hilton was a party to that order is presiding in place of Mr Justice Coldstream. ... the present position has added insult to injury.

The statement concluded, 'We wish to point out that in case Mr Justice Hilton dissociates himself from that order referred to above and gives us an assurance for future orders replaced by some other judge, we are prepared to continue coming to this court, otherwise we shall refuse to attend the court from tomorrow.'[5]

Far from the judges of the Tribunal reaching out to assure these young men that they were being treated with a fair hand, what they did was allow the police free rein over the accused. This had been the case in the Magistrates' Court, and it continued to be the case before the Special Tribunal. Had Justice Agha Haider not been removed, and had he been allowed to continue questioning the prosecution witnesses, the situation would have been different. He alone wished to distance himself from the brutality meted out to the accused in his court and before his very eyes. He alone targeted the approvers, who had been induced and bribed into giving evidence that was clearly suspect and warranted serious investigation. If that had happened, it is likely that Bhagat Singh would not have been sent to the gallows on a 2-to-1 vote. The final judgment of the Tribunal simply would not have possessed either the moral force or the legal foundation upon which a sentence of death could be carried out. In the event, however, the entire hearing process was a litany of crass and blundering errors which negated the essence of a fair trial.

Justice Agha Haider alone emerges from the judicial process with credit, and he does so for all the wrong reasons as he was sacked for upholding the basic principles of justice. It is precisely for this reason that the descendants of Justice Agha Haider on both sides of the India–Pakistan border remember him with such pride and affection today. Such was the impact of Agha Haider's principled conduct that two of his nephews went on to become leading lights in law themselves.

Syed Irfan Habib is a distant relation. He is today a noted historian and public intellectual in India. In his authoritative work he proudly asserts that 'Justice Haider was the only Indian Judge who resigned from the Tribunal in protest against the brutal treatment being meted out to Bhagat Singh and his comrades in the Lahore Conspiracy Case' and that 'it is important to mention this selective amnesia as it conforms to the current trend of religion based nationalism'.[6] No less a claim to the ownership of such a legacy is to be found in Pakistan. Justice Agha Haider himself died on 6 February 1947 without any issue, shortly before the country was engulfed in sectarian carnage, but one of his two sisters, Syeda Masoon Khatoon, went on to marry Mir Syed Hassan Mehdi (later a Major in the Pakistan Army), who was also the nephew of Justice Agha Haider.

Before Partition, Justice Agha Haider's family had adjacent homes in Saharanpur, now in India, in a compound known as Mir Ka Kot, where the *kothi* (manor) of Justice Haider and the *baithak* (seat) of Mir Syed Hassan Mehdi were both located. Living quietly in Gujranwala near Lahore today is an elderly lady by the name of Begum Nafisa Khalid, whose father was the nephew of none other than Justice Agha Haider. A former member of the National Assembly, she fondly recalls having seen Haider in her childhood, when he was always nobly attired in the evenings in '*Mal-Mal kah Kurta, Aur Barreh Paichan Ka Pyjama*'[7] ('a finely-spun cotton long-sleeved tunic, worn with a flared widely-hemmed pyjama' for added comfort). She recalled a tall, handsome man who had tinge of thoughtful solitude about him. He did not smoke or drink alcohol. He was a close friend of the poet Allama Muhammad Iqbal, and would send a car out for him on most days so that the two of them could meet at his house. She recalls him as never once having shown a shred of regret over standing up for Bhagat Singh in the Lahore Conspiracy Case, even though it meant the end of his career and the loss of his knighthood. On the contrary, Agha Haider remained generous to all others around him and gave away much of his lands to the tenants who lived on his properties so that they could build houses of their own. Begum Nafisa drew strength from his example. She would boldly thwart and fend off all attempts to silence or browbeat her when performing in Pakistan's legislative chamber, by reference to her being the inheritor of Justice Agha Haider's intellectual mantle, with the words, '*Merah Taluk Us khandhan Seh Hae / Jiske Bazoorgon neh, Angrez Keh Samneh kalam Tordee thee*' ('Do not threaten me for I hail from that dynasty, whose forefathers did not hesitate, even under orders from their British masters, to break the pencil in their hand, rather than sign an Order which offended against their conscience'). Clearly, to this day there are those on the Indian subcontinent who have not forgotten Justice Agha Haider's role in the Special Tribunal.

Justice Agha Haider's absence was sorely felt given that the main 'approvers' were Jai Gopal, Phonindra Nath Ghosh, Manmohan Banerjee, Hans Raj Vohra and Lalit Kumar Mukerji. These men played a decisive role because a number of the conspirators' secrets were known only to them. Jai Gopal and Phonindra Nath Ghosh even invented false stories, much to the gratification of the police. They escaped the law, but they did not escape the wrath of their former colleagues. Jai Gopal narrowly escaped an attack on him in a court in Jalgaon. Phonindra Nath Ghosh was less fortunate, being killed by Baikunth Shukla, another member of the HSRA. Despite the number of 'approvers', it was only the evidence of Jai Gopal and Hans Raj Vohra that focused entirely on the accused's activities in Punjab. Jai Gopal in particular gave a graphic account of how he had been recruited by Sukhdev, how the killing of Saunders took place, and how the assailants were then arrested. Lalit Kumar Mukerji's evidence was mostly about irrelevant events in Allahabad and Agra. Phonindra Nath Ghosh and Manmohan Banerjee dealt with what went on in Bihar and Calcutta, although the evidence of Phonindra Nath Ghosh included the disclosure of some significant events that took place in Uttar Pradesh, in Delhi, and to a lesser extent in Punjab.

The absence of proper cross-examination facilities proved fatal to the accused. Nothing demonstrates this better than the evidence of the arch-approver Jai Gopal. This should have been subject to intense cross-examination. He began his evidence by expounding upon how it was that in 1926, when he was in the tenth class at the National School in Lahore, he had through his Hindi teacher, Yashpal, come into direct contact with Sukhdev, who was widely accredited as being the most effective recruiter in the Lahore Conspiracy Case. Jai Gopal stated,

> Sukhdev asked me whether being a student of the National School, I had ever thought of serving the country. I said that I would wear Khaddar [i.e. 'pure cotton'] clothes and do Congress work. Sukhdev gave me a lecture urging me to become a member of the secret society the object of which was to overthrow the present government.

Jai Gopal went on to say that 'after that Sukhdev met me in November 1926 and told me that I should become a member of the Secret Society which he had organised. I agreed.' He then recounted how 'Sukhdev used to meet me off and on', and that 'in January 1927, Sukhdev again came to my house and asked me to meet him the next day at Bhatti Gate'. From then on, he began to meet him regularly. He explained that he was given a handbag and told to deliver it to a man who could show him two keys, which Sukhdev held up for his attention. Twenty-five days later, someone called Pandit Jai Chand, a former professor at the National College, met with Jai Gopal and asked him whether he had anything that had been left for him by Sukhdev, to which Jai Gopal said that he had replied that he did not know Sukhdev. At precisely this moment, the ex-professor pointedly held up the two keys that Sukhdev had earlier displayed. Understanding what was expected of him, Jai Gopal then passed the handbag to the ex-professor and was asked to wait outside. He heard the clatter of the handbag being opened. It was then handed back to him. The two keys were not.

Some days passed before Sukhdev returned. When he did, he told Jai Gopal to use a set of keys he possessed to access the National College and to 'procure all kinds of helpful things such as mercury, thermometers, batteries and some books of science. I said I would supply whatever I could.' Gaining trust, he was now assigned further tasks by Sukhdev. Eventually Sukhdev decided that it was time for Jai Gopal to meet Bhagat Singh. This happened in 1927, and afterwards Jai Gopal said he was to be involved in the robbery of the Punjab National Bank. However, due to poor planning this idea was aborted. He claims that he was then present at the meeting in

Mozang House where Chandra Shekar Azad, alias Panditji, proposed the murder of Superintendent James Scott. This was in the presence of Bhagat Singh, Sukhdev, Partap Singh, Rajguru, Kali Charan, Ram Chandar and Hans Raj Vohra. Jai Gopal went on to give detailed evidence about his role, which included observing Scott's movements, and how he stood outside the police station on the day of the assassination, ready to give the signal, as soon as Scott came out of the office. On the day, of course, it was not Scott who emerged but Saunders. Behind him, he explained, strode a tall Sikh constable, fully uniformed, carefully watching the surroundings. This was Chanan Singh. Clearly, all this needed stern cross-examining. It was not.

Jai Gopal carried on to give exhaustive and intricate details. In a blow-by-blow account he said that 'the Sahib had started the motorcycle and taken his seat on it. He moved off slowly.' Rajguru stood ready nearby. Jai Gopal gave the signal from his post that the 'Sahib was coming', and 'Bhagat Singh at that time was close to Pandit Ji [Chandrasekhar Azad] but outside the gate on the road'. Saunders' motorcycle neared the gate on the road. It was then that Rajguru fired a shot as the motorbike approached him. As he was hit by the bullet, Saunders 'lifted up his hands from the cycle and fell on one side of the cycle. The cycle engine went on running. One of the officer's legs fell under the cycle.' It was then that Bhagat Singh made his move. Running towards the officer, who lay on the ground, he pulled out his revolver and shot him several times with his Browning automatic pistol (which was to become exhibit P/480 and lies at Anarkali Police Station). Saunders, still alive, groaned: 'Some sort of sound came out of the officer's mouth as he fell.'

The assailants fled down Court Street. Chanan Singh gave chase, together with the aforementioned traffic inspector, Fearn. Bhagat Singh and Rajguru turned around and shot back at their pursuers. While the firing was still going on, a motor car drove from the direction of the District Courts. The car came to a halt near where Jai Gopal stood. Mr Fearn ducked and fell as Bhagat Singh shot at him. Together with Rajguru, Bhagat Singh then sought refuge in the D.A.V. College, entering through a small gate. Jai Gopal knew all this because he himself went down Court Road with his bicycle. Chanan Singh turned into the compound as well. Sometime after this he was killed.

Bhagat Singh's arrest eventually took place on 15 April 1929 in Kashmir Building, where the culprits were staying. Jai Gopal recalled that it was eight o'clock in the morning when the police arrived. They entered Jai Gopal's room, searched him and then arrested him. Sukhdev pretended to feel sick and left the room on the pretext of getting some water. He was hurriedly brought back in by the officers and searched. As this went on, Sukhdev drew a revolver from his pocket. Sayyad Ahmad Shah, the Deputy Superintendent of Police, quickly snatched it away from him. Jai Gopal subsequently claimed that he asked Sukhdev why he had not fired his revolver, to which Sukhdev apparently replied that he had intended to, and that he had the '*topiwala*' (the one with the police helmet) in mind, but had found no opportunity to do so. The police, Jai Gopal claimed, asked Sukhdev whether his revolver was loaded. He replied that it was. Upon hearing this, the Deputy Superintendent of Police handed the revolver over to Deputy Niaz Ahmad Khan. After searches were concluded, the suspects were then handcuffed. Jai Gopal also claimed that 'Sukhdev then pointed to a box lying above the window saying that it contained a live bomb. The box was opened by the police and the bomb wrapped up in papers was recovered' (it was to become Exhibit P/2 at the trial). The police then searched the premises also. They opened a cupboard by taking the keys from Kishori Lal. There they found bombshells, acids, chemicals and glasses. In total, Kashmir Building yielded eight bombshells, eighteen cartridges belonging to Sukhdev, a revolver belonging to Sukhdev, and five books.

The evidence of Jai Gopal, though detailed and extensive, was not beyond challenge and criticism. It has to be taken with more than a pinch of salt. Indeed, his was not the only evidence that was suspect. Professor Malwinderjit Singh Waraich has shown that when the 'Statements of 457 Prosecution Witnesses were given to all the accused on 30th August 1930 … Sukhdev must have read and re-read the proceedings together while awaiting the final outcome of the case' and that he made notes in the margins commenting on that evidence. Even though 'Sukhdev's Notes, and responses, in the form of underlining, marginal notes etc. seem to have remained unknown to his comrades since none of them had referred to their existence in their memoirs'.[8] they are revealing as to the truth of the evidence against the accused. A. G. Noorani, who painstakingly examined the Record of Proceedings at the National Archives of India, noted some marginal comments written in the hand of Sukhdev at the precise paragraph concerning Jai Gopal's claim that Sukhdev told him 'the Central Body had decided to murder Tassaduq Hussain Bannerjee'.[9] Sukhdev categorically refutes that this was ever the case: 'Wrong. I never told him such.' If this is correct, then the fact that Jai Gopal was not cross-examined at all means that his evidence was never tested. In fact, Sukhdev even claimed, 'I myself handed over the revolver to the police before I was searched.' If, for a moment, one assumes that Sukhdev had no motive to make a false statement on the margin of the official record of the proceedings, whereas Jai Gopal as an 'approver' had every motive to lie, then the failure to cross-examine the account of Jai Gopal is a serious violation of the right to a fair hearing.

Sukhdev had no reason to shoot at a *topiwala* in the way claimed by Jai Gopal. Saunders was shot, in a regrettable case of mistaken identity, because Bhagat Singh and his comrades had reason to do so: they wished to avenge the callous killing of Lala Lajpat Rai. There was no reason for Sukhdev to want to kill a *topiwala* at Kashmir Building on this occasion, just as there was no reason for him not to voluntarily surrender his pistol as he claimed to have done. This is all the more true if, as Jai Gopal claims, Sukhdev warned the police that there was a bomb in a box above the window which had to be safely removed. It has to be remembered that Jai Gopal was arrested on 15 April 1929. Within two weeks, on the 30th, he had accepted a pardon from the authorities on the condition that he turned approver. A. G. Noorani quotes Sukhdev's 'bitter laments' as inscribed in the official record of the trial: 'I believed him too much. Many times I disclosed before him what I should have not ... I have committed the same mistake when I took him to Kashmir Buildings.'[10] This suggests that Sukhdev eventually came to realise that he had been dealing with an imposter all along.

Jai Gopal's evidence was highly suspect in other ways as well. He had stated that those involved in the assassination of Saunders had come to realise their mistake when they saw Scott with his wife the next day. Upon seeing Scott, however, Sukhdev had refused to shoot at him, despite being armed. In his handwritten notes on the official script of the Record of Proceedings, Sukhdev fervently decries any suggestion that he would have shot him without the agreement of his comrades: 'Nonsense. As a member of a body I could not do so.'[11] This also corroborates Sukhdev's claim that he would never have shot at the *topiwala* when the police arrived at Kashmir Building. 'As a member of a body', he was not authorised to act alone.

By far the most significant demonstration of the importance of rigorously cross-examining approver evidence concerns Sukhdev's account of the mistaken murder of Saunders. A. G. Noorani found the following comments scribbled by Sukhdev in the margin of the deposition given by Jai Gopal, who was tasked with giving the signal to fire the fatal shot when Scott left the police office:

Bhagat Singh was to fire first. Rajguru was sent only to guard Bhagat Singh. Pandit [i.e. Chanderashekar Azad] was to guard these both, while escaping. Bhagat Singh remarked that the Sahib is not Scott, so he turned towards Pandit Ji to tell him so. Meanwhile, Rajguru fired which he should not have. He never recognised Scott. Then Bhagat Singh was duty-bound to fire the wrong victim. Thus happened the murder of Mr Saunders.[12]

If Sukhdev's account is the truth, then Jai Gopal was to blame for the wrong person being shot! He was the one entrusted with correctly identifying Scott. Had he done his job, Saunders would not have been shot. Bhagat Singh and his comrades would not have committed murder on 17 December 1928.

Yet, with Justice Agha Haider's continued involvement in the proceedings cut short, it was open season on the accused, who were bereft of a means to challenge the evidence that the prosecution had so unscrupulously arraigned against them. There were gaping holes in the Tribunal's treatment of such evidence, which raised serious questions about the probity of the proceedings. If there had been a right of appeal from the decision of the Tribunal to the High Court, the accused would have been able to draw attention to these material irregularities. That this did not come to pass remains a blot on the justice system of a colonial government that convicted young men barely out of their teens.

It was surely not insignificant that more than one government witness withdrew his statement, so that two of the seven approvers, Ram Saran Das and Brahm Dutt, recanted their statements. Their evidence had to be disregarded. Moreover, the judges knew full well from open evidence given in court that the authorities had interfered with the prosecution evidence and yet chose to do nothing about it. We know that Ram Saran Das had gone so far as to directly accuse the police, both in the Magistrates' Court and before the Tribunal, of altering his statement. Even where the evidence was capable of being taken into account there were serious concerns about the overall weight to be given to it. Thus, of the remaining five approvers – Jai Gopal, Phonindra Nath Ghosh, Hans Raj Vohra, Manmohan Bannerjee, and Lalit Kumar Mukerji – only the evidence of the first three counted for anything against the accused. Of the accused themselves, three of them – Mahavir Singh, Gaya Parshad and Prem Dutt – retracted their confessions, and Kishori Lal's statement was not even recorded. As if all that was not enough to call the trial into question, the Tribunal's preconceived mindset demonstrated its bias against the accused in the way that the undertrials were not referred to in the judgment as 'the accused' but as 'murderers' so that their guilt was predetermined. In fact, the Tribunal's bias is clear from how badly the judgment was drafted.

Thus, early on in the judgment, there is a section headed 'Chronological Account of the Facts Revealed by the Prosecution Evidence without Any Discussion of the Proof of Those Facts'. Yet, the very fact that there was no discussion 'of the proof of those facts' means that they cannot be stated as 'facts' in the judgment. There is background information about Phonindra Nath Ghosh,[13] and from there the judgment proceeds to conclude with the throwing of bombs in the Central Assembly on 18 April 1929.[14] Words like 'possibly', 'probably' and 'presumably' proliferate throughout. Such words foster conditional conclusions. They are hardly proper findings. In a criminal case there have to be findings 'beyond all reasonable doubt'. Bhagat Singh and his two comrades could not possibly have been put to death on this basis. It is no good writing a judgment in terms such as, 'While Mr. Fearn (the Traffic Inspector) was chasing Bhagat Singh and Shivram Rajguru down Court Street, one of the accused, *probably* Bhagat Singh, fired at Mr. Fearn ... Constable Charan Singh was shot in the right groin *probably* by Panditji...'[15] Either Bhagat Singh shot at Mr Fearn or he did not. Either Panditji (Azad) shot and injured Charan Singh or he did not. In a criminal trial it is not enough to convict a person on the basis of what 'probably' happened if only because it is just as probable that what is being alleged did not in fact happen. The Tribunal tried to get around this difficulty by treating the matter as a 'single conspiracy'[16] connected by 'individual incidents'. However, there was still a want of evidence, as the Tribunal openly recognised.[17]

Inevitably, therefore, the Tribunal ended up entertaining evidence that was speculative and impossible to corroborate. An example of this is the September 1928 meeting at the Feroze Shah Kotla in New Delhi, which the Tribunal found to be 'the foundation of the proof that a single conspiracy came into being at that meeting', on the basis of the evidence of Phonindra Nath Ghosh and Manmohan Bannerjee. But when it came to corroborating this, all the Tribunal could bring itself to say was that '[t]he corroboration of the testimony of the Approvers on this point is of different kinds'. The Tribunal had satisfied itself of the evidence of a 'single conspiracy' by finding that 'the same young men' were seen fraternising together. As the Tribunal reasoned, 'In the first place there is the fact that the same young men who were without much money and who had no ostensible business were found associating together in many different places at the same house.' It was a short step for the Tribunal to conclude that even a book shared amongst the same people was tantamount to there being a 'conspiracy'. This enabled the Tribunal to make the following questionable finding:

> The book EX. P. 481, *Roads to Freedom*, was recovered from the possession of Prem Dutt at Gujarat and was seen by Jai Gopal in the possession of Bhagat Singh at Ferozepur. This book has notes written on it, by means of which it is identifiable, and it is noteworthy that Jai Gopal's statement, made to a magistrate *after pardon had been accepted by him*, preceded the recovery of this book from Prem Dutt's possession (emphases added).

The paradox was lost on the Tribunal that Jai Gopal had only made a statement before the magistrate after he had been offered a pardon in return, which he had accepted. This seemed not to have mattered to the Tribunal, steeped as it was in its conviction that the accused were guilty.

In fact, the Tribunal at one stage appears to have dispensed altogether with the need to find the accused guilty on the criminal standard of proof. This happened when two air pistols were recovered. The Tribunal decided that this discovery implicated the accused in a conspiracy against the King, even though 'the two air pistols *cannot be identified beyond all possible doubt* but are sufficiently uncommon articles to be identified with a fair degree of probability'. On this dubious basis it was apparently possible to conclude that '[t]hey were used by the members of the party for target practice'. It is certainly questionable whether pistols were uncommon enough to attribute guilt to the accused, especially given that the Tribunal by its own admission did not possess evidence demonstrating beyond all reasonable doubt that the accused were actually in possession of the pistols. Moreover, without the benefit of cross-examination, it is difficult to see how the Tribunal could in any event have concluded as it did. Nevertheless, the Tribunal decided that:

> Having regard to the various pieces of evidence detailed above and especially to the evidence regarding the bombs and the pink posters and that which concerns the numerous houses at different places *wherein the accused persons are proved to have associated together*, coupled with the testimony of the Approvers regarding the proceedings of the Delhi meeting of September 1928, *there exists full proof of the existence of a single conspiracy dating from September 1928*, and of the

fact that subsequent activities of the various accused persons including the Saunders murder, the throwing of the bombs in the assembly Hall at Delhi, the manufacture of explosives at Calcutta, Agra, Lahore, Saharanpur, and Moulania dacoity were the outcome of the conspiracy.

Yet the only evidence of a 'single conspiracy' comes from recovered books that may or may not have related to the same conspiracy – a matter which could not be definitively proven without cross-examination of the witnesses in question. Thus there is the statement, 'One other matter which gives rise to the inference regarding the existence of a single conspiracy … is the recovery of literature of a revolutionary type from the possession of the various members of the party. For instance, in April 1929, there were found at the Kashmir Building, Ex.P. 25, *An account of the Kabul Revolutionary party…*' The judgment goes on to say, 'From the possession of Prem Dutt in Gujarat were recovered Ex.P. 567, *The seven that were hanged…*' Also noted is the fact that when 'the Mughal Bazar House, Amritsar was searched on 11 May 1929 by Sub-Inspector Chaudhri Saheb Din (P.W.32)' there 'amongst the books found there was EX.P. 170, *Non-Cooperation pushed to its logical consequences.* In the raid on the house at Saharanpur on 13 May 1929, there were found EX.P. 360, *The naming of socialism* and EX.P. 362 *Leninism.*' Even if such books were uncovered, the question remains whether any of these items, belonging to different persons in different locations, would lead to a conclusion that there was a 'single conspiracy' simply by virtue of the fact that all the books recovered at these addresses were related to communism. Viewed from any angle, this is a major stretch of judicial imagination.

This brings us to the evidence against Bhagat Singh. Although in the Tribunal's Judgment this is discussed in no fewer than twenty pages,[18] it is curiously and cryptically encapsulated in the statement that '[t]he important feature of the evidence regarding Bhagat Singh is his ubiquity' because 'he was appointed to be a link between the various provinces'. Neither state of affairs in itself demonstrates his guilt in the single conspiracy. In fact, the Tribunal treated the mere presence of Bhagat Singh at a meeting on Mozang Road in Lahore as confirmation of his involvement in a 'conspiracy'. It is well known that presence alone will not do because in criminal law a conspiracy is an agreement between two or more persons to commit a crime sometime in the future. If the Tribunal could find evidence of presence, it still had to find evidence beyond all reasonable doubt of an agreement to perform an illegal act, and to that end it divided consideration of Bhagat Singh's liability into two sections. One section focused upon his membership of an organised body of individuals intent on acting in a criminal fashion for a robbery in Bihar, which was on the other side of India. The second focused upon his involvement in Saunders' murder, which was in the Punjab. It is worth analysing both of these, for the Tribunal's decision regarding both exhibited serious flaws in fact-finding.

First, let us take the evidence of Bhagat Singh's involvement in a single conspiracy to rob banks across India. This was fundamentally based on the evidence of 'approvers' who were not cross-examined. As the Tribunal explained,

> regarding Bhagat Singh's presence at the Delhi meeting of September 1928, and his appointment at the Central Committee on that occasion, there is the evidence of Phonindra Nath Ghosh and Man Mohan Bannerji, corroborated in an important manner by the testimony of the *chaukidar* [watchman] of the Feroz Shah Tughlak Fort, Bara Singh (P.W. 430), who spoke to Bhagat Singh at the time of the meeting and subsequently identified him in the Court of the Special Magistrate as well as the magisterial parade. That this witness, being the *chaukidar* of the Fort, should have been present on that particular occasion is a natural circumstance and there is no suspicion attaching to his evidence, which should be taken, when coupled with the evidence of the two Approvers, as fully proving Bhagat Singh's presence at the Delhi meeting.

This, however, does not prove Bhagat Singh's involvement in a conspiracy. The witnesses in question, two of whom were 'approvers', were not cross-examined. This is not insignificant given that Phonindra Nath Ghosh and Manmohan Bannerji were only testifying to Bhagat Singh's presence at the Mozang Road meeting in Lahore, and not his involvement in the plans for a robbery in Bihar. Also, as the evidence stood, especially the *chaukidar's* testimony, it only proved Bhagat Singh's presence 'at the time of the meeting'. It does not show what actually took place there. This being so it could not be said to corroborate 'in an important manner' that Bhagat Singh was complicit in plans for a robbery in Bihar. Similar flaws exist in the Tribunal's determination of the question of Bhagat Singh's involvement in a conspiracy to rob the Punjab National Bank in Lahore. Here the evidence relied upon is that of his co-accused, Mahabir Singh. But Mahabir had retracted his confession. Yet, that retracted confession was nevertheless still read in conjunction with statements from a taxi driver, Barkat Ali (P.W. 87), and a Tonga driver, Feroz Din (P.W. 449).

This was despite the fact that neither of these two individuals could identify Bhagat Singh. In that event, it stood to reason that neither of them could actually have corroborated the identification provided by the 'approvers'. Bhagat Singh may indeed have been present at the meeting at a house on Mozang Road. His presence there may have been confirmed by four witnesses, 'all of whom identified Bhagat Singh in the magisterial parades and also in court'. Moreover, this may have been consistent with what was said by the 'approvers'. Nevertheless, the best that can be said of their evidence was that it pointed to Bhagat Singh's 'presence at Mozang House'. The evidence of the four witnesses was no better than 400 if all it did was show Bhagat Singh's presence at a particular place, given that neither the taxi driver nor the Tonga driver could actually identify Bhagat Singh in a way that corroborated what the 'approvers' were saying. A criminal trial, and a criminal 'conspiracy' at that, designed to undertake an unlawful enterprise, required much more by way of proof.

Second, let us take the Tribunal's approach to the finding that Bhagat Singh shot and killed John Saunders. Of course, no one today seriously doubts that Bhagat Singh did indeed shoot and kill Saunders in a case of mistaken identity. Indeed, Bhagat Singh himself did not exactly keep this a secret. There were notices plastered all over Lahore boasting that Lala Lajpat Rai's death had been avenged, and for good measure these were emblazoned with Bhagat Singh's signature. Such audacity on his part, however, did not absolve a fact-finding Tribunal from carrying out its judicial function of setting out to ascertain the facts alleged as being true. In the case of the blatant murder of a young police officer, the evidence may of course have been stronger here, compared to that which existed alleging Bhagat Singh's membership of single conspiracy to undertake a series of robberies, but independent corroboration of the approvers' evidence was still essential even here. This is because only two people – Chanan Singh and W. J. G. Fearn – had seen the murder on 17 December 1928, and the former was shot dead as he gave chase while the latter could not identify Bhagat Singh. Therefore, Bhagat Singh's signed posters announcing that 'Saunders is dead' did not absolve the Tribunal from analysing the evidence. This it did under three headings.

First, there was the 'evidence of various eyewitnesses who claim to have identified Bhagat Singh'. Second, there was 'the evidence of the two Approvers, Jai Gopal and Hans Raj Vohra', particularly that of Jai Gopal, who was not just present at the scene of the crime but was actually a participant. It was said by the Tribunal that Jai Gopal's evidence itself was given 'certain corroboration':

> Mr. Saunders was actually shot by Bhagat Singh, which is furnished by the testimony of Mr. Robert Churchill (P.W. 31) the gun expert of London, who proves that a cartridge case found near the spot had issued from the automatic pistol, Ex. P. 480, which was recovered from the possession of Bhagat Singh by Sergeant Terry (P.W. 18) when he arrested Bhagat Singh on the 18th April 1929, in the Assembly Hall in Delhi.

Third, the Tribunal wrote,

> There are the posters, EXs. P.A.X., P.A.X. /1, P.A.X./ 2. P.A.X./3, P.B.O and P.B.S. all of which are proved by the handwriting expert Mr Scott (P.W. 423) to be in the handwriting of Bhagat Singh and the contents of which are tantamount to a confession on the part of Bhagat Singh of complicity in the murder of Mr Saunders in the interests of the Hindustan Socialist Republican Army. A further admission of Bhagat Singh regarding his participation in the Saunders murder is proved by the confession of Prem Dutt, who mentions that in his presence, probably in January 1929, Bhagat Singh addressing Sukh Dev stated, 'Do you remember how endeavours were made by us to hit the mark accurately, but we used to miss it? When we went to kill Saunders the bullet struck his head and we thought that one of us would be arrested but none was arrested.'

Yet even though seven witnesses had claimed to have seen Saunders being murdered, the fact remains that their testimony did not stand up. There was Traffic Inspector Fearn, but when it came to it he could not identify any of the assailants. Fakir Wahiduddin had disembarked from his cycle to relieve himself in an alley when he had happened to see the shooting take place. Then there was sub-inspector, Gainda Singh. The evidence of the latter two, however, was 'disregarded owing to the fact that neither of these witnesses was prompt in giving information to the authorities about what he has professed to have seen'. When it came to witnesses Muhammad Ibrahim, Constable Habibullah and Kamal Din, the Tribunal found that there were 'certain discrepancies in the testimony of the other witnesses which give rise to some doubt whether these three men should be believed'. That just left one of the seven eyewitnesses. This was 'Abdullah', driver of the car carrying Kamal Din and Habibullah that pulled up on the street as the murder took place. Of this the Tribunal said,

> The evidence of Abdullah (P.W. 34) is, however, satisfactory and reliable. He was the motor driver whose motor arrived, while the firing was going on, at the corner of Court Street near to the position which Jai Gopal had taken up. He afterwards took the body of Mr Saunders to the hospital in his car. He saw the attack upon Mr Saunders and he has identified Bhagat Singh satisfactorily both at a Magisterial parade and also in Court as the taller of the two men who fired upon Mr Saunders. This identification there is no reason to doubt.

Closer scrutiny shows that the Tribunal was quite wrong to regard as 'satisfactory and reliable' the evidence of 'Abdullah', which was given to the Tribunal on 3 July 1930, because his evidence held far more discrepancies than that of his companions, Habibullah and Kamal Din. This is because 'Abdullah' had been quite clear that his statement 'was recorded by the police four days after the occurrence. No police officer took my name and address on the day of the occurrence, nor did anyone take the name and address of Kamal Din or Habibullah in my presence.' Interestingly, in the transcript of the trial proceedings it is clear that the Tribunal was less than enamoured with the circumstances in which 'Abdullah' was now giving evidence. Indeed, it was sufficiently sceptical of him to cast doubt on his evidence. But in the judgment itself, after having had to reject the evidence of the other six witnesses, the Tribunal found itself accepting his evidence as key. This can only be a matter of grave concern.

Third, there were the four student witnesses who 'saw the murderers on the way from the scene of action' passing through the grounds of D.A.V. College. Yet, the first could not identify Bhagat Singh in jail after earlier fingering him in a magisterial parade; the second had only identified Bhagat Singh 'by his back' at the magisterial parade and so unsurprisingly could not pick him out in jail; the third did identify Bhagat Singh both at the magisterial parade and in jail thereafter; and the fourth student, whose bicycle Bhagat Singh had tried to seize, could not identify him at all. The four witnesses bear further consideration. The first witness was Som Nath (P.W. 144):

> Som Nath saw the *three murderers* coming down the staircase from Block B of the D.A.V. College Hostel and noticed that one of them was armed with a pistol. He picked out satisfactorily Bhagat Singh as one

of those three men at a magisterial parade, but the identification of Bhagat Singh in the jail just before giving the evidence in this court was not quite so successful. In the first instance, he picked up another man but immediately corrected himself and picked out Bhagat Singh. His evidence should be regarded as good proof against Bhagat Singh.

The second of the student witnesses was Abnash Chand (P.W. 145) who according to the Tribunal 'saw three members near the Botanical Garden of the D.A.V. College. One of them appeared to be carrying a pistol. He picked out Bhagat Singh as one of those men successfully at a magisterial parade *by his back which is the only part of the man in question that he had seen* on the occasion referred to, but when he went to jail shortly before giving the evidence *he was unable again to pick out* Bhagat Singh. His evidence is, *not therefore, very effective against Bhagat Singh.*' The third student witness was Aftab Ahmed (P.W. 232), who 'was near the Volleyball ground of the D.A.V. College and saw *two of the murderers* pass by, one having a pistol. He satisfactorily picked out Bhagat Singh both at the magisterial parade and in court as the man who was carrying the pistol.' The fourth student witness, Ajmer Singh (P.W. 181), who failed entirely to identify Bhagat Singh, was in many ways the most significant. This was the student whose bicycle Bhagat Singh had endeavoured to snatch as he fled the scene. Surely he would have got as close a look as anybody. And yet, as the Tribunal wistfully recorded, '*He did not succeed in identifying Bhagat Singh* as one of the party who accosted him.'

On the other hand, Bhagat Singh was identified by the bicycle shop owner Ata Muhammad (P.W. 48), from whose premises Bhagat Singh did successfully grab a bicycle. This does raise the question as to why so many witnesses in kindred situations of identification had such different recollections of what they had seen. For the Tribunal, nevertheless, 'the cycle merchant from whose shop bicycle was actually taken but abandoned when the witness gave chase' was the person who 'deposed that one of the three men who passed his shop stopped at a turning while the other would remove the bicycle from a shop. He has satisfactorily identified Bhagat Singh at a magisterial parade and also in court as the man who stopped at the turning and his evidence is good proof against Bhagat Singh. Thus, of the witnesses in this group, Som Nath (P.W. 144) Aftab Ahmed (P.W. 322) and Ata Muhammad (P.W. 48) provide good evidence of Bhagat Singh's participation in the Saunders' murder.' This, however, overstates the position on the Tribunal's own findings of fact. Som Nath, the Tribunal had found, 'was *not quite so successful*' in identifying Bhagat Singh in jail. Aftab Ahmed was the only student who identified Bhagat Singh every time he was asked to. It is true that Ata Muhammad pointed out Bhagat Singh, but Ajmer Singh, whose bicycle Bhagat Singh had tried to collar, singularly failed to do so.

Added to these inconsistencies and ambiguities in the evidence was the fact that the pistol alleged to have been found on Bhagat Singh's person no less than four months later, after the smoke bomb attack at the Central Assembly, was not exhibited at the trial at all! This renders unsafe any conclusion with respect to it. Bhagat Singh's possession of the pistol had not been proved. As Saunders lay dying, a pistol bullet had been retrieved from nearby. Saunders had been shot eight times, and spent shells lay scattered around his body. They were gathered up and transported over to London for forensic analysis. This is how gun expert Robert Churchill came into the picture. He examined the cartridge shells, after which he travelled from London to Lahore to give his expert testimony. In Lahore he gave a rather complex and involved explanation. This was described by the Tribunal as his having made 'an ocular demonstration in court to the Tribunal with the help of micro photographs and a pair of microscopes, with one single eyepiece, in which eyepiece half of each of two bullets to be compared, could be simultaneously compared showing whether or not they had been fired from the same weapon, by relating the lines found on one bullet of those on the other'.

For the Tribunal, this was just what it needed: 'The comparison proved conclusively to the expert and this court that the bullet, EX P. 864/1-1, and the empty cartridge case, Ex-P. 864/1-B, had been fired from the automatic pistol, Ex.P. 480. Had the pistol been removed from Bhagat Singh immediately after the murder, this piece of evidence would have proved by itself that he fired on Mr Saunders. *As it was recovered from Bhagat Singh nearly 4 months later, it cannot be said to amount to more than corroborative evidence of the statement of Jai Gopal*, but as corroborative evidence it has a very high value.' The Tribunal went on to conclude that, 'taking all the above evidence together, it is conclusively proved that Bhagat Singh took part in the murder of Mr Saunders and actually fired at him with the pistol, EX P. 480'. However, this did not follow quite as night follows day, because 'the pistol, EX P. 480', with which Bhagat Singh is alleged to have shot Saunders, was not even exhibited at trial before the Tribunal.

Ineluctably, the Tribunal moved to convict the accused. It explained how, a few months after the murder, Bhagat Singh went to the Central

Assembly chamber and threw smoke bombs on 18 April 1929. Its conclusions now ranged far and wide:

> To sum up, Bhagat Singh was a leader of the revolutionary party which was formed at Delhi in September 1928, and had already taken part in revolutionary activities before the party was formed. He was the active member of the Punjab Branch of which Sukh Dev was the organising member and from the time of the Delhi meeting Bhagat Singh was selected as a link between the various provinces and in this capacity was constantly travelling from place to place between the Punjab and Calcutta. As a member of the Central Committee he also took part in the important deliberations and plans of the party and was generally found participating in the active side of the movement.

This was not all. The Tribunal was in little doubt that

> he took part in the project to raid the Punjab National Bank of Lahore, he was a protagonist in the murder of Mr Saunders and it was he who entered into negotiations that J.N. Dass should teach bomb-making to the members of the party. He actually took part in the bomb-making at Agra, in the rescue party of Jagdesh Chander Chatterji and in the journey to Jhansi to test a bomb and finally he was selected to throw a bomb in the Assembly Hall, Delhi, in April 1929.

That, then, was how Bhagat Singh finally came to be arrested, arraigned first in the Magistrates' Court in committal proceedings before Pandit Shri Krishna and then before the Special Tribunal of Justice Hilton and of Justice Coldstream, before finally being convicted and sentenced to death by hanging. Kala Masih of Shadra, near Lahore, carried out the execution late on the evening of 23 March 1931, ending the lives of Bhagat Singh, Rajguru and Sukhdev in Lahore Central Jail. To this day, this location is wrongly identified as what has for the most part been known as Fawara Chowk, south of a large flowing watercourse, where once the 'Female Penitentiary' stood some distance away from a lunatic asylum. This complex was torn down in the 1960s, and Lahore Central Jail, where Bhagat Singh was hanged, was actually close to Shadman Gardens, where Shadman Market is today located alongside a plaza of glittering shops, but not Fawara Chowk.

The Lahore Conspiracy Case was a big trial, and people had to be rewarded for their participation. A. A. Lane, an Indian Civil Service officer, together with G. T. Hamilton Hardinge, Acting Superintendent of

Police in Lahore, supervised the execution. Also present at the gallows to watch were Lieutenant Colonel F. A. Barker, Inspector General of Prisons, and G. C. Stead, Inspector General of Punjab Police. All were honoured by the British government after the hanging. When the bodies of Bhagat Singh, Rajguru and Sukhdev were taken down from the gallows, they were disposed of by Deputy Superintendent of Police Sudarshan Singh. He too had to be rewarded, so he was quickly promoted to the post of Additional Superintendent of Police in Kasur, a town not far from Lahore. By the time he retired in September 1942, he was Superintendent of Punjab Police.

The four main 'approvers' – Hans Raj Vohra, Jai Gopal, Phonindra Nath Ghosh and Manmohan Bannerji – were amply rewarded. Vohra in particular was smart. He refused monetary rewards and instead opted for a sponsorship from the Punjab government to take up studies in the UK at the renowned London School of Economics. He eventually returned to India and became a prominent journalist before emigrating to Washington in the 1960s. He died there in July 1995. Jai Gopal was rewarded with Rs 20,000. Phonindra Nath Ghosh and Manmohan Bannerji were both given a largesse of 50 acres of land in their home area of Champaran in Bihar.

Two days after the executions, Major P. D. Chopra, the jail superintendent at the time of the Lahore Conspiracy Case, was promoted to Deputy Inspector General of Prisons for the Punjab. On the other hand, Khan Sahib Mohammad Akbar Khan, the Deputy Jail Superintendent, had broken down and wept bitterly after watching the execution of Bhagat Singh and his two companions. For this display of unmanly human infirmity he was suspended from his post, although he was later reinstated as Assistant Jail Superintendent. Nevertheless, the government made sure that he would not escape reprimand. Accordingly, on 7 March 1931, he was stripped of his coveted honorific 'Khan Sahib'. Lieutenant Colonel Barker, meanwhile, received a knighthood – one can safely assume that he did not lose his composure during the hangings.[19]

A few days after the execution, Lieutenant Colonel N. R. Puri, the District Inspector General of Prisons in the Punjab, assumed the position of Inspector General of Prisons for the Punjab. Khan Bahadur Sheikh Abdul Aziz, who as Superintendent had been the investigating officer in the Lahore Conspiracy Case, was rewarded handsomely with 50 acres of land in Lyallpur. This was in addition to being promoted to a higher grade at once, and then three years later to the highest rank. In this way, he became the only person during the entirety of British rule in India to join as a head constable and reach the rank of District Inspector General. Indeed, his eldest son, Masood Aziz, was appointed as Deputy Superintendent of Police in November 1931 in the Punjab Police. All the constables and head constables who accompanied the Inspector General of Prisons, G. C. Stead, received 'appreciation letters' recognising their service. Another who received a letter of appreciation was the Special Magistrate, Rai Sahib Pandit Sri Kishen. He was soon fast-tracked to the position of Additional District Magistrate.

A. G. Noorani has made it only too clear that '[t]oday, no historian contests the fact that Bhagat Singh and Rajguru did, indeed, fire the fatal shots at Saunders'.[20] However, what is equally clear is that the legal proceedings in the trial of Bhagat Singh were monstrously flawed. The court did not convict the accused on the basis of a fair procedure and due process of law. Legally, they could not have been hanged. Military tribunals of today fall into the same error. Then it was a case of coercive legal colonialism. Today, it is a case of coercive legalism in the ill-conceived 'War on Terror'.

9

Priviligium in the Privy Council

Jaan ke sab kuchh, kuchh bhii na jaane, hai.n kitane a.njaane lohg /
aaye hai.n samajhaane lohg /hai.n kitane diivaane lohg

Those who are in the Know / still deny all knowledge
How accursed is this world / in which we venture to persuade others
Kunwar Mohinder Singh Bedi Sahar

It was not Bhagat Singh but the Bhagat Singh Defence Committee which decided that the Tribunal's judgment in Lahore must promptly be appealed to the Privy Council in London. Led by Lala Dunni Chand and Dr Gopi Chand Bhargava, its progress was keenly watched from all over India, where lawyers Pran Nath Mehta and Motilal Nehru supported the appeal. Motilal Nehru, the father of India's first Prime Minister, Jawaharlal Nehru, a counsel of national eminence, could only watch the appeal from afar as he lay sick in bed. He did, nonetheless, muster enough strength to send a message from Simla, where he was convalescing. He tragically passed away on 6 February 1931, just five days before the date of the Privy Council hearing, which did not even do him the honour of admitting his petition to a regular hearing. From the outset, the omens for Bhagat Singh were not good.

The task of arguing the appeal in London fell to a left-wing lawyer known as D. N. Pritt. Born in London in 1887, Denis Nowell Pritt started life as a conservative but drifted inexorably leftwards as he surveyed the world around him. This started with his first joining the Liberal Party in

1914 and then the Labour Party in 1918. For most people in life it is the other way around – they start off with leftist leanings and gradually become more and more conservative. Pritt was different, and he had plenty of reason to be. He attended boarding school at Winchester College, and then joined the Middle Temple in 1909, graduating from London University with a law degree in 1910 and took Silk in 1927. However, towards the end of the 1920s he got himself embroiled in defending a number of seemingly disreputable Indian rebels and renegades. He was said to have a remarkable assiduity in his work and a wonderful capacity for the retention of facts, such that he had developed 'a huge practice within a short period of time'.[1] In 1929 he began defending several trade unionists in British India, including three Englishmen, who had been arrested for organizing an Indian railway strike. This case, which dragged on for many years, has been immortalised as the Meerut Conspiracy Case. Pritt was forty-three years old when, two years later, on 11 February 1931, he stood up for Bhagat Singh before the Privy Council. By then he was rubbing shoulders with the leading lights of the Labour movement, having joined the Society for Socialist Inquiry and Propaganda (SSIP), which had been set up by G. D. H Cole. This later became known as the Socialist League, and included such stalwarts as Harold Laski, C. H. Trevelyan, Stafford Cripps, R. H. Tawney, Clement Atlee, Ernest Bevin and Michael Foot. The Socialist League was so left-wing that in 1933, members G. D. H. Cole, R. H. Tawney and Frank Wise unsuccessfully urged the Labour Party in a written letter to support the Communist Party of Great Britain. D. N. Pritt strongly endorsed this action, but it was not to be.

Pritt won major victories in the UK, such as the trial for sedition of the veteran socialist Tom Mann in 1934 and damages on behalf of the National Unemployed Workers' Movement against the police the same year, and went on to act for the National Council for Civil Liberties in later years (the precursor of the present-day Equality & Human Rights Commission). In 1935 he won a Labour Party seat for Hammersmith North. Five years later he was expelled from the Labour Party for defending the Soviet invasion of Finland, after which he began to sit as an independent in Parliament. Pritt was a Russophile, and his transformation became complete when in August 1936 he went to Moscow to see the Moscow show trial known as the Trial of the Sixteen. He came away convinced that Joseph Stalin was right to eradicate his opponents and defended this attitude in his work *The Zinoviev Trial*. This was unsurprising for someone who had been described as 'a long-term opponent of imperialism and a lawyer of outstanding international reputation'.[2]

The Lahore Conspiracy Case was the first of the big cases which D. N. Pritt took on for anti-colonialists fighting against British imperialism. It was on any view the most difficult of all his cases. It must have left him scarred, for he never spoke of it nor wrote of it again. He isn't even accredited with its defence anywhere in the mainstream literature. It is as if the appeal never happened. There are reasons for that, and they are to do with Pritt's mistreatment at the hands of the judges in the Judicial Committee of the Privy Council in 1931 and the contemptuous dismissal of the first-rate arguments which he so painstakingly deployed before the Board. It was not long before he was vindicated in his view of the law by other judgments from Britain's apex courts, but this came too late for the intensely political Lahore Conspiracy Case, during which he was given short shrift.

Pritt went on to defend Ho Chi Minh, whose extradition from Hong Kong the French government had demanded in 1931–32. A few years afterwards he took up the case of Jomo Kenyatta – who became independent Kenya's first President in 1952 – when he was charged as one of the 'Kapenguria Six' along with Bildad Kaggia, Kung'u Karumba, Fred Kubai, Paul Ngei and Achieng Oneko. Dudley Thompson, a Jamaican Rhodes Scholar who had studied at Merton College Oxford, and was on the team of lawyers defending Kenyatta during the 'Kapenguria Six' case, wrote of D. N. Pritt that '[t]hroughout the case he showed such superiority in his knowledge of the law over that of the judge that it produced a striking and pathetic picture'.[3] Those who would have seen him perform in February 1931 before a Board of five judges of the Judicial Committee of the Privy Council in Bhagat Singh's case would surely have echoed Dudley Thompson's sentiments. Pritt's mastery of law and his grasp of the facts towered over that of the judges. Such was his contribution in the case of the 'Kapenguria Six' that in Nairobi today there is a Dennis Pritt Road. A few years after the 'Kapenguria Six' case, Pritt found himself in Singapore leading another team of lawyers in the 'Fajar Trial' of May 1954, during which he defended members of the left-wing University Socialist Club in what was the first sedition trial in post-war Malaysia and Singapore. On Pritt's team was a young lawyer called Lee Kuan Yew, who would go on to become Singapore's first Prime Minister.[4] Thereafter, in the mid-sixties, Pritt served as Professor of Law at the University of Ghana. Pritt was said to have suffered 'social and professional ostracism as a result of the work which he did', but also because his 'views … always remained closer to the Communist Party than to the mainstream liberal views', even though 'he was the product of an establishment milieu from which he sprang'.[5] Despite such a varied and illustrious legal career, his work on the Lahore Conspiracy

Case is almost forgotten. When he died in 1972 at his Hampshire home, his record of having defended anti-colonial leaders from Ho Chi Minh to Jomo Kenyatta was emblazoned in headlines in *The New York Times*[6] – but there was no mention of Bhagat Singh or the Lahore Conspiracy Case.

What the patrician D. N. Pritt rose to challenge before the Privy Council was the very legality of the Lahore Ordinance No. III of 1930. The petition was heard on 11 February 1931, four months after the Tribunal had given its judgment in Lahore. The Board of the Privy Council on that day certainly had an impressive range of experience and expertise to draw upon. Nevertheless, what no one has ever asked is why these distinguished judges were the ones sitting in on an appeal from a Special Tribunal constituted by a Governor-General in India. Their own political backgrounds and affinity to the corridors of power in London smacked of a lack of judicial independence. Before the Human Rights Act 1998 incorporated the European Convention of Human Rights 1950 into British law, their being able to sit in judgment in this manner was unfortunately all too permissible. Certainly, if a similar situation were to arise today one can expect there to be a challenge to the judge and a demand that in the circumstances he recuse himself from hearing the appeal.

First on the Board was the Scottish politician and judge Viscount Dunedin, who had served as Solicitor-General for Scotland in Lord Salisbury's Conservative administration before being promoted to Lord Advocate and then Secretary of State for Scotland, with a seat in the Cabinet. His was a very political appointment. Then there was the Irish statesman Charles Russell, Lord Russell of Killowen, the first Roman Catholic to be appointed Lord Chief Justice of England in the last few centuries. His ancestors had borne the brunt of Roman Catholic persecution in the seventeenth and eighteenth centuries, and his three sisters had become nuns while his remaining brother became a Jesuit priest. Charles Russell had fought for the right of Catholics to resist forced proselytism by organised groups in Ireland's Protestant counties. Despite failing to graduate from Trinity College Dublin, he was said to have a masterful character as a lawyer, judge, and parliamentarian, which he combined with a loyalty to his faith and country, earning him a rare and widespread popularity. Ultimately, he was reputed to have succeeded in combining a sensibility of temperament, a spirit of helpfulness and comradeship, and a dreamer's devotion to ideals. Also on the Board was the Anglo-Indian lawyer and judge Sir George Lowndes, who had practised law before the Bombay High Court before returning to Britain where he had the remarkable luck to be appointed to the Judicial Committee of the Privy Council in

1929, just in time to hear Bhagat Singh's appeal. He would retire before long in 1934. Then there was Lord Thankerton, a Scottish Unionist Party politician educated at Winchester College and Jesus College, Cambridge, from where he graduated with a third-class degree. He held the office of Solicitor-General for Scotland before being appointed as Lord Advocate and then promoted to Lord of Appeal in Ordinary, which position he held until his death in 1948. Lord Thankerton had a penchant for knitting. He would practice even while hearing cases, although it is not clear whether he did so during the hearing of Bhagat Singh's appeal. Finally, there was the Indian judge Sir Dinshah Mulla, one of the most distinguished Indian jurists of his day. A Privy Counsellor from 1930 and the author of some important legal texts, he also possessed considerable political clout as an erstwhile member of the Central Assembly in India.

Despite this wealth of talent, only one judge gave a written judgment – an exceedingly short one at that – and it inattentively dismissed the petition of Bhagat Singh in the case of *Bhagat Singh v. The King-Emperor*. This is significant. Single decisions from the highest judicial tribunal in the realm are not, generally speaking, carefully considered. In an appeal against a sentence of death this was doubly important. The matter is highlighted in a speech in 2007 by Lord Bingham, Britain's most senior and highly respected law lord. In a lecture on the rule of law,[7] he echoed the view of fellow Supreme Court judges 'that the quality of single Privy Council judgments has on the whole been inferior from the point of view of developing the law' because 'a well-constituted committee of five or more can bring to bear a diversity of professional and jurisdictional experience which is valuable in shaping the law'. One only has to look at the short and highly dismissive solitary judgment of the Board of the Judicial Committee of the Privy Council in the Lahore Conspiracy Case to see that shaping the law is one thing that this august judicial body did not have on its mind at that time. Nor was it concerned with analysing the dictates of the rule of law. The two-page judgment, penned by Viscount Dunedin, ran to a paltry eight paragraphs. The other judges had nothing to say.

Viscount Dunedin said the entire case was a matter of discretion for the Governor-General of India. Lord Bingham, however, aptly reminds us that '[t]here is in truth no such thing as an unfettered discretion, judicial or official, and that is what the rule of law requires'.[8] The entire saga has served only to expose the 'noble lie'[9] of the rule of law. The notion of a 'noble lie' can be traced all the way back to Plato's *Republic*[10] and conveys the idea of a myth or untruth that is knowingly propagated by an elite to maintain the social harmony of its community or to advance its own elitist agenda. So it has been also in the law. In *Liversidge v. Anderson*,[11] Robert Liversidge (born Jacob Perlzweig), a Jewish pilot officer in the Royal Air Force Volunteer Reserve, had been arrested on a warrant issued in 1940 by Secretary of State Sir John Anderson on the vague grounds of 'hostile associations'. The majority accepted that in times of national emergency such as the Second World War, the judiciary could effectively give such assistance to the executive as was required, for instance interning individuals suspected of posing a security risk. Lord Atkin dissented in this case, bravely attempting to uphold the rule of law. The majority on the court initially prevented him from giving his speech, in which he accused them of being more executive-minded than the executive itself. When he gave his judgment, it became the most celebrated judicial dissent in English law. Indeed, so corrupted is the rule of law that in another essay Lord Bingham acknowledged how it 'is a principle routinely invoked by the leaders of illiberal and authoritarian regimes, who rely on it as meaning that people should obey the laws which the government makes, and be punished if they disobey'.[12]

The paradox is that this is surely how Viscount Dunedin's judgment in Bhagat Singh's appeal now stands to be interpreted. Discrimination against perceived non-nationals has a long history. As one writer has explained, in modern times, '[v]irtually every significant government security initiative implicating civil liberties – including penalizing speech, ethnic profiling, guilt by association, the use of administrative measures to avoid the safeguards of the criminal process, and preventive detention – has originated in a measure targeted at noncitizens'.[13] It was against this legal backdrop that, on 11 February 1931, a balding, bushy-browed and exuberantly moustachioed Viscount Dunedin scornfully sneered through his dismissal of the appeal of Bhagat Singh and his comrades.

Pritt's approach throughout had been unflappable, tenacious and assiduous, however. When Viscount Dunedin asked whether Pritt was able 'to make out that Section 72 does not authorise what was done', Pritt's nifty answer was that 'it is a section which has been in the statute for some time; it is a section of an Imperial Act of Parliament; there is no doubt whatever of its force and validity, but I do not think anyone would deny that it creates a somewhat striking power, and is one, at any rate, which any court will construe with care.' To this Viscount Dunedin quite wrongly responded that 'it creates an absolute power', whereupon he had to be reminded by Pritt that this was only 'when the conditions are fulfilled'. In fact, Pritt had to explain to Viscount Dunedin that 'the power it creates is a limited power of delegated legislation' which is what the Ordinance was:

The Governor-General *may*, in cases of emergency, make and promulgate ordinances for the peace and good government of British India or any part thereof, and any ordinance so made shall, *for the space of not more than six months* from its promulgation, *have the like force of law as an Act passed by the Indian legislature*; but the power of making ordinances under this section *is subject to the like restrictions as the power of the Governor-General* in legislative Council to make laws.

As Pritt adroitly explained, there were three conditions which had to be satisfied before the Governor-General could pass any Ordinance 'for the peace and good government of British India or any part thereof' under what was initially Section 72 of the Government of India Act 1915, and then the Act of 1919 of the same name. First, 'there must be a case of emergency', whatever 'emergency' may mean. Second, 'that the ordinance must be an Ordinance falling within the description that it is an Ordinance for the peace and good government of British India, or some part thereof'. Third, 'that it must, in addition to being for peace and good government, fall within the restrictions of the legislative powers of the Indian Legislature, which are to be found mainly, if not wholly, in Section 65'.[14]

What this meant was that 'something must happen before the power comes into force at all', and that 'when it has come into force, that is to say when there is an emergency and the Governor-General must do something, there are two limits'. These two limits were that 'it is necessary to establish affirmatively that there is a case of emergency; it is not for the executive, if I may so describe the Governor-General, to say there is an emergency; it must be proved; like any other question of fact lying at the root of the jurisdiction, it has to be established before the courts, in my humble submission'. This is because the issue here was the use of a 'very striking power'. After all, as D. N. Pritt stoutly proceeded to explain, 'the courts in British countries are places where facts are decided. At the root of the Governor-General's right to make an Ordinance lies in every case the question of fact: Was there an emergency? If it becomes material to know whether there was an emergency or not, that is a matter which has to be proved before the court.' Viscount Dunedin mocked him pathetically by asking, 'Is it your proposition before the Governor-General can promulgate an ordinance he would have to bring a *declaratory action* in the courts for a declaration?' This was patently absurd and served only to demonstrate how the learned lord was descending into an unedifying act of self-parody. In fact, when Pritt responded that this was not his proposition, Viscount

Dunedin was churlishly condescending, asking, 'What do you mean by "the Courts?"' as if that was a question that warranted a serious answer.

With impeccable clarity, Pritt cautiously elucidated what he was purporting to set out: '[T]hat anybody, however eminent, who has power to act when certain facts exist, must make up his mind whether they exist or not, and then act, and that when his power is challenged and it is suggested that those facts did not exist, the question whether those facts exist or not is a question *like any other question lying at the root of any jurisdiction* and must be *decided by the courts*.' Giving the impression of feigned ignorance, Viscount Dunedin now wanted to know whether Pritt's contention was 'that this Board, which is the only place to which you can come, *shall have an inquiry into facts* and review the view of the Governor-General that there was a case of an emergency', quite forgetting that 'an inquiry into facts' is what courts do all the time when facts are under question. Unruffled, Pritt submitted that this was 'in the same sense as happens *when any other executive makes up its mind* that there is a riot and exercises powers which it has when there is a riot, and which it does not have when there is not a riot'.

Viscount Dunedin, who was never interested in legal arguments in the first place, could not resist a chance to scoff at Pritt. With a mirthless smile on his face, he haughtily boomed, 'I am not aware of any clause in an Act of Parliament like Section 72 which has to do with riots.' A more serious approach from the highest judicial tribunal in the realm would not have gone amiss. It was, after all, hearing a death sentence appeal from the outer reaches of the Empire. Viscount Dunedin was making pitifully light of the situation. Perhaps these unfortunate young men and their lawyers and advisers had expected too much. Seasoned and hard-bitten lawyer that he was, however, Pritt remained unfazed and undaunted. In fact, he too saw his chance. In a brilliant put-down, he calmly and assuredly proceeded to inform Viscount Dunedin with devastating effect that 'it is a question that often arises in English common law'.

Next, it was Lord Thankerton's turn. Very smart and well turned out, clean shaven, with slicked hair neatly parted down the middle, Thankerton came to the aid of his brother judge. Pritt was asked what he meant by his assertion that 'this is a pure question of fact'. Such a proposition, it was put to him, was questionable, bearing in mind that 'the trouble about an emergency is what it may lead to' rather than 'what has already happened', and it is this which leads the court to 'assume somebody having an opinion not as a question of fact'. It was a fair point, and incisively put. Pritt rose to the occasion. In a quick-wittedly astute reply, he explained that this made no difference whatsoever. Whilst it may be 'a very difficult question of fact', he said, the principle involved remained unaltered because 'even a question of opinion is a question of fact'. The logic was impeccable and unassailable. Lord Thankerton had to concede. He concurred with Pritt: '[I]t is so treated by the Courts, I agree.' However, there remained the question of 'who is the proper person to judge it', because 'it is not the ordinary question of fact'. This, too, was a fair point. Today, when courts grapple with government decisions after ministers decide a situation raises particularly intractable national security issues, this question still exercises the minds of the court.[15] Pritt's artful but no less effective riposte was to remind His Lordship of the age-old common law adage that 'the state of a man's mind is as much a fact as a state of his digestion'. But that would not do in this case. This was a political trial where Bhagat Singh and his comrades had first assassinated a policeman in broad daylight and then gone on to attack the legislature in Delhi, creating mayhem. They also remained unrepentant. Furthermore, they sympathised with the architects of Russia's revolution of 1917.

Lord Thankerton therefore remained unconvinced. It was surely a question for the government of the day to decide, he thought, what actions were conducive to the safety of the country. He accordingly put it to Pritt: 'This is a question of administration, is it not?' Pritt pointed out that the answer to that question quite simply lay in the law as enacted. The legislature had passed a primary law by statute. As an Act of Parliament, it could not be challenged because it is for Parliament to make statutory laws. The courts could only interpret such laws. The legislature had, however, allowed for the Governor-General to enact a subsidiary and secondary form of legislation, by way of an Ordinance, provided that he could show that there existed an 'emergency' and the Ordinance was necessary for the 'peace and good governance' of India. This meant that the Courts, in order to remain true to the parliamentary intention in the Government of India Act 1915 and now 1919, had to ensure that there did indeed exist as a matter of fact an 'emergency', because otherwise the Governor-General would be going beyond the scope of his authority as intended by Parliament. Accordingly, Pritt had no hesitation in stating that 'Section 72 is not a matter of administration; it is a matter of substituted legislation', thus reminding the Board that the power in question was not one arising from parliamentary legislation but from delegated legislation.

Next came Lord Russell of Killowen, with his receding white hairline, clear light-brown eyes, full lips and heavy jowls. He wanted to know if Pritt was right that it was for a court of law to decide the question of whether an 'emergency' existed. If so, he asked, 'What is the test to be applied in ascertaining whether an emergency exists?' Pritt was unshaken in his resolve to defend the principle at stake. He replied that it was 'the usual test as to whether Johnson has told a lie, or drove a car negligently'. It was as simple as that. Fortunately, Viscount Dunedin did not see fit to quip that this was not a case involving 'Johnson' or a car being driven 'negligently'! However, Lord Russell, like Lord Thankerton, was intent upon treating it as 'more a question of opinion' and asked, 'Who is best qualified to form an opinion?' Pritt explained that his submission could be put in two ways: '[F]irstly, that merely construing that section, the words "in cases of emergency" meant not that the Governor-General is the sole judge as to whether there was an emergency or not, but that there *had* to be an emergency.' Secondly, that 'a proper method of construing one section of a statute is to see what words it uses in other sections, and a comparison of this section with half a dozen other sections in this act makes it overwhelmingly clear that the Imperial Parliament, when confirming *this very great power* by Section 72 *on one individual*, however eminent in the Executive of British India, was deliberately refraining from entrusting to him the right to decide, either as fact or opinion, whether there was an emergency or not.'

It was now Sir George Lowndes' turn to take Pritt to task. For his part, having heard three of his brethren on the Board, he simply preferred to overlook the words of the statute. He ventured to suggest to Pritt that 'I should have thought there was a personal element here'. Pritt remained unshaken. For him, principles were principles. They did not change as a matter of constitutional law simply because the decision came from a Governor-General of India. He nimbly responded that 'many personal elements have to be decided by a court afterwards. There is a personal element in every running-down case.' With these words, Pritt went on to address the Board as follows:

> May I call your Lordships' attention to Section 67(b) of the Government of India Act: 'Where either chamber of the Indian legislature refuses, or fails to pass in a form recommended by the Governor-General, any Bill, *the Governor-General may certify that the passage of the Bill is essential for the safety, tranquility or interests of British India or any part thereof.*'[16]

In Pritt's submission, these were words which left the matter in the hands of the Governor-General alone. So much so, he explained, that if one looks at Section 67(b)(2) of the Government of India Act, this makes clear that 'every such Act' – that is the bill turned into an Act – '*shall be* expressed to be made by the Governor-General, and shall, as soon as practicable after being made, be laid before both Houses of Parliament, and shall <u>not</u> have effect until it has received His Majesty's assent'.

Proceeding with clinical precision, Pritt asked the judges to look lower down the provision of Section 67(b)(2) because what was said here was, '[U]pon the signification of such assent by His Majesty in Council, *and the notification thereof by the Governor-General,* the Act shall have the same force and effect as an Act passed by the Indian legislature and duly assented to.' In circumstances where the Governor-General had to act still more quickly and expeditiously, however, there remained the added proviso that '[p]rovided that where *in the opinion of the Governor-General a state of emergency exists which justifies such action,* the Governor-General may direct that *any such Act shall come into operation forthwith'.* Having laid this out, Pritt made his point clear:

> [T]here are at least eight other passages in that Statute of varying strengths and varying kinds ... in which it is shown overwhelmingly that the Imperial Parliament, when it wants to entrust the matter to the Governor-General, has sufficient command of the English language to be able to put it beyond the range of doubt. Section 72 has existed for a long time, and some of the other sections in which the sort of thing is dealt with have existed for a considerable time ... the Governor-General has power here to substitute himself to a certain extent for a short period of time for the legislature in order to move more swiftly than the legislature can in legislative matters...

Eventually, faced with such well-thought-out and measured submissions before the Board, Viscount Dunedin was forced to concede: 'I quite understand the point.' However, he now wished to know 'what is the remedy according to you'. Pritt explained that 'the remedy for the subject is that when an Ordinance is sought to be applied to him' he is entitled to put it to the courts that 'here is the Crown doing something which I say it has no power to do'. Pritt was not wrong here, because the power in question was not primary legislation but delegated legislation. It was what Pritt had earlier called 'substituted' legislation. On that basis, Pritt made the following distinct submissions to the Board: 'The first thing I shall say to the board is: I challenge this Ordinance: it is made under a definite *limited* power; I say that *the conditions of the exercise of the power do not exist,* and never have existed.' When Viscount Dunedin interrupted to ask him what would happen if this was the case, he answered,

The power is limited; in order to show that it has been *validly exercised* and that *the conditions are fulfilled*, there must be *some proof that there was a case of emergency*. I have challenged that, once before this very tribunal and once before the High Court at Lahore and in neither instance did the Crown produce one tittle of evidence that there had ever been a case of emergency.

Viscount Dunedin affected to concede the argument: 'Then you would say that the matter must be gone into, I suppose?' Pritt felt emboldened – and who could have blamed him given the abject failure of the government to make good its case? He went one better: 'I am not sure I should not take a hard line and say: "*The Crown having had two opportunities to establish that they had this power because there was an emergency, and having refrained on both occasions from adducing any evidence...*"' This was too much for the Board. Viscount Dunedin cut Pritt short at precisely this point, even though his point followed logically. The government was fraudulently maintaining that an emergency existed, and seeking through an Ordinance to set up a Tribunal outside the normal courts of law in the form of a military court, so that it might try Bhagat Singh and his comrades without regard for procedural niceties. It would then have them sentenced to death, and there would be no right of appeal to the High Court in Lahore. In the face of this, all Viscount Dunedin could muster was to ask whether 'the ordinance had been promulgated long before this'. He was politely reminded by Pritt that '[t]his ordinance was promulgated six or seven months after my clients first stood their trial'. By this he meant that Bhagat Singh and his two comrades had already been undergoing criminal law proceedings for half a year before a proper magistrate, Rai Sahib Pandit Sri Kishen, from where they had a full right of appeal to the High Court, when these proceedings were mystifyingly aborted in favour of a Tribunal. Allowing a court case to be prised away from a magistrate in this way had no previous precedent. It was entirely irregular and contrary to the rule of law.

For Viscount Dunedin, none of this mattered because the Ordinance 'was promulgated before the trial took place before the Special Tribunal' and so there could be no unlawfulness in how Bhagat Singh's trial was manipulated by the state. But Pritt drove home his point, arguing, 'We challenged it by habeas corpus proceedings, and the Crown produced no evidence of any description.' Viscount Dunedin remained unpersuaded, retorting, 'And you failed in that?' Pritt offered an explanation, namely that 'leave is now being applied for to the High

Court at Lahore to appeal from that judgment'. The fact still remained, as Pritt implored the Tribunal,

> that the Crown, having twice had the opportunity of establishing a case of emergency and not having even attempted still to do, that the decision of the court ought to be declared by your Lordships to be entirely void, whereupon the condition of my clients, as I understand it, would be that my clients would be people as to whom there had been a preliminary hearing before the Magistrate, if that is the right description at Lahore, which was entirely void and they would be people whose trial was entirely void; and they could, if it was thought right, be rearrested and *tried according to the ordinary process of law* which was *mysteriously interrupted* at the beginning of last May.

Pritt was not finished. He had one further card up his sleeve: he could show that the Governor-General's own disclosed justification for the Ordinance shows that there was no 'emergency'. The procedural irregularities were accordingly compounded by the failure of the government to identify the 'emergency' which had led the Governor-General to take such a baffling, aberrant and grotesque course. So, Pritt now argued, 'Let it be granted that I am wrong in asserting that it is for the Governor-General to establish that there was a case of emergency.' In that event, the Board may say, 'I see a statement by the Governor-General; the Governor-General is so important a person that if he says something in his Gazette, I would take it as evidence', but the problem with this is that *'we only have to look at the Governor-General's statement to come to the conclusion that there was no emergency.'* Lord Thankerton looked as if he had been struck by a bolt of lightning. Drawing in his breath, he wheezed, 'That is to say, we are to come to the conclusion that the Governor-General was wrong?' It was too much to take. An incredulous Lord Thankerton went on the attack. He put it to Pritt that 'the preamble of the Ordinance gives the reasons, does it not? You say he should not have come to the conclusion that there was an emergency.' But Lord Thankerton could not have been more wrong. Pritt had to remind His Lordship,

> It is not the preamble. One must be very accurate here. The preamble does say something about an emergency. It appears in the same number of the Gazette as a statement by the Governor-General; but in my very humble submission, in spite of the eminent position of the Government General, *the statement by him proves nothing.*

Caught out, Viscount Dunedin attempted to come to the rescue of Lord Thankerton, and tried a different tack. It was no less unedifying a spectacle in a court of law. Pressing Pritt further, he suggested one of two possibilities open to the court:

> Either you look at his statement and say: Those are his reasons and he has come to a wrong conclusion that there was an emergency; or else you say: Those are not his reasons; I do not know what his reasons were; how can I say whether there was an emergency or not in the opinion of the Governor-General?

By now it must have been painfully clear to Pritt that no matter what he said, the Board was committed lock, stock and barrel to throwing out the appeal. Nevertheless, Pritt tried to explain even more clearly:

> In the first place, I say there must be proof of an emergency; secondly, if it is suggested that is evidence, then I say, when it is looked at, there must be some limits to the word 'emergency', and that he can only act within those limits.

He even went on to remind the Board that 'one or two courts in India ... have laid down expressly that is for the court to make up its mind and investigate the questions of fact whether there is an emergency or not'. Accordingly, 'if leave to appeal was granted' to him he could show in this case that 'there was no evidence' of an emergency here because '[t]his depends upon a consideration of the facts of the case and a consideration of the meaning of the word, "emergency"', although this 'is not the whole argument that I would desire to put before your Lordships'. Thereafter he gave his reasons:

> I rely very much upon the definition of the power, or rather the definition of the power to legislate under circumstances of this sort, that it must be for the peace and good government of British India. I do not presume to challenge the proposition that, 'the peace and good government of British India' is a very wide phrase, but at some stage in my submission to your Lordships I do want to put it very strongly that this particular ordinance is a priviligium of a very terrible description; *whether it could possibly conduce to peace is a matter of some difficulty; that it could conduce either to good government or to government at all, I would invite your Lordship should consider very carefully indeed.* My submission is that on the

true construction of Section 72 it is plainly intended to empower the governor general in cases of *general emergency* or cases of a *particular emergency* area.

Indeed, such was the travesty at hand that it was something which 'in every Roman law country any jurisprudent would indignantly deny to be legislation at all'. When asked by Lord Thankerton why this should be so, Pritt replied,

> Because *it is a priviligium*. It makes no law that any man has to obey, except the civil service of the Crown and the members of the tribunal. It lays down no liberty to any man to do anything; it lays down no provision by way of criminal law or anything else that any man shall not do anything.

It is useful to note here the sheer eccentricity of the very concept of 'priviligium'. It was derived from Roman law, and its purpose was to allow the Roman Emperor by special constitution to bestow on a single person of his choosing either an obligation or a punishment in a manner which was entirely anomalous or irregular. This is what Pritt was referring to. Viscount Dunedin was taken aback at this. 'What about the old acts of Attainder?' he asked. Dunedin could not have been serious. Acts of Attainder are today entirely forgotten, and deservedly so. They are hardly ever commented upon in England because they are seen as a blot on the legal system. This is because they were the scandalous use by the legislature of a practice popular in the fifteenth century by which a person was declared guilty of a crime and then subjected to punishment without any judicial oversight or trial, all with the active consent of the monarch.[17] In this case, because the law in question was 'passed by the supreme imperial parliament', Pritt explained that what was relevant here was that

> this is delegated legislation, and all that the Governor-General can do is to make and promulgate Ordinances for the peace and good government of British India or any part thereof, which are to have the force of law for six months. *That is a Priviligium*, and I submit *that cannot in any view be called legislation at all for peace, order and good government*.

The reason why the Lahore conspirators were being subject to a priviligium was because they were purportedly being tried under a Governor-General's own legislation, namely, the Lahore Ordinance 1930 which specifically named the twenty-four defendants in the Schedule to be tried, but without stating what offences they had committed, and this was being done before a specially constituted three-member tribunal, on evidence that was entirely dependent on what the 'approvers' said, as and when they turned up.

The fact that Viscount Dunedin himself drew Pritt's attention to Acts of Attainder is highly significant. It demonstrates that the Privy Council itself was acutely aware of the enormity of the untrammelled and undefined power which the Governor-General was arrogating to himself in this Ordinance. Bhagat Singh and his comrades were being accused of a crime with no details provided, and then subjected to a penalty of death, with the court providing no judicial surveillance whatsoever. When Pritt remarked that this was a 'priviligium', Viscount Dunedin's response was effectively that it had been done in the past over a period of many decades and across the reign of many monarchs in England. This is the clearest judicial admission of the fact that Bhagat Singh was essentially being subjected to an Act of Attainder proceeding.

Yet, all forms of Acts of Attainder (also known as bills of Attainder) had been abolished in England by the nineteenth century following their gross abuse. Henry VIII, for example, used one against his fifth wife, Kathryn Howard, whom he had married when he was forty-nine and she was nineteen years of age. Describing her initially as the 'very jewel of womanhood' and a woman without a thorn, within a year he had accused her of infidelity. He did not want her to stand trial, fearing as he did that she might divulge disconcerting details of their marriage while giving evidence on the stand. Careful not to be accused of instigating his wife's execution, Henry VIII was the first monarch to delegate the power of execution in this way to Parliament. The last bill of attainder in England was against Lord Edward Fitzgerald for leading a rebellion in Ireland in 1798. He was condemned to death by an Act of Parliament. Here in the Ordinance was something dangerously reminiscent of this hideous monstrosity from a distant past long considered to have been barbaric. Its reprehensible shadow ought not to have been cast in the Privy Council on this occasion – but Viscount Dunedin had named it.

This is why Pritt was immediately afterwards asked by Lord Russell if he thought 'that under Section 65 of this Act the Indian legislature could not have passed an act in these terms'. Unmoved, Pritt was resolute in his conviction that the Indian legislature could not have done so. This is because, as every lawyer knows, legal provisions in an Act of Parliament rarely stand alone. They have to be read with other provisions in the Act, because more often they interlock with them to give the Act its precise meaning. The legislature has to balance out the different rights, interests and values at stake, and the draftsman uses carefully chosen words to do so. Ultimately, however, the courts must determine the true meaning of the words by looking at the broad purposes of the Act. So, in this case, as Pritt reminded Lord Russell in what was the most important passage in Pritt's submission before the Board,

Section 65 is not the only section which has been looked at in order to discover the power and restrictions of the Indian legislature, but it is much the most important. I concede reluctantly that the Indian legislature could have done this but then the legislature is allowed to legislate within clauses (a) to (f), whether it is for the peace, order and good government of British India or not. It is, in my humble submission, right to bear this in mind, that what the statute actually does is this. It says:

'Here are a number of men; they are all in custody; they are not running about; they are under trial; that is to say, preliminary proceedings are being carried forward against them on specific charges. They have at the moment the right of citizens in British India who have a *prima facie* case made out against them, before they are tried to know what that case is. They have a right to be tried before the ordinary Sessions Judge with assessors or a Jury, and after the trial to appeal to the established High Court at Lahore, with which court this Ordinance cannot interfere; that is another point to which I will come in a moment. The authorities say by this priviligium, in which there is not a word about other men, not a word about other offences, *not a word about means of preserving law and order and peace and good government,* we say that these particular individuals shall be deprived of the right to know the case against them, shall be deprived of the right to have a *prima facie* case made against them, shall be deprived of the right of trial before a Sessions Judge and a jury or assessors, shall be deprived of the right to go to the High Court at Lahore on appeal; and *we say they shall be tried before a Special Tribunal without knowing what the case is against them* except as and when it comes out of the mouth of Approvers or independent witnesses, as the case may be. At any moment the Tribunal may change its personnel, and when they come to the end of the case, it may be that these people will be sentenced to death without appeal by three gentlemen who, by reason of the changes in personnel, may none of them have seen a single one of the witnesses, and they may sentence these men to death on evidence of Approvers whose demeanour they never have had the opportunity to observe.'

I submit to your lordships that on any reasonable meaning of the word 'legislation' this is not legislation at all.

In this way, Pritt highlighted how the government of the day was acting in an entirely unconstitutional manner by passing the Lahore Ordinance of

1930. The 'legislation' in question in that Ordinance was only so called; in truth it was nothing more than an illicit and illegitimate attempt to resurrect the old Acts of Attainder.

The Lahore Ordinance was a twentieth-century caricature of what sixteenth- and seventeenth-century sovereigns and potentates used to get rid of troublesome individuals on a whim. It is worth setting out what was at stake. The accused in the Lahore Conspiracy Case are all men who (i) were detained in custody; (ii) had not absconded and were not at large; (iii) were already undergoing a trial under a properly constituted court and an appointed magistrate; (iv) were being required to answer specific charges in preliminary proceedings, such that they had the constitutional right together with any other British citizen to have the prosecuting authorities demonstrate the existence of *a prima facie case* against them; (v) had the right, before they were put to trial, to know what the case against them was, rather than the case they have to answer coming directly out of the mouths of 'approvers'; (vi) have to face evidence of 'approvers' who are wrongly kept in police custody beforehand, and who then give evidence in the presence of the police officers in court and within the earshot of prosecution counsel, who are able to suggest the evidence to them; (vii) are deprived of a trial by jury before the ordinary sessions judge by being put before a Special Tribunal which may reconstitute itself as it goes along by changing anyone of its three judges at any moment and without any cause being shown; (viii) have no right of appeal to the established High Court in Lahore against a sentence as final and as irrevocable as one of death, (ix) are in a Tribunal where none of the three judges may have heard the evidence upon which an appeal is founded where changes in judicial personnel had occurred, or even have seen a single one of the witnesses in question, thus not knowing what their demeanour was when they gave evidence as 'Approvers'; and (x) undergo a process where the normal trial proceedings are impeded, obstructed, or in any way hindered, by the Governor-General's passing of an Ordinance.

At the same time, the Ordinance contained (i) no mention of any other men involved in a conspiracy; (ii) no mention of other offences having been committed; and most importantly (iii) no mention of the preservation of law, order peace and good government – which was the very *raison d'etre* of how any such Ordinance could have been passed in the first place! So, here now were Bhagat Singh and his comrades, being tried before a Special Tribunal with the power to put them to death, without knowing the charges against them. What was this, Pritt rhetorically asked, if it was not a priviligium?

10

Repugnant Law

aaj bazar mein pa-ba-jaulan chalo
chashm-e-nam, jaan-e-shoreeda kafi nahin

Let us walk in the bazaar in shackles
wet eyes and restless soul is not enough

Faiz Ahmed Faiz

When arguing the case of *Bhagat Singh v. The King-Emperor* before the
Board of the Privy Council on 11 February 1931, Denis Nowell Pritt was not
content with simply calling Lahore Ordinance No. III of 1930 'a privilgium
of a very terrible description'. If it was a 'priviligium', then the next logical
argument was that it could not in any normal sense be understood as 'law'.
This indeed is what Pritt went on to argue. In doing so, he raised the stakes
even higher for the judges. The Ordinance in question, under which a Special
Tribunal had sentenced three young men to be hanged with no right of
appeal to the High Court in Lahore, he argued, could not even be described
as legislation. That did not please the Board. 'Why is it not legislation?'
Lord Thankerton had asked waspishly. 'You may think it is bad legislation.
You have admitted that under Section 65 the Indian legislature could have
passed such an Act. Would you have said that was legislation?' The question
must have left Pritt mystified, as it was so basic to the understanding of what
we mean by 'law'. Pritt calmly and assuredly explained himself again:

[T]o an Englishman brought up with the idea of Parliaments with
unlimited powers and of subsidiary parliaments with very limited powers,
that would be an administrative Act disguised in the form of legislation, but
which is perfectly lawful, but when one comes to a Section which does not

say the Governor-General shall be invested with all the legislative powers of Section 65, *but does say that he may make and promulgate Ordinances for the peace and good government of British India, that means that the Governor-General may make legislation which provides what people ordinarily call law;* **which provides something which applies to more than one person or one group of persons.** Legislation that it shall be unlawful to wear a particular kind of hat that is insulting to one's fellow citizens would not be legislation but an administrative act disguised as a piece of legislation dealing *ex post facto* with the trouble which has already arisen in the case of the certain individuals who are to be tried for specific offences. In my humble submission, if legislation is used in any ordinary sense or if it is used as a power to make and promulgate legislative Ordinances for the peace and good government of the country, *my clients ought to be given the opportunity to put before this Board on a full appeal the argument that such an ordinance is invalid* and cannot fall within the words 'Ordinances for the peace and good government' of anything.

What Pritt was making abundantly plain to Lord Thankerton was that the Governor-General was a subsidiary legislature subject to the sovereign Parliament in London, and he had not been invested with absolute power to do as he wished if any regard was to be given to Section 65 of the Government of India Act 1915.[1] Any power to make legislative Ordinances for peace and good governance is subject to the right of the individual to challenge it, just as any other subordinate-delegated legislation in the form of an Ordinance can be challenged, on the basis that it is invalid because it does not in any sense promote peace and good government of British India.

To elaborate on his arguments further, Pritt went on:

[T]he restrictions imposed by this Act upon the power of the Indian legislature to make laws must also be proved. Your Lordships will probably know there is one case that has been challenged on the broad proposition whether this type of Ordinance offends against the unwritten law or constitution of the United Kingdom of Great Britain and Ireland. I do not think I can advance that argument to your Lordships; that seems to be precluded; but there is another ground here, and that arises out of the consideration of Section 84 and a later one, I think Section 113. Section 65 is the main section imposing the power and placing restrictions on the power. Section 84 is in a department called, 'Validity of Indian laws.' The only one that matters here is: *'A law made by any authority in British India and repugnant to any provision of this or any other Act of Parliament shall, to the extent of that repugnance, but not otherwise be void.'* This is partly an enabling section, but it prevents pregnancy destroying the whole thing, but in my submission the effect of that is this: *If any act of the British Indian legislature be challenged, and therefore if any ordinance under Section 72 be challenged, as operating repugnantly to any provision of this Act of Parliament, it will be void.* My submission is that this is repugnant to the provisions of this Act of Parliament, so it will be void. My submission is that this is repugnant to the provisions of this Act of Parliament **because it deprives the High Court at Lahore of jurisdiction in the matter.**

Pritt pressed on relentlessly with the ineluctable force of his argument:

May I refer your lordship's to Section 113:
'His Majesty may, if he sees fit, by letters patent, establish a High Court of Judicature in any territory in British India, whether, or not included within the limits of the local jurisdiction of another High Court, and confer on any High Court so established any such jurisdiction, powers and authority as are vested in or may be conferred on any High Court existing at the commencement of this Act; and where a High Court is so established in any area included within the limits of the local jurisdiction of another High Court, His Majesty may, by letters patent, alter those limits and make such incidental, consequential and supplemental provisions as may appear to be necessary by reason of the alteration.'
... my submission on that point ... is simply this: **The right to confer jurisdiction on what is now the High Court at Lahore is committed by this Imperial Statute to His Majesty to be done by letters patent.** If the Indian Legislature, being a subordinate Legislature, seeks by any act of its own to deprive the High Court at Lahore, established by his Majesty's letters patent of jurisdiction, in whole or in part, the argument is the same. It is offending against Section 113, which has conferred upon someone else, and someone higher, namely, His Majesty, by the executive act of letters patent, to create the High Court. This particular Ordinance, in order to be valid, has to be such as not to infringe Section 113. *If this particular ordinance took away the whole jurisdiction of the High Court at Lahore, it would, in my humble submission, equally offend against Section 13.*

Such impeccable logic even startled Sir George Lowndes, who, having been jolted from his slumber, rather disinterestedly asked, 'Is that provided for specifically in the Act?' He had quite forgotten that it need not have done so, because, as Pritt properly explained, 'Section 65 is the general section which gives the power to make laws', and 'Section 65 and Section 84 have to be read together' because 'Section 65 confers a very wide, but nevertheless not universal, power on the Indian legislature, and that Section 84 says: "*A law made by any authority in British India and repugnant to any provisions of this or any other act of Parliament shall, to the extent of that repugnance, but not otherwise be void.*"' Faced with this onslaught of intellectual rigour, Lord Russell hissed dismissively at Pritt, 'I'm not sure that I follow your repugnance yet. Where is the repugnancy?'

It had evidently escaped his lordship's mind that the repugnancy was the very issue that Pritt had been so painstakingly describing to the Board just a moment ago – how the creation of the High Court at Lahore by His Majesty through imperial statute in London was being abrogated by a subordinate Indian legislature in Delhi, which made it void to that extent. Pritt therefore ventured once more to make his point in plain English:

> The repugnancy, I suggest, is this: Whereas His Majesty alone can create the High Court at Lahore, or limit, or amend, or alter, or take way from its powers, before this Ordinance was passed the High Court at Lahore had jurisdiction to hear my clients on appeal and that has been taken away by the ordinance which has said they shall not have an appeal.

To this Lord Russell reposed, 'The Ordinance has constituted a Special Tribunal to try particular people.' He was quite overlooking the fact that the Special Tribunal still has to have included in its rules an appeal to the Lahore High Court, which had already been constituted by letters patent by the imperial statute in London, if it was to avoid repugnancy with that statute.

It should have been quite obvious to Pritt by now that the Board was prepared to put the proverbial Nelsonian telescope to its blind eye and willingly disregard the truth of what was being argued before it. Indeed, Lord Russell proceeded to ask Pritt, 'Is that repugnant to Section 113?' with the incredulous remark, 'I do not see it.' Pritt, not for the first time, had to reiterate his point:

> Yes, because my clients, when the Ordinance was passed, were people who were being prosecuted on charges that were *being formulated in the ordinary course,* and the High Court *had jurisdiction at that moment to hear an appeal*, and the Ordinance has entirely destroyed that exceedingly important portion of the jurisdiction of the High Court at Lahore.

When Sir George Lowndes suggested that under Section 65(3) there existed power to 'limit' the jurisdiction of the High Court without abolishing it altogether, Pritt pointed out that this was a distinction without a difference because 'the Indian Legislature cannot abolish any High Court existing *when the statute was passed, neither can it interfere with the operation of Section 113*, which says that His Majesty can appoint a new High Court and deal with its jurisdiction'. The discussion then turned very legalistic. Pritt pointed out that 'this matter was sufficiently in the minds of the draftsmen of the letters patent', given that the letters patent were made on 21 March 1919 for what was 'a relatively recent High Court' in Lahore. This was in the wording of clause 37 of the letters patent that established the High Court in Lahore.

It was now time for the only Indian member of the Board of the Privy Council to speak up. Sir Dinshah Mulla was one of the most distinguished jurists of his day. He had served as Attorney-at-Law of the Bombay High Court and had been a Professor of Law at Government College Bombay. He became a Privy Counsellor in 1930 and started sitting on the Judicial Committee from January 1931. Although he was a Parsee, he had written *Principles of Mahomedan Law* on the application of sharia law in India and Pakistan. More impressively still, he was the assistant editor of the prestigious Sir Frederick Pollock's Commentaries on the law of contract in India. Nevertheless, for all his undoubted qualities, the choice of this particular Indian judge to sit on the Board of the Privy Council to hear the petition of Bhagat Singh was invidious. It was not done in the interests of diversity or equal opportunities back in 1931, of that one can be quite sure. On the contrary, the point was to have a compliant native try one of his own. If the truth be told, Sir Dinshah Mulla ought not to have been sitting in on this appeal at all. Not long before, on 14 September 1929, this was the very man who had voted against the adjournment motion on the Hunger Strike Bill. The avoidance of apparent bias in the rule, '*Nemo judex in causa sua*', stood for the principle of natural justice that no person can judge a case in which they have an interest. It is one of the oldest edifices of English common law.

Sir Dinshah Mulla had so far escaped notice because he had remained quiet, but he had been waiting for his moment. He now mustered up the courage to tell Pritt that this was not the only time that the jurisdiction of the High Court had been interfered with in this way; there was a previous case of 'a very old High Court' in Calcutta, much older than the one in Lahore. He read out clause 44 in the Calcutta letters patent, explaining, 'The Letters Patent of the Calcutta High Court have been re-drawn.' The amending letters patent of 11 March 1919 had substituted clause 44 with a new clause 37. Sir Dinshah Mulla proceeded to enlighten Pritt and his fellow Board members: 'The Calcutta letters patent is of 1869 and what is done is to substitute the section of the Government of India Act of 1915 in the case of the Lahore High Court.' Pritt could only quietly agree: 'Yes; that is obviously what has been done.' However, just because this had been done did not mean that it had been done lawfully. An imperial statute was still the parent statute. Section 84 still read that a law that is 'repugnant to any provisions of this or any other act of Parliament shall' be void 'to the extent of that repugnance'. It was for the Privy Council to look into this.

Pritt nevertheless moved on quickly to the question of the 'emergency', drawing attention to 'some of the authorities upon the subject of the powers of the Court to investigate the question whether there was a state of emergency'. In his opinion, '[t]here is no very direct English authority, although there is one which I think it would be right to refer your Lordships to'. He explained,

> There are several in India where the matter has been expressly discussed, and the trend of Indian decisions is that the courts have power to investigate that question, and must investigate it. They must investigate the question and see whether there was any reason on which the Governor-General could arrive at his conclusion.

Viscount Dunedin was concerned only to know whether these were specifically 'cases which arose under Section 72'. Pritt explained that 'the particular one that I want to draw your Lordships attention to is as recent as the 1st September last, and was a case in the High Court of Bombay, which dealt with Section 52'. This happened to be a case of which the Board was well aware. Sir George Lowndes quipped, 'Is that the *Sholapur* Case?'

The counsel for the government in the appeal, A. M. Dunne, finally found an opportunity to make himself useful. He pointed out that he had, from the government side, prints of the judgment in court already. At his instigation, these prints were promptly handed out. This made Pritt's task somewhat easier, for he was able to take the Board through 'the judgment of Chief Justice Beaumont' wherein Beaumont had discussed 'the Defence of the Realm Act and the state of siege in France'. The relevant part, Pritt pointed out, was the section which applied 'in cases of emergency'. The court had there explained,

> The question whether the determination as to the existence of an emergency is an administrative act is to be decided by the governor general alone, or

whether it is a question of fact which can be enquired into by the course has been discussed by the High Court of Lahore in the case of *Desraj v. Emperor*, and the learned judges who decided that case differed upon the point. In my opinion the judgment of Mr Justice Bhide is correct, and *the question whether an emergency exists or not is one of fact which the courts can enquire into*. But inasmuch as the Governor-General is the person who must, in the first instance, decide whether or not there is an emergency upon which he ought to act, and inasmuch as he may frequently have information which, in the public interest, he may be unwilling to disclose, and which no court can compel him to disclose, I think all that the court can do is to enquire whether there is evidence upon which the Governor-General may reasonably conclude that an emergency exists. If the question be answered in the affirmative, there is an end of the matter.

What is particularly noteworthy about this citation of legal authority is that the Board had before it a quite recent decision from the High Court of Bombay by the name of *Sholapur* which had determined that the question of an emergency was 'one of fact which the courts can enquire into' on the basis of 'whether there is evidence upon which the Governor-General may reasonably conclude that an emergency exists'. This meant that the courts were not excluded from a consideration of the question. It was nothing new that a Governor-General might only be able to include so much of the information that he had as was compatible with the public interest in the form of peace and good government. The initial burden was on him. He had to make out a *prima facie* case that, for the enumerated reasons, there was a case of emergency in existence. The court could not just assume this; it had to have had the rudiments of such a case laid out before it by the Governor-General.

Yet, despite there being a court case drawing upon the development of emergency jurisprudence law even as early as the 1930s, Lord Thankerton took the opposite stance, asking Pritt whether it was not the case that '[t]hat involves an enquiry into what the government general does not want to disclose'. Pritt promptly answered that this was only true in the sense that 'there is in the first place the Governor-General: he may disclose to the court what he thinks is enough'. Before he could develop the point, Viscount Dunedin, determined to frustrate Pritt's argument, cut him off. He now changed tack completely, telling Pritt, 'The first point is whether the judgment of Mr Justice Bhide is correct.' He asked if Bhide gave any reasons for his judgment, and Pritt must have lost his composure here because he wrongly replied that he did not. It is plain from the extract cited above that reasons are given for the conclusion.

Indeed, Justice Bhide is clear about four things in his judgment: i) the question whether an emergency exists or not is one of fact; ii) as a matter of law it is the Governor-General who must, in the first instance, decide whether or not there is an emergency; iii) the Governor-General may be unwilling to disclose all the information that he has in the public interest, and if this is so then no court can compel him to disclose more; iv) the court can nevertheless 'enquire whether there is evidence upon which the Governor-General may reasonably conclude that an emergency exists'. Those are reasons if ever there were reasons.

The court already had copies of the decision, so Viscount Dunedin must have been equally aware that reasons were given by Justice Bhide. Faced with Pritt's mistaken admission that no reasons were given, however, Viscount Dunedin relished the opportunity to inform him, 'Therefore, there is no argument about that.' Pritt protested that 'it was obviously very fully argued', to which Viscount Dunedin retorted that 'there was no argument in his judgment except to say: "I think Mr Justice Bhide's judgment is correct." Therefore it does not help us upon the point.' With respect, this is fallacious. It did not prevent the Board from answering for itself the question – which had, of course, been fully argued before the Chief Justice – of whether the conclusion reached by the Chief Justice was correct or not. Pritt must by now have been under no illusion that his words were falling on deaf ears. He had no hope left. Never one to give up, he tried in vain to explain that 'the argument that leaps to mind ... is adopted by this learned Chief Justice'. Viscount Dunedin simply told him, 'It does not help us, except the fact that he says so.' He must have known this was not the case. Viscount Dunedin now moved to close off any further argument by Pritt. He had just got the upper hand, and felt secure and certain of his ability to quash any further discussion. The words flowed naturally now. 'I do not think you need go into this matter,' he drawled at Pritt with barely concealed derision.

Always consummate, determined and fearless, Pritt was not finished. He still had some more good arguments up his sleeve. Under the Government of India Act 1919, he now returned to the argument that the Governor-General did not have the authority to pass Lahore Ordinance No. III of 1930. This is because, unlike legislation in India, 'the validity of Statutes of Parliament cannot be questioned in the Courts of British India' since 'Section 72 of the Government of India Act empowers the Governor-General to pass such Ordinances in cases of emergency' only. However, 'the omission of any such words as "in the opinion of the Governor-General" after the words "emergency" suffices to enable us to consider whether there was such an emergency as to justify the passing of the Ordinance and further to examine also its provisions to see how far they make "for the peace and good government of British India"'. Pritt pointed out that '[t]wo learned judges of the Lahore High Court have considered the former question in the case of *Desraj v. Emperor*' and that '[t]heir difference of opinion seems to be more apparent than real'. He elucidated why this was so:

> Section 72 as a whole hardly empowers the courts to consider whether the Governor-General was right or wrong in his conclusion that an emergency existed, much less to examine how far the provisions of the Ordinance tend to the peace and good government of the country. That responsibility the statute has laid on the Governor-General and not on the Courts. *Unless the Governor-General thought that there was an emergency, and he alone under the Section is a judge thereof, he would not promulgate the Ordinance to meet that particular emergency*. That statute does not require that the Legislative Assembly should not be sitting as a necessary precedent to the exercise of the power of passing an Ordinance. Therefore the fact that in some cases the Act of Indemnity has been passed by the Central Legislature and not by way of Ordinance by the Governor-General is immaterial.

However, the unfortunate Pritt was once again thwarted in his attempts to introduce this as a second plank to his arguments. Lord Thankerton balked, snapping at him that 'there is no law against it'. Pritt's terse response was that '[t]here is no law in England against a priviligium', implying that this did not necessarily mean that it was not unlawful if it was to all intents and purposes nothing short of a 'priviligium', conferring upon a single person – in this case the Governor-General – an anomalous or irregular obligation to act in this way in India. In determining whether there was an emergency within the meaning of Section 72, Pritt argued, the court is entitled to require its satisfaction that the Governor-General was privy to information that, if true, might reasonably lead him to conclude that an emergency existed. This is because Section 72 does not say if it is in 'the Opinion of the Governor-General' that an emergency exists; it states that '[t]he Governor-General of India may, in cases of emergency, make and promulgate Ordinances for the peace and good government of British India'. Indeed, the language is not mandatory but permissive. Provided that an emergency exists, the Governor-General is permitted by the use of the word 'may' to make Ordinances. He is not mandated by words such as 'shall' or 'will' to be compelled to do so. The reason is obvious. The act of passing an Ordinance is drastic given that it has 'the like force of law as an

Act passed by the Indian legislature'. The Governor-General accordingly has to be sure that he is acting only 'in cases of emergency'.

Viscount Dunedin persisted in misunderstanding the argument, replying, 'The only way to do that would be by examining the Governor-General.' Pritt had to remind him,

> He cannot be compelled to come into court; he can please himself and do the middle one of three things. The first, which he would be very reluctant to do, is to say: Never mind the public interest; I am challenged; I will give you every fact. *If that were his only course, there will be a difficulty.* His second course would be to say: *I can reconcile the general public interest and the particular interest of maintaining the Ordinance; I will show you quite enough to prove an emergency without showing you everything I know.*

Obviously, if any respect was paid to the individual interests of those in custody undergoing trial, or to general interest in public safety, this second course of action would have been preferred. Certainly it was Pritt's favoured option. The Governor-General would only have had to show that reasonable grounds existed for him to decide what he did as a question of fact. But Viscount Dunedin could not resist the temptation to bait Pritt at this stage, absurdly suggesting to him, 'In order to do that he would have to be made a party to the case?' Pritt pointed out that which must have been perfectly clear to Viscount Dunedin, namely that 'in direct criminal proceedings, it would be the Crown' that would be a party to the proceedings, and 'in habeas corpus proceedings it would be the Crown again', because it is the Crown which is the body 'having access to public information'.

Unperturbed, Pritt soldiered on, explaining that there was an even better option for the executive in a case such as this:

> The third course which the Governor-General could adopt is a course which is adopted by the Executive in this country whenever a difficulty arises. He can go to the legislature and say: I had to act in an emergency which I say is an emergency; I am not going to publish my facts to the court in the disturbed state of this country at present. Give me an Act of Indemnity.

Pritt explained that if this course of action was followed then the Act of Indemnity would be given to the Governor-General long after the emergency. For a moment, Lord Thankerton seemed genuinely interested and began probing the intricacies of this argument. He asked a most pertinent question: 'Do you say if the Governor-General does not disclose the reasons, the Ordinance is bad? If he does disclose the reasons, it may prove another emergency. The court must either be seized of the whole of the facts or none of them.' Pritt could not believe his luck. He wheezed, 'I respectfully agree.' Viscount Dunedin too appeared to genuinely entertain the arguments being made: 'Have you any other authority besides this that you can show us?' Pritt responded by saying that there was, of course, this particular habeas corpus case. Viscount Dunedin was not, however, altogether terribly interested in this particular case, observing, 'I think we know that.' Pritt now gave a crushing answer:

> May I say in answer to Lord Thankerton I see the difficulties of the Executive. It would be impertinence on my part to say that I sympathise with them. The answer is: I did not draft this Constitution. This Constitution has said, in my humble submission, in the plainest possible terms that the Governor-General may do this very striking thing in cases of emergency, and *he may do it in cases where he is of opinion there is a state of emergency for any time. Before he does it, there must be a state of emergency.* That is the kernel of the case.

Pritt must have thought that he was finally getting the Board to listen to him. Excited by this, he was not going to let the opportunity slip:

> Your Lordships remember the line of cases under the Defence of the Realm Act, one or two of which went to the House of Lords. This covers two points of my argument; it covers a question who is to decide a question of fact like this question of whether there is an emergency, and also the question of what is legislation in the direction of peace and good government.

If Pritt was thinking of taking the Board's attention to the cases in the House of Lords, he was scuppered in that design by Viscount Dunedin's clever repartee: 'We will listen to any case you choose to give us, but I do not myself see how any case would be much use, unless there was something equivalent to Section 72, which, so far as I know, there is not.' It was clear that Pritt was facing nothing but a closed mind on the part of the learned judge, so he answered by stating that there was 'a true analogy' to be drawn nevertheless and that 'the analogy is complete in this sense':

> I submit they are both cases of subordinate legislation, and it came from the same body. In the one case, the Imperial Parliament has said

certain persons may pass subordinate legislation for securing the safety of the Realm for the better prosecution of the war – I have forgotten the exact words for the moment – in the other case, the same Imperial Parliament has said in cases of emergency certain persons may pass legislation for the peace and good government of British India. The essence of the cases in which I wanted to rely – indeed, perhaps it is sufficient to state it – is that *there is an efficient body, the High Court or the Court of Appeal* and, I think I may say, the House of Lords *in this country*, dealing with the Defence of the Realm legislation *to see whether the legislation passed falls within the four corners of the Section of the Imperial Statute.*

To this Lord Viscount airily replied, 'Obviously.' Yet, in this answer lies the acid admission that different standards applied in the colonies, with its different races and peoples. Pritt nevertheless proceeded to explain: 'The analogy is this: it is the duty of whatever court becomes concerned with the Lahore Conspiracy Case to construe whether the legislation passed by the Governor-General to establish this particular court falls within the four corners of Section 72.' Viscount Dunedin was patronising and not a little disdainful: 'No doubts about that.' Pritt pushed the point home: 'The question is: Is there a case of emergency, and is it legislation for peace and good government?' When Pritt suggested that 'that argument is supported by some English authority', Viscount Dunedin cut him off again in no uncertain terms: 'I do not think they help us at all.' Legal authority in a court of law is, however, everything – as Viscount Dunedin well knew. An advocate cannot make a legal submission without citation of legal authority. And no case before the Board of the Privy Council required this more in 1931 than the Lahore Conspiracy Case. In fact, Viscount Dunedin himself acceded to the principle that 'obviously it must be within the four corners of the Section', a principle more aptly summarised by what immediately followed in Lord Russell's aphorism: 'It must be *intra-vires*.' How the citation of authority could be considered superfluous in these circumstances is mystifying. Pritt hurried on doggedly: 'Yes, and the *vires* depends on whether there is an emergency and whether the legislation is for peace and good government.'

In short, the fact that the Board was at one with Pritt (and *ad idem* as lawyers say) on the principle that the Governor-General must act 'within the four corners of the Section' meant, as Pritt sought to establish, that there must be evidence of an emergency and evidence conducive to the maintenance of peace and good government. If either or both components are missing but the

Governor-General has still passed an Ordinance, then he has acted 'outside his power' and jurisdiction, and engaged in an *ultra vires* act. It was for the court to scrutinize his actions. If, having done so, they found that the Governor-General had acted to faithfully promote both these components, as delineated by Section 72, then he had acted 'within his power' and jurisdiction. He had engaged in an *intra vires* act and his actions were perfectly lawful.

Asked imperiously by Viscount Dunedin whether '[t]hat is your argument', Pritt conceded that it was, at which point he was thanked by Viscount Dunedin. Remarkably, notwithstanding Pritt's erudite and far-ranging legal submissions, long before the law of judicial review properly developed some forty years later, Viscount Dunedin did not call upon counsel for the government, Mr Dunne, to respond at all. He must have felt robbed. It was landmark case, but the Board did not wish to hear from the government lawyer at all. That was truly remarkable, and entirely revealing of the Board's collective mind. It was the ultimate insult to Pritt that his submissions were not even worthy of a reply from the government lawyer. Instead, Viscount Dunedin turned towards Mr Dunne. Solemnly and quietly he told him, 'Their Lordships need not trouble you, Mr Dunne.' This is an accolade given only to those who have been presented with no case to answer by their opponent. That was not all. Viscount Dunedin wasted no time in giving the decision. Both sides were instantly told in open court that, as far as the Board was concerned, '[t]hey are unable to advise his Majesty that leave to appeal be granted in this case for reasons which will be given later'.

The reasons followed on 27 February 1931. There was just one judgment given, and it was given by Viscount Dunedin alone. With that, the appeal of Bhagat Singh was thrown out. He was to be hanged as sentenced. No wonder that Kuldip Nayar, when describing the Privy Council appeal, wrote, 'My feeling is that crucial files have been destroyed or kept back. Secret telegrams or papers must be somewhere to show that the British establishment was determined to hang Bhagat Singh...'[2]

Two observations can be made. First, in his seminal work on *The Trial of Bhagat Singh*, A. G. Noorani has a separate chapter on whether the outcome in the Privy Council would have been any different if Lord Atkin were on the board.[3] He even notes that 'Atkin is very relevant to the story' because,

On March 24th, 1931, only a month and more after Dunedin's judgment on February 11, Atkin pronounced judgment in a landmark case which differed significantly from Dunedin's or the doctrine of a judicially unreviewable opinion of the executive when it exercises power which is conferred on it by the legislature on condition that it 'is satisfied' that a particular set of circumstances exist.

This is because Atkin held that the courts are not precluded from ascertaining whether a reasonable person can honestly say that a condition in question 'is satisfied'.[4] However, be that as it may, this assumes the absence of the practice of 'coercive legalism' by the British courts in the colonies. The fact is that for much of the hearing, during which Pritt raised complex arguments about the nature of the power at hand (amounting, as he put it, to a 'priviligium) and the reach of the reviewing power of the courts in relation to the satisfaction of a condition precedent of the existence of an 'emergency' before an Ordinance under Section 72 could be promulgated, all that Lord Dunedin did was mock him.

This is despite the fact that the very arguments Pritt was deploying had been raised successfully both in India in *Des Raj v. Emperor* (delivered in July 1930, just seven months earlier) before Justice Bhide and the Chief Justice, and before the highest judicial tribunals in the UK under wartime legislation which also required the satisfaction of a 'condition precedent'. Thus, after asking Pritt at the outset if he could 'make out ... that Section 72 does not authorise what was done' in this case, Viscount Dunedin quickly realised that Pritt had mounted a formidable argument, which was driving a coach and horses through the exercise of power under Section 72. That is why Viscount Dunedin had put it rhetorically to Pritt whether '[y]ou mean really the Court is to have the power of reviewing the view of the Governor-General that there was a case of emergency'. This was something he simply was not prepared to do. When Pritt replied that 'the Courts in British countries are places where the facts are decided' and that 'at the root of the Governor-General's right to make an ordinance lies in every case a question of fact' – namely whether or not there was an emergency – Viscount Dunedin could contain himself no longer. After ridiculing Pritt with the absurd query as to whether this meant that Governor-General 'would have to bring a declaratory action in the courts for a declaration', he had proceeded to ask Pritt what he meant 'by "the courts"'.

When Pritt had explained that the question before the courts was really no different from what happens 'when any other executive makes up its mind that there is a riot and exercises powers', Viscount Dunedin had sneered that he knew of no clause in an Act of Parliament like Section 72 concerning riots. Clearly, Viscount Dunedin was not bothered by the fact that three young men were waiting upon the decision of the Board, having been sentenced to the gallows, in a wholly exceptional use of executive powers, without even a right of appeal to the High Court of their own country. As Pritt proceeded with his immaculately crafted argument that 'even a question of opinion is a question of fact', Lord Thankerton surely gave it all away when he jibed, 'This is a question of administration, is it not?' Eager to relinquish all judicial control, this was indeed how the Board was determined to see the matter. This is also why Lord Russell's question about what test should be applied in ascertaining whether an emergency exists was met with the response from Pritt that it is 'the usual test as to whether Johnson has told a lie, or drove a car negligently'. Lord Russell could then only quibble that it seemed 'more a question of opinion', which was clearly wrong if it implied that the courts could not go into the question at all. Added to this is Viscount Dunedin's refusal to look at any authority at all. Given that some person had to exercise the power of 'emergency', Viscount Dunedin's conviction was unshakeable:

> It is more than obvious that that someone must be the Governor-General and he alone. Any other view would render utterly inept the whole provision. Emergency demands immediate action, and that action is prescribed to be taken by the Governor-General. It is he alone who can promulgate the Ordinance.

It is certainly not the case, however, that being able to review the decision of the Governor-General renders 'utterly inept the whole provision' given that the provision needs to be interpreted to determine the exercise of power under it in the first place. Nor is it the case, even if it is the Governor-General 'alone who can promulgate the Ordinance', that the question of the existence of an 'emergency' as an *a priori* fact cannot be determined by a judicial body. Otherwise, how else can it be said, as Viscount Dunedin was prepared to concede, that '[o]ne is obviously prepared to concede you the proposition that obviously it [i.e. the power] must be within the four corners of the Section', or, as Lord Russell immediately added, 'it must be *intra vires*'?

Despite this, Viscount Dunedin was scathing in his denunciation of Pritt's argument: 'In fact, the contention is so completely without foundation on the fact of it that it would be *idle to allow an appeal to argue about it*.' After having heard the full arguments, he was unwilling to accept Chief Justice Beaumont's adoption of Justice Bhide's conclusion that the Governor-General's decision about the existence of an emergency was reviewable.

Even more bizarre, however, was Viscount Dunedin's categorical assertion that no reasons were required from the Governor-General himself:

> Their Lordships must add that, although the Governor-General thought fit to expound the reasons which induced him to promulgate this Ordinance, *this was not in the Lordships' opinion in any way incumbent on him as a matter of law.*

So wrong was this decision that it astonished even seasoned legal officers serving in India, such as Sir Edward Maynard Chamier, who had been Chief Justice of the Patna High Court (1911–1915) and before that a government advocate in the North West Frontier Province (1875). He had keenly observed the Privy Council proceedings from the wooden chairs overlooking the dusty courtroom in Downing Street as the current legal adviser to the Secretary of State for India. As soon as the Privy Council dismissed Bhagat Singh's petition, he lost no time in writing with much relish to David George Mitchell, joint secretary in the Legislative Department:

> I was agreeably surprised to find that Lord Dunedin presiding over the Board which heard the petition in the Lahore Conspiracy case – *with any other President I think the petition would have been admitted to a regular hearing* – but Dunedin took a *very strong line from the start*...

Upon receiving this letter on 24 February 1931, Mitchell promptly forwarded it to Home Secretary H. W. Emerson, who would have been no less gratified to receive such an absolute and unqualified endorsement of the Governor-General's position on determining when an 'emergency' comes into existence and how one should deal with it.

On 24 March 1931, just over a month after Viscount Dunedin handed down his judgment, Lord Atkin, in a differently constituted Privy Council Board, arrived at a completely different decision in *Eleko*.[5] The question in this case was whether an executive officer's decision on whether he 'is satisfied' is reviewable before a court of law. In an appeal from the Supreme Court of Nigeria, Lord Atkin (sitting with Lord Blanesburgh and Sir Lancelot Sanderson) held that a habeas corpus petition would lie against the Governor of Nigeria in the exercise of powers conferred by Section 2(2) of Deposed Chiefs Removal Ordinance – in favour of a Nigerian chief who had been deposed and banished from a specified area – even though those powers were far wider than those reposed in Section 72 of the Government of India Act 1919! Lord Atkin considered the

Governor of Nigeria's power to order a chief's removal from a specified area enshrined in the words, 'If the Governor shall be satisfied that it is necessary for re-establishment or maintenance of peace, order and good government in such area…' In light of this, he made clear his opinion:

> Their Lordships are satisfied that the opinion which has prevailed that the Courts cannot investigate the whole of the necessary conditions is erroneous. **The Governor acting under the Ordinance acts solely under executive powers, and in no sense as a Court.** As the executive he can only act in pursuance of the powers given to him by law. *In accordance with British jurisprudence no member of the executive can interfere with the liberty or property of a British subject except on the condition that he can support the legality of his action before a court of justice.* And it is the tradition of British Justice that judges should not shrink from deciding such issues in the face of the executive.

Lord Atkin continued with the explanation that 'under the legislation in question, if the Home Secretary deported a British subject in the belief that he was an alien, the subject would have the right to question the validity of any detention under such order by proceedings in habeas corpus, and that it would be the duty of the Courts to investigate the issue of alien or not'.

Unlike in the case concerning Bhagat Singh, the decision of the Privy Council in the *Eleko* case has stood the test of time, being quoted in cases ever since. It was cited in landmark cases like *Zamir*[6] in 1980, confirming that the exercise of a power depends upon the precedent establishment of an objective fact. In such a case it is for the court to decide whether that precedent requirement has been satisfied.[7] It was cited as recently as 2006 by Maurice Kay LJ in *AN*.[8]

Had Viscount Dunedin decided as Lord Atkin did in *Eleko*[9] just a month later, not only would Bhagat Singh and his comrades have had a retrial in the regular Sessions Court, but this would have been followed with a right of appeal to the Lahore High Court. The Governor-General would not have been allowed to interfere with individual liberty. The tradition of British justice, that judges should not shrink from deciding such issues in the face of the executive, would have been resoundingly upheld. *Bhagat Singh v. The King-Emperor*[10] would have been continuously affirmed and reaffirmed in British courts today. As it is, Viscount Dunedin may have made quick work of D. N. Pritt before him but so ignominious was the decision that it is today entirely forgotten, nowhere cited, and not even remembered by any lawyer of any note anywhere in the world.

565-w
4-4-31
Three Death warrants

WARRANT OF EXECUTION ON SENTENCE OF DEATH.

Section 381 of the Criminal Procedure Code.
Sections 8 and 11 of Ordinance No:III of 1930.

In the Court of the LAHORE CONSPIRACY CASE TRIBUNAL,
Lahore, constituted under Ordinance No: III of 1930.

TO THE SUPERINTENDENT OF THE CENTRAL JAIL AT LAHORE.

WHEREAS Bhagat Singh, son of Kishen Singh,
resident of Khawasrian, Lahore, one of the prisoners
in the Lahore Conspiracy Case, having been found
guilty by us of offences under section 121 and section 302 of the Indian Penal Code and also under
section 4(b) of the Explosive Substances Act read
with section 6 of that Act and with section 120-B
of the Indian Penal Code at a trial commencing from
the 5th: May, 1930, and ending with the 7th October,
1930, is hereby sentenced to death.

This is to authorise and require you, the said
Superintendent, to carry the said sentence into
execution by causing the said BHAGAT SINGH to be
hanged by the neck until he be dead at Lahore on the
27th: day of October, 1930, and to return this
warrant to the High Court with an endorsement certi-
fying that the sentence has been executed.

Given under our hands and the seal of the Court,
this 7th day of October, 1930.

Authorisation to the Superintendent of the Central Jail, Lahore, 'to carry the said sentence' of death 'on the 27th day of October 1930', although the three men were actually hanged on 23 March 1931 at 7 p.m., rather than at dawn.

11

Pritt Vindicated

Baad marne ke meri qabr pe aaya wo 'Mir', Yaad aai
mere Isa ko dawa mere baad

What use is to visit my grave afterwards as a Messiah 'Mir',
if when I was alive you were not there for me?

Mir Taqi Mir

Ever since the trial had begun, *The Tribune* in Lahore had been reporting on it with meticulous punctuality. It is no surprise, then, that its editors wasted no time in publishing a leading article on Lord Atkin's judgment on 17 June 1931. On the matter of executive action, Lord Atkin had declared that the court should not 'shrink from deciding such an issue in the face of the executive', whereas Viscount Dunedin had said precisely the opposite and shown supine subservience to the executive. Lord Atkin's judgment deeply troubled the colonial government back in India. Two days later after the piece in *The Tribune*, on 19 June 1931, H. Williamson, director of the Intelligence Bureau of the Home Department, wrote to the Home Secretary, H. W. Emerson, about Lord Atkin's approach. He did not mince his words:

This ruling seems to conflict with that of the Privy Council in their recent decision regarding Bhagat Singh's case but it is unwise to make deductions from extracts of judgments. I think that the Legislative Department might be asked to compare this judgment regarding the Nigerian deportee with that regarding Bhagat Singh. From the extracts quoted by *The Tribune* it would appear that *a High Court can challenge all executive orders for detention under Reg. III of 1818 and other such laws or Ordinances.*

When Emerson hastily forwarded the file on to home member Sir James Crear, the latter shoddily attempted to distinguish the two judgments on the basis that 'the decision in the case of Bhagat Singh was not on the point of habeas corpus', unlike the Nigerian decision, quite forgetting that Lord Atkin had held that in his judgment 'the whole of the necessary conditions' were amenable to judicial oversight because 'the Governor acting under the Ordinance acts solely under executive powers, and in no sense as a Court'. Remarkably, the same mistake was made by law secretary Sir Lancelot Graham, who next looked at the file, because he too conveniently overlooked what was glaringly obvious, preferring instead to suggest that there was nothing whatsoever in common between the two cases:

> No student of law could suppose for a moment that the authors of the report in the Nigerian case would not have referred to the report in Bhagat Singh's case if it was thought that there was anything in common in the subject matter of the two. A perusal of the two judgments or rather reports makes it quite plain that whereas in Bhagat Singh's case it was held that *the decision as to whether an emergency had arisen was not a justiciable issue, because in the words of Lord Dunedin a state of emergency is something that does not permit of any exact definition*, in the Nigerian case, on the contrary, there were three perfectly plain and obviously judiciable issues; the first, whether the party concerned was a Chief within the meaning of the Deposed Chief's Removal Ordinance, the second whether he has been deposed or removed from this, and the third whether it was the native law and custom that if a chief had been deposed, he should be required to leave the area in question. All these are plainly questions of fact on which the Court is capable of coming to a decision. So far as I see the case, then, *we need have no grounds of apprehension* as to the validity of ordinance issued by the Governor-General in so far as the question of emergency is disputed.[1]

Yet, this is plainly wrong because Viscount Dunedin had accepted that the stipulated power 'must be withing the four corners of the Section'. In fact, precisely because the existence of an 'emergency' does not permit of an exact definition, a judicial tribunal should have been especially alert as to how the executive power may have been misused in routine public order matters, and for that reason to have been doubly concerned to protect the liberty of its British subject. Moreover, the fact that Chamier had immediately written to Mitchell that '*with any other President I think the petition would have been admitted to a regular hearing* – but Dunedin took a *very strong line from the start*' only serves to highlight how wrong Viscount Dunedin's decision was known to be as a matter of law even then amongst people who knew something about the law. It was a clear case of coercive colonial legalism.

Yet, one need only look at the decision of Justice Bhide to realise why Viscount Dunedin decided as he did. Justice Bhide would have been another unsung hero of Indian origin if only he had been sitting as a judge on the Bhagat Singh case, but it is worth noting the repercussions his judgment had following *Des Raj v. Emperor*. A. G. Noorani, who undertook his research in the National Archives of India, observes in his book how the record in 'File N. 250 – Political of 1930' reveals the extent to which Justice Bhide's judgment caused panic among officials in the Punjab government. As early as 29 August 1930 there was a request to the Central Government to have the 'defect' in the law removed by the actual amendment of Section 72 itself! Home Secretary Emerson, who had played a role in the debate on the Hunger Strike Bill in the Central Assembly, expressed his concern that the way 'the courts can go into the existence of an emergency ... reveals a joint in one armour of which we were previously not aware and which may be the cause of very serious embarrassment'. This is why a minute of 6 August by the Home Secretary suggested an amendment to the law, so that 'in the meantime it would appear advisable to sit tight until the danger is more serious than at present'.

On this basis, the matter was referred to the Legislative Department of the Law Ministry, where George Hemming Spence (later to become a legal adviser to the Nizam of Hyderabad) was more circumspect in the advice that he gave. His minute of 30 August 1930 would have taken Emerson aback:

> I find it very difficult to refute Mr Justice Bhide's view that as the law now stands, the courts have jurisdiction in a proceeding challenging the validity of an ordinance to enquire, to the very limited extent indicated, into the existence of the emergency which must exist before an ordinance is made. It was conceded by Mr Justice Broadway, *and is fully established by the previous case law*, that the courts have

jurisdiction to examine an ordinance in order to decide whether it was lawfully made and promulgated. *It is plainly necessary to the law for making a promulgation of an ordinance that there should be an emergency*, and *prima facie* the only possible conclusion is that *the courts have jurisdiction to satisfy themselves that an emergency existed.*[2]

Spence was clear that 'the existence of an emergency is a necessary condition to the valid exercise of the legislative power conferred thereby and consequently that the admitted jurisdiction of the courts to examine an ordinance in order to decide whether it was lawfully made necessarily carries with it a jurisdiction to enquire into the existence or otherwise of an emergency'.[3] Spence forwarded his file to D. G. Mitchell in the Legislative Department. As A. G. Noorani records,[4] law member Sir Brojendra Lal Mitter was personally opposed to taking any 'immediate steps', as is clear from his own note of 18 August 1930. Emerson was nevertheless determined to press ahead with a legislative change to avoid the implications of Justice Bhide's judgment, and therefore recorded a week later that he had spoken with Mitter and found that he favoured an amendment to the law 'when the act next comes up for revision', the effect of which would be that the Governor-General's view would be the final word on the matter whenever an Ordinance was promulgated under Section 72.

Home member James Crear's request that the Reforms Office, which dealt with amendments to the constitution, should be asked about any proposed amendment to the Government of India Act 1919 was met with opposition from William Hawthorne Lewis. His minute on 27 August 1930 is to the effect that 'the view taken in this office is that mention in the Reforms Dispatch of the need to amend Section 72 might attract undue, perhaps undesirable, attention to a point of detail. It is suggested that the wishes of the honourable home member may best be met by passing through the amendment simply as a drafting point, when the present act is revised.' Section 72 was to stand. This only serves to prove how right D. N. Pritt was when he stood up to plead for Bhagat Singh a few months later.

There was some comfort, nevertheless, for D. N. Pritt. His arguments did in fact succeed before Lord Atkin in another case which has become a landmark in British constitutional law. This was a decade later at the high point of the Second World War. In the now celebrated judgment in *Liversidge v. Anderson*,[5] given a few weeks before Lord Atkin's seventy-fourth birthday, the relationship between the courts and the state, and in particular the assistance that the judiciary should give to the executive in times of national emergency, was brought into sharp relief. More than half a century later, in the words of Lord Bingham, we learn how '[t]his was the time when France had fallen. The British army in France had been destroyed or captured except for the remnant which escaped by the skin of its teeth through Dunkirk. German invasion was expected daily. It was the gravest national crisis in the life of anyone alive in the UK then or since. There was high anxiety about the risk of German collaborators in the United Kingdom.'[6] In these circumstances, the deportation provisions of Regulation III of 1818 were part of the repressive colonial armoury of laws which the British used to deal with insurgents and revolutionaries every bit on par with detentions, beatings and executions.

Thus it was that when the United Kingdom Parliament enacted the Emergency Powers (Defence) Act 1939, it empowered Parliament to issue any controls or regulations that the government felt were necessary to secure public safety, defend the realm, maintain public order and enable the efficient prosecution of the war. Under Regulation 18B of the Defence (General) Regulations 1939 (UK), the Secretary of State was empowered to direct that a person be detained 'if satisfied with respect to any particular person' that their detention was necessary 'with a view to prevent [that person] from acting in any manner prejudicial to the public safety or the defence of the Realm'. Lord Atkin declared, 'In this country, amid the clash of arms, the laws are not silent. They may be changed, but they speak the same language in war as in peace.'[7] For Lord Atkin, '[t]he matter is one of great importance both because the power to make orders is necessary for the defence of the realm, and because the liberty of the subject is seriously infringed'. Importantly, as he pointed out, 'the order does not purport to be made for the commission of an offence against the criminal law'. On the contrary, as in the case of Bhagat Singh, 'it is made by an executive minister and not by any kind of judicial officer'. This is all the more relevant in Bhagat Singh's case, as 'it is not made after any inquiry as to facts to which the subject is party, it cannot be reversed on any appeal, and there is no limit to the period for which the detention may last'.

Lord Atkin had no doubt that '"reasonable cause" for an action or a belief is just as much a positive fact capable of determination by a third party as is a broken ankle or a legal right'. In fact, referring to the 'powers given by statute to arrest for suspicion or belief of offences or intentions to commit offences' he was in no doubt that 'the constable is in exactly the same position as in respect of his common law power to arrest on reasonable suspicion of felony'. This being so, 'there is an "objective" issue in case of dispute to be determined by the court'. Moreover, this was a case where the legislators 'have shown themselves to be fully aware of the true meaning of the words' and that, being so, they 'have clearly appreciated the difference between having reasonable cause to believe and believing without any condition as to reasonable cause, and have obviously used the words "reasonable cause" in order to indicate that mere honest belief is not enough'. With a swipe at other judges who were not with him – such as Lord Maugham, who gave the majority decision to the contrary – Lord Atkin decried in his thunderous dissent 'the attitude of judges' who 'show themselves to be more executive minded than the executive'.[8] This entirely vindicates Pritt in Bhagat Singh's case.

Yet, if Pritt was so confident in his legal stance, why did he never speak about it? A. G. Noorani rightly expresses disappointment at the absence of any reference whatsoever to the trial of Bhagat Singh in Pritt's own autobiography given his commendable advocacy before the Privy Council. There is, however, a good reason: Pritt was gravely disappointed by what he saw in the Privy Council. He had fought tenaciously to save the lives of three young men. He failed, and they were sent to the gallows. He was given short shrift by Viscount Dunedin in an application that was not even given a full hearing. So clever was Pritt that his arguments foresaw the future development of judicial review, particularly in national security cases, by at least half a century, but Viscount Dunedin's decision at the time to not even call upon government counsel to reject Pritt's arguments must have been deeply hurtful and humiliating. This is why there is no mention of Bhagat Singh's case over the three volumes of Pritt's autobiography. In fact, Bhagat Singh's case is not mentioned in the biographies of any of the British judges of the Board either. It is as if they were ashamed; as if they knew that they had not done right by sending three men to the gallows without due process and in the absence of a fair hearing – the right of every citizen of British India. It is as if they knew that coercive colonial legalism should not have been endorsed by the Privy Council 8,000 miles away in London.

The Privy Council's decision in *Bhagat Singh v. The King-Emperor*[9] continued nevertheless to haunt the courts of the common law world for decades to come. Nearly half a century later, the proclamation of an emergency under Article 150 of the Federal Constitution by the Government of Malaysia was challenged in the case of Stephen Kalong Ningkan[10] on the grounds that it was not made *bona fide* but *in fraudem legis*. Relying on two Privy Council decisions from India, one of which was that of Bhagat Singh,[11] the Federal Court of Malaysia held that the court could not inquire as to whether His Majesty, the Yang di-Pertuan Agong, had been satisfied that a state of emergency existed in the state of Sarawak. The Chief Justice of Malaysia, Tan Sri Azmi, 'based his decision entirely on the authority of two Privy Council cases from India, where it was held that the Governor-General of India was the sole judge as to whether a state of emergency existed'.[12] One judge, Ong F. J., dissented, to no avail.

Pritt's legacy did not die, however. He took his revenge from the grave. His barrister's silk gown, so lovingly and adoringly presented to him by the defendants in the Meerut Conspiracy Case, which concluded in 1933, was passed on to one of the greatest civil rights lawyers of his generation in the 1960s. This was Sir Stephen Sedley, who practised from Cloisters Chambers, the leading civil rights barristers' set in the country. Sedley cherished Pritt's silk gown, and for no idle reason. Born in 1930 to a father who was a lifelong communist, Sedley revolutionised the understanding of modern constitutional law in case after case with his involvement in groundbreaking cases on employment rights, sex and race discrimination, prisoners' rights, coroners' inquests, immigration and asylum, as well as in freedom of speech cases. His consummate skill and devotion to the liberty of the individual against the overweening powers of the state proved irresistible for a conservative Lord Chancellor, who appointed him, much to his astonishment, to the High Court in 1992. From there he moved on to the Court of Appeal in 1999 as a Lord Justice of Appeal, quickly becoming the most senior public law judge. He even went on to sit on the Judicial Committee of the Privy Council and as a judge *ad hoc* of the European Court of Human Rights. When Lord Justice Sedley heard the Chagos Islands case of *Bancoult*,[13] which was destined to become 'the longest Supreme Court case ever heard',[14] he decisively ruled 'that the power of a colonial legislature is not unfettered because it will be limited by its own constitutive instrument and by the principle of territoriality':

> One can readily accept that the colonial use of the peace, good order and good government of the prerogative power is for the most part beyond the reach of judicial review, but not that it is always or necessarily so … even if its subject-matter is incontestably the colony, it is capable of being rendered invalid by jurisdictional error or malpractice…[15]

Moreover, the exercise of such power by a colonial legislature 'must also be open to challenge if its subject-matter, on examination, is manifestly *not* the peace, good order and good government of the colony'.[16] On this basis, 'the use of the prerogative power of colonial governance enjoys no generic immunity from judicial review'. On the other hand, '[w]hat are immune ... are prerogative measures lawfully enacted and rationally capable of addressing the peace, good order and good government of the colony'.[17] These distinctions were truly demonstrative of the rule of law at its best. They vindicate Pritt, who must have smiled from his grave.

The *Bancoult* case arose in circumstances which are worth recalling in some detail as they are of direct relevance to the manner of the determination of Bhagat Singh's appeal. In 1965, Britain created a separate colony out of the Chagos Islands, which had been ceded to it after the Napoleonic Wars by France in 1814, and called it the British Indian Ocean Territory (BIOT), to which were added Mauritius and certain other Indian Ocean dependencies. The method of governance of such colonies was essentially through the exercise of the prerogative power of the Crown, by virtue of which Orders in Council are made. And so the situation remained until, at height of the Cold War in the 1960s and 1970s, the Chagossian people were exiled through the use of prerogative powers because the USA wanted to use Diego Garcia, the principal island in the archipelago, as a military base. The freehold interest in the entire territory of the BIOT was then acquired by the Crown in 1967. The way in which the compulsory removal of the Chagossians was effected was by the Commissioner for the BIOT acting under the Immigration Ordinance of 1971, which confined the Chagossians to Mauritius. In 1983, the BIOT was declared Crown land.

In 1999, Oliver Bancoult challenged the expulsion under the 1971 Ordinance made by the Commissioner. He did so because, long before, in 1967, when he was just three years old, his parents had taken him together with his infant sister from the island of Peros Banhos in the Chagos Archipelago to Mauritius. A cartwheel had run over the leg of his little sister, and they had to go to Mauritius to get her urgent medical treatment. When they tried to return, however, they were forbidden by the British authorities. Now, more than thirty years on, Bancoult remarkably found himself succeeding before the Divisional Court in London in November 2000 (comprising Laws LJ and Gibbs J.), which quashed the 1971 Ordinance. The court held that the exclusion of an entire population from its homeland could not have been authorized by the parent Order in Council, the British Indian Ocean Territory Order 1965, which was limited to the governance of the population. It did not encompass its expulsion.

Remarkably, however, on 10 June 2004, two Orders in Council were placed by ministers before Her Majesty for approval. These were the British Indian Ocean Territory (Constitution) Order 2004 and the British Indian Ocean Territory (Immigration) Order 2004. The first declared that no person has the right of abode in BIOT nor the right without authorisation to enter and remain there. The Chagossians were thus effectively exiled. In the Court of Appeal thereafter, the government argued that the effect of the Colonial Laws Validity Act 1865 was that once the royal prerogative is exercised, then any attack on the validity of a colonial Order in Council is precluded. This was no different to the government's argument in Bhagat Singh's case. Further, since the government of a ceded colony by Order in Council is a sovereign act of the Crown, it can only be challenged on the basis of its incompatibility with imperial legislation. Sedley LJ at the outset quipped that '[i]f either argument is right, the executive will have accomplished by Order in Council what it was prevented by the first Divisional Court decision from doing by Ordinance', such was the enormity of its implication. Here again one is reminded of Pritt's argument that imperial legislation setting up the Lahore High Court cannot be undermined by subordinate legislation in India taking away the right to appeal to that very same High Court. The Government in *Bancoult*, however, argued that no colonial law could be challenged unless it was 'repugnant to any Order or Regulation made under Authority of such Act of Parliament, or having in the Colony the Force and Effect of such Act', as stipulated in the Colonial Laws Validity Act 1865, the purpose of which was precisely that it should be 'an Act to remove Doubts as to the Validity of Colonial Laws'. The government argued that 'an Order in Council is placed by the 1865 Act on a par with the Act of a colonial legislature and placed beyond challenge save for repugnancy to an imperial statute'.

Sedley LJ, however, found a way of limiting governmental power by suggesting that local colonial courts could nullify legislation that was *ultra vires* the imperial statute law, so that

in my judgment the rule created by the 1865 Act is one of priority, not of powers: a colonial law, albeit validly enacted, is to be inoperative to the extent, but only to the extent, to which it conflicts with imperial statute law. That there exists a judicial power so to decide is assumed by the legislator: it is not a power created by the 1865 Act. Nor is the power of a colonial legislature unfettered: it will be limited by its own constitutive instrument and by the principle of territoriality, so that colonial judicatures remain able notwithstanding the 1865 Act to strike down local legislation which transgresses these limits. Likewise, *those colonial Orders in Council made under statutory powers continued to be open to challenge not only for repugnancy to imperial legislation but, if they exceeded the powers which they purported to be exercising, for invalidity.*

Pressing forward with his impeccable logic, Sedley LJ added, 'Repugnancy as a legislative term means an irreconcilable conflict between two laws.' But here, 'if an unconstitutional colonial statute is not law – as manifestly it is not – no question of repugnancy arises'. Once again, it may be noted here that Pritt too had argued that what one was dealing with in Bhagat's Singh's case was not a law at all but a *priviligium*. As such Sedley LJ explained,

> The present dispute, equally, is not about whether the Constitution Order is repugnant to a superior statute or other legal provision but about whether it is law. It is accordingly not barred by the 1865 Act.

In this way, Sedley LJ decided that Section 9 of the Constitution Order, together with the Immigration Order, was not lawfully made, as it was *ultra vires*, being unconnected with the governance of the BIOT; and that, alternatively, it fell to be quashed for irrationality or for breach of the Chagossians' legitimate expectation of a right of return; and that it also breached the principles of public international law. This is because the phrase in Section 9 of the Constitution Order of 'peace, order and good government', which, as Sedley LJ explained, 'has a long legislative pedigree, has become a term of art in the sense that it is regularly used without further explanation to denote the delegation of large but undefined powers to a nominated rule-maker'. It was, however, 'a power of the greatest importance carrying commensurate responsibilities' since 'at its fullest it can bring about the creation of independent states'. Nevertheless, 'it has limits, even if these are self-imposed'. These are 'directed to the wellbeing of a dependent territory and its population' as a way of deciding 'what is best for a colony and to affirm that, like every discretion, it is limited by and to its own expressed objects'. As far as the courts were concerned, 'it is their constitutional function to decide whether what has been enacted (or what it is proposed to enact) is rationally and legally capable of providing for a colony's wellbeing. If it is not, then it falls outside the prerogative power.'[18]

Quoting from what Laws LJ had said in the High Court in 2000, Sedley pointed out how 'S.4 of the Ordinance effectively exiles the Ilois [i.e. Chagossians] from the territory where they are belongers and forbids their return. But the "peace, order, and good government" of any territory means nothing, surely, save by reference to the territory's population. They are to be *governed*.'[19] One may here wonder again whether Governor-General Irwin's Lahore Ordinance of 1930 was actually setting out to 'govern' its Indian territory in any way. Sedley LJ also made a distinction between the 'mother country' and the colonial territories in that '[t]he governance of each colonial territory is in constitutional principle a discrete function of the Crown' and '[t]hat territory's interests will not necessarily be the interests of the United Kingdom or of its allies'. These words represented a marked break from the Bhagat Singh case, in which the interests of Her Majesty's Government were considered to be paramount.

Such laws were subject to the following two provisos. First, only a colonial law which is in any respect 'repugnant to ... any Act of Parliament extending to the Colony ... shall, to the Extent of such Repugnancy, but not otherwise, be and remain absolutely void and inoperative'.[20] Here Pritt had said that one cannot exclude a High Court appeal. On the other hand, the second thing to note was that 'no Colonial Law shall be ... void or inoperative on the Ground of Repugnancy ... *unless the same shall be repugnant to the Provisions of some such Act of Parliament*, Order, or Regulation as aforesaid'.[21] What the House of Lords faced, when the appeal finally ended up there in 2008, from the government was the argument that since the territory in question was a colony with its own legislature – the Commissioner – and since the Constitution Order is a law made for the colony by Order in Council and therefore a 'colonial law', it 'cannot be void or inoperative by reason of its repugnancy to English common law doctrines of judicial review'.[22] In the Court of Appeal, however, Sedley LJ had already rejected this archaic argument. He had held in 2007 that the 1865 Act was concerned with the repugnancy of otherwise valid colonial laws to the law of England, but that was not to say that the principles of judicial review could *not* be used to determine whether the Order in Council was valid in the first place. If the Order in Council was beyond the powers of Her Majesty in Council to make, then 'no question of repugnancy arose, as there was no colonial law which could be repugnant to anything'.[23] This meant that in the case of Bhagat Singh it was unnecessary to delve into the question of 'repugnancy' because the essential issue was whether the Governor-General was properly exercising his powers – and, even if he was, whether in the exercise of those powers there was evidence of jurisdictional error or evidence of a malpractice.

In the House of Lords in 2008, the court in *Bancoult* was split. This is because it was being forced to countenance the possibility of the prerogative of colonial governance falling under the 'shadow of the rule of law',[24] as Mark Elliott and Amanda Perreau-Saussine state – rather than the rule of law itself. While Lord Hoffman took the view that the government had acted lawfully, Lord Bingham held that Section 9 of the Constitution Order could not be enacted,[25] and Lord Mance said that only the proper governance of the territory could justify the Order in council.[26] Lord Hoffman held the prerogative's exercise by the Crown to be 'in the interests of her undivided realm, including both the United Kingdom and the colony',[27] whilst Lords Rodger[28] and Carswell[29] suggested that it was a matter for the Crown and not the Court. But they then also held that the question of whether the power was exercised rationally was a justiciable question.[30]

The saga did not end there. A decade later, in 2016, *Bancoult* returned to the Supreme Court (which had previously been called the House of Lords), this time on the question of whether the return of the Chagossians to their homeland was practically possible. The judges in the country's leading judicial tribunal were even more startling on this occasion. Pritt would nevertheless have smiled with satisfaction. Lord Mance (who alone had also sat on this case ten years earlier in 2008), giving the leading judgment, was clear that judicial review was indeed the main legal remedy[31] (as Sedley LJ had also ruled). Although the majority for the time being decided in favour of the government, the dissenting judgment of Lord Kerr was unmistakeably clear that 'a decision to remove the Chagossians from their homeland' was 'one for which compelling justification would be required'.[32] This is because '[t]he fact that their removal was unreasonable cannot ... be left out of account in assessing whether the subsequent decision to perpetuate the Chagossians' exile was rational'.[33]

Even stronger criticism of the government came from the redoubtable Lady Hale, who referred to an academic article by Frost and Murray written in 2015 which mentioned the competing forces of 'liberal imperialism' and 'utilitarian imperialism'. Lady Hale used this to express her powerful dissent of the majority judgments. She went so far as to say that back in 2008, 'Lord Hoffmann acknowledged that a choice between the liberal and utilitarian faces of imperialism did rest with the court, and decisively affirmed the utilitarian importance of the imperial interests at stake'.[34] For her, however, there is every reason to now doubt whether this 'utilitarian' view of imperialism, about 'how best to appropriate colonial possessions for the benefit of the imperial power' will prevail over the 'liberal' view of imperialism, which is to do with 'the civilising nature of empire and focuses on the good governance of colonies'.[35]

The government may have won in 2016, but it was a pyrrhic victory. In the words of Lady Hale, 'Courts have ... to do justice according to law ... and the people to whom it is of such momentous importance are entitled to expect the highest standards of decision-making and the most scrupulous standards of fairness *from the institutions of imperial government*.' What a far cry this was from the words of Viscount Dunedin in the Lahore Conspiracy Case. In a rare judicial statement highlighting the central role played by judicial personalities in hard cases arising before the courts, Lady Hale also added that these questions ultimately have 'to be answered objectively rather than by reference to the particular judges who were then sitting on the case'.[36] This is a salutary reminder of the importance of people and personalities. They cannot be divorced from the great events of history. In Bhagat Singh's case it was the judicial personalities that mattered. From Lord Atkin down to Justice Bhide and Justice Broadway in India there was one view, and it favoured the existence of the judicial review of the executive power under which Bhagat Singh and his comrades were going to be executed. On the other hand, there were the hostile views of Lords Dunedin, Thankerton and Russell, who sat in London with Sir George Lowndes and Sir Dinshah Mulla. There was one remarkably short judgment, without a full hearing of the appeal, where the government lawyer was not even called upon to make good his case – and that too in a capital punishment trial marred by glaring procedural and substantive irregularities.

If all this was not shocking enough, there was one thing more which has so far not been recognised in the passage of almost a hundred years since Lahore Conspiracy Case was heard in the Privy Council in 1931. Bhagat Singh, Sukhdev and Rajguru were unlawfully executed by an Act of Attainder! By virtue of something that was not law.

In the meantime, the cold chill of colonial litigation continues with *Bancoult* in the UK's highest courts in a way that is eerily reminiscent of colonial repression – and coercive colonial legalism still lingers on in the empire even today.

Appendix

The Lahore Archives

The carefully compiled Index to the Lahore Conspiracy Case 1929 has the documents set out under:
   (1) Serial Number (Sr.)
   (2) Description of Documents
   (3) Remarks.

Sr. 13 is the Poonch House Lahore Conspiracy Case File of the miscellaneous applications filed by the accused and correspondence (pages 1-266).

Sr. 14 is a file containing admission forms for one year class of D.A.V. College, Lahore. (For the year 1927).

Sr. 15 is the Lahore Conspiracy Case No. 1/2 Crown v Prem Dutt, Sukh Dev and Bhagat Singh etc. U/S 302/120, 109, 121, I.P.C. File containing police papers and challan etc. (handwritten in Urdu and English).

Sr. 16 is a Lahore Conspiracy Case, File containing petition U/S 497 Criminal Procedure Code from Jai Dev and Dharm Vir etc. dated 13 May 1929.

Sr. 17 is a Lahore Conspiracy Case, File containing exhibits admitted in evidence by Judge Special Tribunal Lahore (Prem Dutt accused).

Sr. 18 is Lahore Conspiracy Case File containing exhibits P.E.A. regarding Dyal Singh College, Library, Lahore.

Sr. 19 is Lahore Conspiracy Case, File containing exhibits P.F.A. etc. and papers regarding identification parade held on 4-7.1929 by Chairman Mushtaq Ahmad M.I.C. Lahore.

Sr. 20 is a Lahore Conspiracy Case, File containing exhibit P.J./2 etc. regarding Recovery list of accused involved in the case.

Sr. 21 is a Lahore Conspiracy Case, File containing statement of P.W.164 – Manmohan Banerji, approval on S.A. dated 18–1–1930.

Sr. 22 is a Lahore Conspiracy Case, File containing statement of P.W.147- Hans Raj Wohra approval on S.A. dated 2-12.1929.

Sr. 23 is a Lahore Conspiracy Case, File containing the Police Journal Vol. II, No. 7 regarding the forensic examination of firearms and projectiles by Robert Churchill, along with a film negative copy (exhibit B.P.A.).

Sr. 24 is a Lahore Conspiracy Case, File containing the photos of bombs prepared by the accused (exhibits P.F.C. 1.2.3.4.).

Sr. 25 is a Lahore Conspiracy Case, Judicial File No. 2/3 Crown v Shivram Raj Guru etc. (16) persons, U/S 52 Act. 9 1894 No. Register General No. 26 No. Goshawara 1771 dated of Order 12.12.1930 passed by A.D.M. Lahore.

Sr. 26 is a Lahore Conspiracy Case, Judicial File No. 447/3 Crown v Shir Ram, Raj Ghuru etc. U/S 52 Act, 9 of 1894 No. Register General 23 No. Ghoshawara 1776 dated of Order 12.12.1930 passed by A.D.M. Lahore.

Sr. 27 is a Lahore Conspiracy Case, Judicial File No. 5/3 Crown vs Bhagat Singh etc. U/S 52 Act, 9 of 1984 No. Register General 28 No. Ghoshawara 1773 Date of Order 12.12.1930 passed by A.D.M. Lahore.

Sr. 28 is a Lahore Conspiracy Case, Judicial File No. 1/3 Crown Vs Bhagat Singh etc. U/S 52 Act. 9 of 1894 No. Register General 25 No. Ghoshawara 1770 date of Order 12-12-1930 passed by A.D.M. Lahore.

Sr. 29 is a Lahore Conspiracy Case, Judicial File No. 4.3 Crown Vs Shiv Ram, Raj Ghuru etc. U/S 52 Act. 9 of 1894 No. Register General of 27 No. Ghoshwara 1772 date of Order 12-12-1930 passed by A.D.M. Lahore.

Sr. 30 is a Lahore Conspiracy Case, Judicial File No. 6/3 Crown Vs Bhgat Singh etc. U/S 52 Act. 9 of 1894 No. Register General 31 No. Ghoshwara 1774 date of Order 12-12-1930 passed by A.D.M. Lahore.

Sr. 31 is a Lahore Conspiracy Case, Judicial File No. 451/3 Crown Vs Bhagat Singh etc. U/S 52 Act. 9 of 1894 No. Register General 24 No. Ghoshwara 1777 date of Order 12-12-1930 passed by A.D.M. Lahore.

Sr. 32 is Lahore Conspiracy Case, Judicial File No. 1 Crown Vs Shukh Dev etc. (18 persons) U/S 302, 120(B), 109 I.P.C. Register General No. 1697 Ghoshwara No. 1384 date of Order 7-10-1930 passed by Special Tribunal Lahore.

Sr. 33 is a Lahore Conspiracy Case, File No. 93/94 list of exhibits produced in the Lahore Conspiracy Case Tribunal.

Sr. 34 is a Lahore Conspiracy Case, list of exhibits produced in the Special Tribunal Lahore Conspiracy Case (27-10-1930).

Sr. 35 is a Lahore Conspiracy Case, Misc; Case No. 134 of 1930 Des Raj s/o Ram Kishar Vs The Crown Petition U/S 491 and 561-A Criminal Procedure Code filed in the Court of Judicature at Lahore date of Order 16-7-1930.

Sr. 36 is a Lahore Conspiracy Case, Crown Vs Bhagat Singh etc. U/S 302/121/120 etc. I.P.C. Decided by the Special Tribunal Lahore on 7-10-1930 (warrants only executed and printed copies of the Privy Council Judgment in the case noted above).

Sr. 37 is a Lahore Conspiracy Case, Criminal Misc. Case No. 290 of 1929 The Crown Vs Shukh Dev. and Others Petition U/S 561-A Criminal Procedure Code. Date of Order 31-1-1930 passed by the High Court of Judicature at Lahore.

Sr. 38 is the Lahore Conspiracy Case cash book of Dwarka Dass Library (Servants of the People Society Lahore for the year 1927 to 1929).

Sr. 39 is the Lahore Conspiracy Case Lecture Register of the second year class of DAV College Lahore 1928.

Sr. 40 is the Lahore Conspiracy Case register of expenditure produced by Fazal Abbas, Rawalpindi.

Sr. 41 is the Lahore Conspiracy Case register for daily visitors of the Dyal Singh Library and reading room (27 August 1929).

Sr. 42 is the Lahore Conspiracy Register of Create Indian Peninsula Railway regarding daily return of black card and papers, tickets (1928).

Sr. 43 is the Lahore Conspiracy Case register of expenditure produced by Fazal Abbas of Rawalpindi (16 January 1928 to 31 March 1928.

Sr. 44 is the register of meal etc. produced by Baboo Ramaish Chander Ch. Proprietor, Eastern Home Hotel, Calcutta.

Sr. 45 is the general diary of the official of Superintendent Police Saharanpur for the year 1929.

Sr. 46 is the register of visitors to Arya Samag Guru Mall Section, Rawalpindi produced by Secretary Arya Samag, Rawalpindi.

Sr. 47 is register for expenses of kitchen number 1 store system for the year 1928 to 1929 Guru Datt Bawan, Lahore. Produced by Superintendent Guru Datt Bharmbharam.

Sr. 48 is the daily issue book of Tilak School of Politics Gari Mohal City Branch, Lahore.

Sr 49 is a register produced by the Manhat Ram s/o Bhagwan Das Khatri Manhat Prem Bhojan Shalla, Barham Chari Neehru Hotel, Gawal Mandi, Lahore.

Sr. 50 is the registered kitchen produced by Natho Ram s/o Chajjoo Ram of Guru Datt Baan Hostel, Lahore.

Sr. 51 is a register of kitchen (number 1) written in Hindi.

Sr. 52 is the attendance register of Bombay Cycle and Motor Agency Ltd Lahore.

Sr. 53 is a register of Eastern Indian Railway for collection of tickets to Cawnpur.

Sr. 54 is the admission of withdrawal register of Victoria Diamond Jubilee, Hindu Technical Institute at Lahore.

Sr. 55 is the attendance register Grami Gram School, Amritsar.

Sr. 56 is the Urdu Appendix A at page 1 to 1290 (these statements were transferred from the records of the Special Magistrate to the Tribunal).

Sr 57 is the English Appendix A Crown v/s Bhagat Singh etc. charges under Section 302/102, 109 I.P.C. pages and 1 to 1662 (these statements were transferred from the records of the Special Magistrate to the Tribunal).

Sr. 58 is the Urdu records (Part A) Case Crown v/s Bhagat Singh etc. charges u/s 302/120, 109, I.P.C. pages 1 to 402.

Sr. 59 is the Urdu record Part C Crown v/s Bhagat Singh etc. charges u/s 302/120, 109, I.P.C. pages 1055 to 1500.

Sr. 60 is the Urdu record Part D (statements) Crown v/s Bhagat Singh etc. charges u/s 302/120, 109 I.P.C. pages 1501 to 2060.

Sr. 61 is the Urdu record (statements) Part E v Bhagat Singh charges u/s 302/120, 109, I.P.C. pages 2061 to 2534.

Sr. 62 is the Urdu statement Part II Crown v Bhagat Singh charges u/s 302/120, 109, I.P.C. pages 477 to 1142.

Sr. 63 is the Urdu record (statement) Part III Crown v Bhagat Singh charges u/s 302/120, 109, I.P.C. pages 1143 to 2080.

Sr. 64 is the English record (statement Part II) manuscript notes of the Honourable President (Mr Justice Hilton) Lahore Conspiracy Case, Special Tribunal Poonch House, commencing from 21 June 1930 and ending with 7 October 1930 (pages 1 to 1042).

Sr. 65 is the English record (statement) Part I notes of the Honourable President (Mr Justice Hilton of the Tribunal) (pages 1 to 940).

Sr. 66 is the Crown v Bhagat Singh u/s 3021 to 0109 I.P.C. original English record of the Lahore Conspiracy Case Part I pages 1 to 876 decided on 7 October 1930.

Sr. 67 is the original English record of the Lahore Conspiracy Case Part II pages 877 to 1852.

Sr. 68 is the original English record of the proceedings of the Lahore Conspiracy Case Special Tribunal Part II P.W.49 to P.W.288 (pages 1853 to 3050).

Sr. 69 is the index to the proceedings of the Lahore Conspiracy Case Part IV statements of prosecution witnesses pages 305 to 3675.

Sr. 70 is the Urdu record relating to the proceedings inspection police statements of P.W. (pages 2081 to 3071).

Sr. 71 which is serial number 71 is proceedings of the Lahore Conspiracy Case Part V statements of prosecution witnesses pages 3677 to 5331.

Sr. 72 is the Marathi translation of the proceedings on 1 June 1930 to 15 July 1930 i.e. up to printed page 502 complete pages 1 to 457.

Sr. 73 is a file containing summons to witnesses except of pages 1 to 562.

Sr. 74 is a file containing summons to witnesses at dockets issued from the Special Tribunal (pages 469 to 927).

Sr. 75 is a file containing summons to witnesses and dockets issued from the Special Tribunal pages 99 to 1371.

Sr. 76 is a file containing summons to witnesses and dockets issued from the Special Tribunal. Warrants of execution on the sentence of death in respect of Bhaghat Singh etc. pages 1373 to 1813.

Sr. 77 is a file containing summonses to witnesses and Rob Karskrs issued by the Special Tribunal.

Sr. 78 is the original records in the case of Crown v Bhagat Singh and B.K. Dutt u/s 55 of the Prisons Act. Which were apparently obtained by the Punjab Government for the perusal of the solicitor to the Government of India, Part I pages 1 to 695.

Sr. 79 is the original records in the case of Crown v Bhagat Sing and B.K. Dutt u/s 52 of the Prisons Act. Which were apparently obtained by the Punjab Government for the perusal of the solicitor to the Government of India, Part II, pages 697 to 1645.

Sr. 80 is a Crown v Sukh Dev and Others u/s 302/120-B, 121 I.P.C. file of the exhibits relating to the court room witnesses (pages 1 to 48).

Sr. 81 is the Photostat copy of judgment in the Lahore Conspiracy Case, 1930 (pages 1 to 282).

Sr. 82 is the Photostat of judgment in the Lahore Conspiracy Case, 1930 (pages 1 to 282). There are also newspapers so,

Sr. 83 contains newspapers of The Tribune from 10 February 1928 right the way through to 27 December 1928. There is also the Swtentrn which is a Hindi daily dated 6 June 1929. There are furthermore other newspapers like the Vir Bharat an Urdu newspaper for 16 January 1929 right the way through 27 February 1930 and a special issue for 8 December 1930.

Sr. 85 is a register box regarding Rooznamcha Police Station, Old Anarkali, Lahore.

Sr. 86 is the copy book containing particulars etc. of the persons admitted into the court room to attend the proceedings of the Lahore Conspiracy Case.

Sr. 87 is the admission and the fall register of Bharat Motor Company and Training College from 1 November 1927, Rai Sahib M. Gulab Singh and Sons, Lahore.

Sr. 88 is a daily attendance register of the Bharat Motors Co and Training College from 18 September 1927.

Sr. 89 is a file containing statement of Tulsi Ram (P.W.).

<u>Sr. 90</u> is the file containing particulars of identification proceedings.

<u>Sr. 91</u> is the file containing risk note form (A) of the Great Indian Peninsula Railway.

<u>Sr. 92</u> is a file containing post-mortem report etc.

<u>Sr. 93</u> is a file containing the list of contents of the steel trunk number 111 sent to the chemical examiner, Agra.

<u>Sr. 94</u> is the file containing Hindustan Socialist Republic Army Notice.

<u>Sr. 95</u> is a file containing photocopies of the correspondence of the Himalaya Assurance Company Limited, Lahore.

<u>Sr. 96</u> is a file containing photocopies of the documents regarding identification parade held in Central Jail, Cill Block Number XIV.

<u>Sr. 97</u> is a file containing notification in respect of Mr R.C. Jefferys, SSP Lahore.

<u>Sr. 98</u> is a file containing photocopies of the correspondence of Preem Dutta Varma.

<u>Sr. 99</u> is a file containing correspondence between SP and Chemical Examiner Governor, Government of Punjab.

<u>Sr. 100</u> is the Lahore Conspiracy Case file containing extract on the criminal intelligence consent UP dated 17 April 1930.

<u>Sr. 101</u> is a file containing a statement of the accused, Prem Dutt Verma.

<u>Sr. 102</u> is a file containing a statement of the Residence of College Hostel.

<u>Sr. 103</u> is a file containing statement of residence of D.A.V. College Hostel.

<u>Sr. 104</u> is a file registered correspondence between the Chemical Examiner to Government (CUP Agra) and District Magistrates Saharanpur.

<u>Sr. 105</u> is a Lahore Conspiracy Case file regarding deputation of magistrate.

<u>Sr. 106</u> is a file containing the appeal against transportation for life.

<u>Sr. 107</u> is an envelope containing the maps of the size involved in the case.

<u>Sr. 108</u> is the simple index of B. Nar Singh Das.

<u>Sr. 109</u> is a simple index of Mohammad Ali.

<u>Sr. 110</u> is a simple index of Sant Singh.

<u>Sr. 111</u> is a statement of attendance in the Hindu Hotel Lahore for February 1929.

<u>Sr. 112</u> is a statement of attendance in the Hindu Hotel Lahore for March 1929.

<u>Sr. 113</u> is a statement of attendance in Hindu Hotel Lahore for the year 1929.

<u>Sr. 114</u> is the attendance in Sherma Hindi Hotel Ferozpur City.

<u>Sr. 115</u> is attendance register produced by the owner Eastern Home Hotel Lahore.

Sr. 116 is a loose paper file.

Sr. 117 is an envelope plan of Assembly Chamber containing two plan.

Sr. 118 is a file nominal role of convicts who have completed fourteen years in jail.

Sr. 119 is a file regarding descriptive role of the prisoner for transfer from the Lahore Central Jail to Maini Central Jail.

Sr. 120 is a file containing statements of the accused regarding search of their room etc.

Sr. 121 is a file containing statements of Mahindra Nath Ghosh as Crown witness.

Sr. 122 is a file containing papers of 'The Sanjiwan' Delhi and Hindu monthly magazine.

Sr. 123 is the file containing a report of the Chemical Laboratory.

Sr. 124 is a file containing search list of accused.

Sr. 125 is a file containing the proceedings of All India Youth Congress Third Session 1928.

Sr. 126 is a file regarding the verification of the statement of accused Phanindra Nath Ghosh, Crown witness.

Sr. 127 is a file containing the proceedings conducted in Lahore Fort.

Sr. 128 is a file containing the application of accused Bhagat Singh to have an interview with his father.

Sr. 129 is a file containing the papers 'Servants of the People Society' 2 Court Street, Lahore and Dwarka Dass Library.

Sr. 130 is a file containing the sketch plans of the house number 1784 Soot Para, Agra etc. and source of Crown witness.

Sr. 131 is a file containing post-mortem report by Mr J P Sanders.

Sr. 132 is a file containing the risk note form (A) of the Eastern Indian Railway, Agra City.

Sr. 133 is a file containing papers of search of the houses of the accused.

Sr. 134 is a file containing the statement of Jai Gopal before D M Lahore.

Sr. 135 is a file Number A-1 facilities given to the accused confined in jails in the matter of interviews with their relatives.

Sr. 136 is a file number A-2 admission of lawyers into the Tribunal, engagement of lawyers for the accused, appointment of prosecutors etc.

Sr. 137 is the Lahore Conspiracy Case file number dict money advance for witness in the Crown in the case Crown v Bhagat Singh etc.

Sr. 138 is a file number F-1 supply of Ver. Forms (Criminal) by the Central Jail, Lahore and Government Printing Press.

<u>Sr. 139</u> are miscellaneous papers.

<u>Sr. 140</u> is file number P-1, passes and photos.

<u>Sr. 141</u> is file number P-2 printing of the Special Tribunal proceedings by the Government Printing Press.

<u>Sr. 142</u> is file number – D-i dict money etc. paid to the witness who appeared in the case Crown v Bhagat Singh.

<u>Sr. 143</u> is a register catalogue of the office file of the Office of Special Tribunal Lahore Conspiracy Case Lahore.

<u>Sr. 144</u> account register of the money received from the District Nazir Lahore on account of dict money etc.

<u>Sr. 145</u> is one copy produced by Hussain Bux s/o Fazal Din shopkeeper Mozang, Lahore for house rent (Hindi).

<u>Sr. 146</u> is the bahai produced by Abdul Jabbar shopkeeper regarding purchase of rice.

<u>Sr. 147</u> is bahai produced by Ram Saroop Sweet Meet Maker for purchase of milk.

<u>Sr. 148</u> is the bahai written in Landay.

<u>Sr. 149</u> is a laundry book by the owner of Komi Washing Factory, Gwalmandi, Lahore.

<u>Sr. 150</u> is a two postman books.

<u>Sr. 151</u> is a receipt book from number 5501 to 6000.

<u>Sr. 152</u> is a receipt book of the 'The Bharat Motor Co Lahore'.

<u>Sr. 153</u> is a receipt book regarding payment of house rent.

<u>Sr. 154</u> is a receipt book of Master Amir Kanhay Lal regarding house rent.

<u>Sr. 155</u> is a bill book for the chemical etc. from Beli Ram and Brothers Lahore.

<u>Sr. 156</u> is a drama 'Bay Zaban Dost' alias 'Zakhmi Punjab'.

<u>Sr. 157</u> is a novel 'Sultana Dakoo'.

<u>Sr. 158</u> is a drama called 'Gunga Watram'.

<u>Sr. 159</u> is a novel 'Gunga Das Dakkoo'.

<u>Sr. 160</u> is a final order dated 7 October 1930 in the case known as Lahore Conspiracy Case, 1929 (Photostat copy of the printed judgment' Crown v Sukh Dev and Others.

Finally it is to be noted that most of the documents are simply one copy and many of them are preserved in a box, for example documents 1 to 3 are preserved in the iron safe.

The index runs to 35 pages and consists of 160 serial numbers.

The post-mortem report on the gruesome murder of the young J. P. Saunders, with descriptions of his external appearance upon arrival at the mortuary. Previously unpublished.

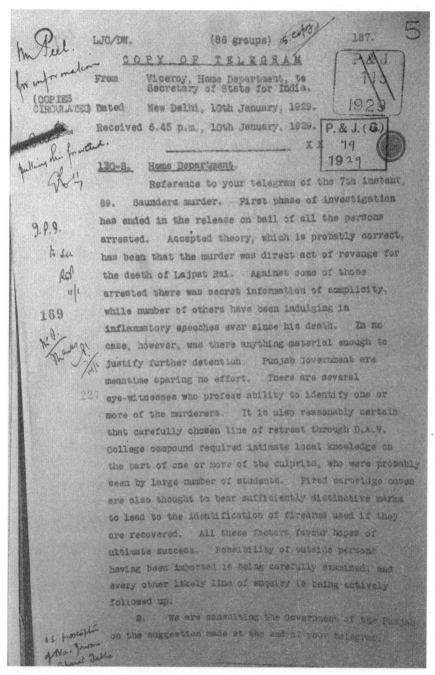

Although it was quickly realised by the authorities that the chilling murder of J. P. Saunders was a 'direct act of revenge for the death of Lajpat Rai', they initially faced considerable difficulty in identifying the assailants, and Bhagat Singh was not even in the frame. Previously unpublished.

FCN/ETP/WMC   (33 words.)   5955

C O P Y   O F   T E L E G R A M   5250

From   Viceroy, Home Department, to Secretary
        of State for India.

Dated   New Delhi, 18th December, 1928.

Received   18th December, 1928, 5.45 a.m.

P. & J. (S.)

7 9

1929.

IMPORTANT.
_____

D.3249-Police.   Following from the Government of the

Punjab, dated the 17th December, is repeated for your

information. Begins:- Regret have to report that

Saunders, Assistant Superintendent of Police, was shot

down and killed this afternoon by 2 youths, who escaped

into Dav College and thence (? into) country on bicycle.

Pursuit immediately organised, but no arrest yet made.

Munshi who pursued also killed. Ends.

_____

Note:-

        Owing to the urgent nature of this telegram,
    figures, doubtful passages and corrupt groups
    have not been checked. This will be done
    later.

An urgent telegram from the Viceroy's Office referring to the death of J. P. Saunders
at the hands of '2 youths' who were as yet unidentified. Previously unpublished.

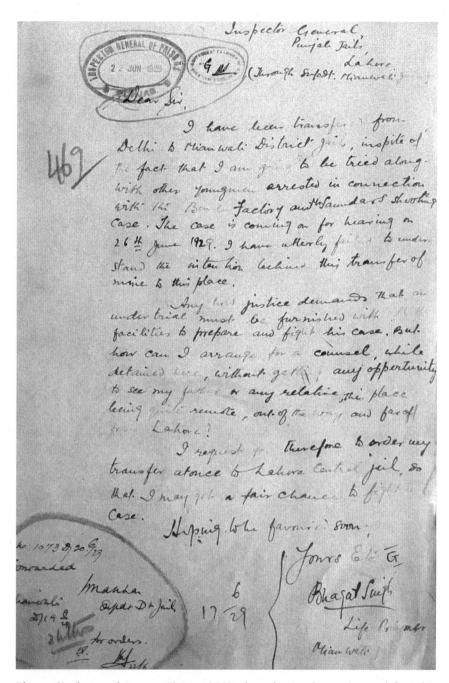

Bhagat Singh complains on 17 June 1929 about having been separated from his fellow conspirators by being whisked off to Mianwali Jail, while the others were in Lahore, on the basis that this prevented the adequate preparation of his defence.

to help the country in any way, for example in the building of schools or the raising of the education amongst my people.

Requests and appeals by the Indian people as a whole has been sent to the King Emperor of India and his government and have had no effect upon them. Therefore the time has come when the people of India must stand up and show those vultures of British Imperialism that no longest (sic) must they bleed and deprive the people of my beloved land but use and utilise the products and profits of the country for the benefit of the people without class or creed prejudice.

SHEET "B"

This is a medley of English, Gurmukhi and Urdu. It concludes with the words used by Udham Singh when he addressed the Court and which were interrupted by the Judge.

The first few lines consist of a poem in Urdu, which is signed 'Bawa', this being the name by which he was commonly known to his associates. The following words of this poem have been deciphered:

O God! into what hardships have the people of India fallen! Our guests have begun to exercise oppression over us; Let the enemies stand on our heads, the dagger be poised at our throats ......
The times are all gone wrong and oppression has appeared before our sight!

Further down appears the following in Urdu:

Hitherto God has not changed the condition of that nation which has no idea of (impending) change.

There follows a stanza of a Gurmukhi poem on Indian martyrs. The words 'Bhagat Singh', 'Dutt', 'Tilak' and 'Lajpat', all well-known figures in the Indian national struggle, appear in this poem.

Next come a few words in English:

I am not afraid to die. I am proud to die for such a glorious cause to help to free my native land and I hope when I am gone that in my place will come thousands of my country-men to drive you vultures until you not only free our country but also clear to hell out of it.

The first few words of this tirade the prisoner shouted from the dock when sentence of death was about to be passed.

Sheet "B" concludes with the following violent attack on British rule in India:

I anticipate and hope for the downfall of British imperialism by which India would automatically be freed, for Hitler and Stalin would not take India even if given to them.

Long live Mahatma Gandhi VIVA India and Subas Bose. Down with the British democracies. VIVA INDIA. Down with Britain. Down with the British democracies. Indians do not have peace. What we have got is slavery. Greedy Britain English. For generation your so called civilization has brought forth everything (?)filthy and degenerate known to the human race. It's not for me to point out or debate on any one particular point. All you have to do is to read

The words used by Udham Singh when addressing the court following his death sentence refer to Bhagat Singh and Lala Lajpat Rai together with others involved in the Indian national struggle before his declaration that, 'I am not afraid to die. I am proud to die for such a glorious cause to help free my native land and I hope when I am gone that in my place will come thousands of my countrymen.' Previously unpublished.

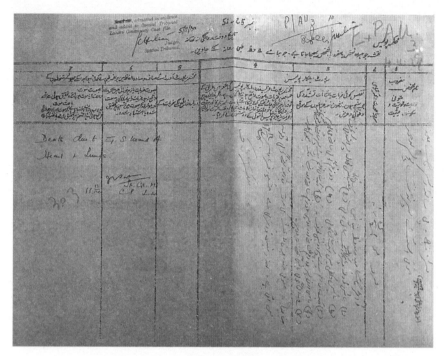

'Matter No. 25–51: Body recovered by the Police of Mr. J. P. Saunders, male aged 25–26 years, one gunshot identified in the left bicep, another two in the abdomen, one on the left, another two above the knee.' Previously unpublished.

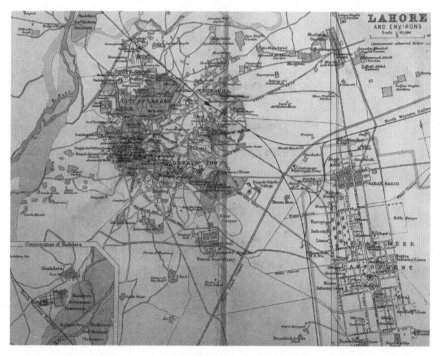

Map of Lahore showing the Central Lahore Jail complex which is clearly not anywhere near Shadman Chowk, where Bhagat Singh day is celebrated today.

D.O.No. 5.755-Jas

Punjab Civil Secretariat,

Lahore, dated the 14th Feb. 1930.

My dear H~'s

With reference to your confidential D.O. No. D-3351, dated the 1st February 1930, to Emerson's address, I am desired to point out with reference to your second paragraph that no decision was arrived at at the Conference on jail administration held on the 9th and 10th December 1929 on the treatment to be accorded to under-trial prisoners and that only two of the Lahore Conspiracy Case accused are convicts. The Punjab Government's view was that no change was required and that the present rules whereby under-trial prisoners are allowed to supplement their diet at their own expense and to use, subject to certain restrictions, their own clothing, bedding and utensils are sufficiently liberal to meet the requirements of those who are of a superior social status. Certain other provinces held the view that there should also be a special class for under-trials, but it is not yet known what decision has been come to by the Government of India on this question. If the Punjab view holds, then the Lahore Conspiracy Case accused are receiving altogether exceptional treatment. They are supplied at the charge of Government with cots, simple furniture and a special diet costing Rs.-/12/- a day, and certain newspapers are also provided for their use free of cost. If on the other hand a special class for under-trial prisoners is created, it seems certain that the concessions at present given to these prisoners would be considerably in excess of those which may be ultimately granted to any such class. The two convicts (Bhagat Singh and Dutt) are also receiving far greater concessions than those contemplated for convicts admitted to the proposed new or 'B' class. With reference to

Before the government issued its press communique on the Jail Rules, there was this confidential confirmation on 14 February that 'the present rules are sufficiently liberal' because 'under-trial prisoners are allowed to supplement their diet at their own expense'! Previously unpublished.

LAHORE CONSPIRACY CASE.

The Lahore Conspiracy Trial opened in July, 1929, after considerable amount of searching of the houses of known members of the revolutionary nationalist movement had taken place. Most of the people placed in the dock were accused and betrayed by police informers. Bhagat Singh and Dutt, two of the accused, were sentenced for life for throwing a bomb in the Assembly in June, 1929, and arising from the evidence given during the trial, they were accused of the murder of Mr Sanders, a Government official, in 1928. The history of this so called trial unparalleled in the history of political persecution, is characterised by the most inhuman and brutal treatment which is the outcome of a frantic desire on the part of the Labour Imperialist Government to strike terror into the hearts of an oppressed people.

Much indignation has been shewn in India at the inhuman treatment meted out to these revolutionaries. An All-India "Dutt and Bhagat Singh Day" was observed in July 1929, when thousands of Indians demonstrated upon the streets in sympathy, exhibiting banners bearing the slogans "Long live the Revolution" and "Down with Imperialism". Hunger-striking was resorted to by practically every one of the prisoners as a protest against the inhuman and brutal treatment of political prisoners. At last one of the accused, Jatin Das, after a period of 63 days paid the price of his heroic gesture by death. Jatin Das had become paralysed, blind, and his blood circulation only operated in the near vicinity of his heart. He had in the process of hunger-striking been focibly fed until such forcible feeding became a danger to his life. His body had been reduced by 60 lbs in weight and only weighed 19 lbs at his death. His body was carried through the streets of Lahore, followed by a huge procession of 50,000 shouting "Long live the Revolution" - "Long Live Das".

On September 14th, the day after the death of Das, the Meerut prisoners demonstrated in Court. As they were brought in they shouted "Down with the White Terror"- Down with the British Government". One of the Meerut prisoners, Sharkat Osmani addressed the others as follows:

"Comrades, Jatin Das is dead. He laid down his life in the cause of his country. We have to pay our homage to the departed patriot, and we should sing the "Red Flag" bareheaded and standing".

All the Meerut prisoners then stood and sang the "Red Flag" bareheaded.

Many of the prisoners, in spite of the brutal methods of forcible feeding refused food for periods of over 6 weeks and both Bhagat Singh and Bk. Dutt refused food for over 10 weeks. But in spite of the terrible state of physical weakness caused by the hunger striking, these comrades were brought into court on stretchers handcuffed and fettered.

Many of the prisoners in October 1929 were brutally beaten in court by the police because they refused to be handcuffed. Unheard of brutalities were perpetrated upon the prisoners after Dutt had flung a slipper at a police informer, Jaigopol, whilst he was giving evidence. The Magistrates, therefore instructed the jail authorities to bring the prisoners to court in handcuffs.. The

Above, overleaf spread: A detailed account by the Communist Party of Great Britain as to how the hunger strike by the accused in the Lahore Conspiracy Case led to the death after sixty-three days of Jatin Dass, and how 'in spite of the terrible state of physical weakness caused by the Hunger Striking, these comrades were brought into court on stretchers, handcuffed and fettered'. This account of 5 March 1931 expresses the fear that, as with the Lahore Conspiracy Case, so also now with the Meerut Conspiracy Case, there was a very real danger that the accused would be tried under special Ordinance 'for the peace and good will of British India' of the thirty-one who now stood accused for 'conspiracy against the kings' and subject to 'judicial murder' by the government of Ramsay Macdonald. Previously unpublished.

-2-

following morning, the handcuffed prisoners refused to leave the
police lorry unless the handcuffs were removed. The jail
superintendent ordered the prisoners to leave the lorry and this
they refused to do unless their request was granted. He therefore
advised the Magistrates to adjourn the case because of the attitude
of the prisoners. He ordered that the prisoners should return to
jail and while on the journey back they were beaten unmercifully
by the police. One, Raj-guru, became unconscious and Bejoy was
found to be bleeding. Dutt was sentenced to three months' solitary
confinement.

The following day the prisoners were again brought to court
handcuffed and again they refused to leave the lorry. The police
therefore forcibly removed the prisoner and so brutally did they
carry out their rask that the "scene in court was unbearable", some
of the prisoners lying on the floor unconscious. The prisoners
asked the Magistrate to record their statement in the evidence as
to the brutal treatment. This the Magistrate refused to do. Bejoy
asked for medical treatment as some were unable to walk, one passing
blood with urine, whilst all had acute pains all over the body.

One Indian paper describes the tortures as follows:-

"Each prisoner was assaulted by at least 20 to 25 policemen, the
method of assault being most inhuman. One method employed was the
penetration of fingers into the rectum and kicking of testicles.
The assault continued for more than one hour after which five
prisoners got fever; all others had acute pains in different parts
of the body. Canes were frequently used and marks can be actually
seen on these prisoners. Mahabi Singh and Rajgures fell down senseless on the spot. "

Under such circumstances, this political "frame up" lasted
for over nine months, the butchers of Imperialism had thought it
necessary to call some 600 witnesses in order to prove their charges
The Government could not see the end of this great farce under such
conditions, and the whole population had been incited against the
barbarous treatment afforded to these prisoners, so it was necessary
to hasten the proceedings.

The Viceroy therefore, used his despotic powers and on May 1st
1930, issued the Lahore Conspiracy Case Ordinance, and a statement
of the Viceroy which accompanied the promulgation of this Ordinance
contained the following:-

"After anxious consideration I have come to the conclusion that
neither the end of justice nor the interest of the accused are served
by allowing these proceedings to drag out to a length which cannot
at present be foreseen..."

" Public policy clearly demands that the grave charges against the
accused should be thoroughly scrutinised and finally adjudicated
upon with the least possible delay by a tribunal of indubitable impartiality and authority and that the preliminary proceedings which
have already extended over nine months and the end of which is not
yet in sight, should be terminated. It is also necessary to ensure
that obstruction shall not further interrupt the course of justice.
I have accordingly decided to avail myself of the authority conferred
upon the Governor-General under Section 72 of the Government of
India Act, and to issue an Ordinance which has the effect of entrusting the trial of the case to a Tribunal to be constituted by the
Chief Justice of the High Court of Judicature at Lahore, and consisting of three Judges of the High Court, and to invest this
Tribunal with powers to deal with wilful obstruction. By these means
the accused will be assured of a trial before a Court of the highest
possible authority, and it may be expected that a final and just
decision will be reached with no unnecessary delay.".

-3-

Under this new Court of three judges "of the higest possible authority", the trial began again on May 5th, 1930, and after 25 of the witnesses for the prosecution had been examined, two new ~~~bers of the Tribunal were appointed in place of two of the members who had been originally appointed.

But this did not matter,- the trial proceeded for the "peace and good government of British India" and the change in the personnel of the Tribunal did not matter to the ultimate finding of the Court of the "highest possible authority".

The Court on October 7th 1930, for the "peace and goodwill of British India " sentenced three - Bhagat Singh, Shivram Rajguru and Akh Dev to death. Kishorilal, Mahbir Singh, Bejoy Kumar Sinha, Sheo Yarma, Gya Parshad, Jai Dev and Kanwal Nath Tewari to transportation for life, -Kundan Lal to seven years rigorous imprisonment,

Against these savage sentences, there is to be no appeal in law. The judicial Committee of the Privy Council have refused the appeal of the accused and only the pressure of the international working class can save these heroic comrades being sent to the gallows and to that living death "transportation for life".

A similar set of circumstances surround the trial of 31 comrades now proceeding at Meerut in India who have been accused of "Conspiracy against the King" and have been kept in jail since March, 1929 undergoing trial.

These comrades have all taken some prominent part in the organisation of the working class movement in India and this in itself is regarded as "Conspiracy Against the King". It has taken the Labour Government of Britain nearly two years and some thousands of pounds to fake this trial,- yet in the interests of imperialism, it must proceed.

Unless the workers are prepared to stop this butchery the Meerut Trial can at any time be transferred in the interests of "peace and goodwill in British India" to a special Court of Highest Authority, in order to bring about a speedy conviction.

The Lahore Conspiracy political frame up and the Meerut Conspiracy political frame up were initiated by the Baldwin Government but conducted by the brutal imperialist butcher, MacDonald. Judicial murder is their slogan in order that British Imperialism may retain its stranglehold on the bodies of the Colonial peoples. The overthrow of imperialism is the task of the international world proletariat under the leadership of the Communist International.

DOWN WITH THE WHITE TERROR !

DOWN WITH IMPERIALISM AND

THE 2ND INTERNATIONAL BUTCHERS. !

FORWARD TO WORLD COMMUNISM. !

To,

The Commissioners
The Special Tribunal
Lahore Conspiracy Case
Lahore.

Sirs, On behalf of six of my comrades including myself
We the six undersigned accused in this
I case feel it necessary to make the following
statement at the very commencement of the trial
and wish that it be retained on the record.

We do not propose to take any part
in the proceedings of this case because we do not
recognise this Govt. to be based on justice or
established by law.

We believe and do hereby declair that

"Man being the source of all the
authority no individual or Govt.
can be entitled to any authority
unless and until it is directly
derived from the people."

Since this Govt. is an utter negation of these principles
its very existence is — not justifiable. Such Govts.
as are organised to exploit the oppressed nations have
no right to exist except by the right of the sword
(i-e brute force) with which they try to curb all the
ideas of liberty and freedom and the legitimate
aspirations of the people.

We believe all such Govts. and
particularly this British Govt. thrust upon the helpless
but unwilling Indian nation to be no better than
an organised gang of robbers and a pack of
exploiters equipped with all the means of carnage
and devastations. In the name of "law and order"
they crush all those who dare to expose or oppose
them.

We believe that imperialism is the
nothing but a vast conspiracy organised with
predatory motives. Imperialism is the last stage
of development of insidious exploitation of
man by man and of nation of nation.
The imperialists with a view to further

Above, opposite, overleaf spread: On the very day that the Special Tribunal took over the conduct of the trial from the magistrate, the accused on 5 May 1930 made it quite clear that they did not wish to 'take any part in the proceedings of this case because we do not recognize his Government to be based on Justice established by law' and thus challenged the jurisdiction of the Tribunal to try them at all, as this previously unpublished document makes clear.

their piratical designs not only commit judicial murders through their law courts but also organise general massacres, devastations and other horrible crimes like war. They feel no hesitation in shooting down innocent and unarmed people who refuse to yield to their depradatory demands or to acquiesce in their ruinous and abominable designs. Under the garb of custodians of 'law and order' they break peace, create disorder, kill people and commit all conceivable designs.

"We believe" that freedom is undeniable birth right of all people, that every man has the inalienable right of enjoying the fruits of his labour and that every nation is indisputably the master of his resources. If any Govt. deprives them of these primary rights it is the right of the people — nay it is their duty to destroy that Govt. Since the British govt is a negation of these principles for which we stand it is our firm conviction that every effort made, every method adopted to bring about a Revolution and to destroy this Govt. is morally justified. We stand for a change, a radical change in the existing order of affairs in social political and economic spheres and the complete replacement of the existing order by a new one rendering the exploitation of man by man impossible and thus gauranteeing full liberty to all the people and in all the spheres. We feel that unless the whole social order is changed and socialistic society is established the whole whole world is in danger of a disastrous catastrophe.

As regards the methods – peaceful or otherwise – to be adopted for the consummation of the revolutionary ideal, let us declare that the choice rests with those who hold power. Revolutionaries by virtue of their altruistic principles are lovers of peace — a genuine and permanent peace based on justice and equity, not the illusiory peace resulting from cowardice and maintained at the point of bayonets. If the revolutionaries take to bombs and pistols it is only as a measure of terrible necessity as a last recourse."

We believe that

"Law and Order" is for man
and not man for "Law and order"

As the supreme juris consil of Revolutionary France has well expressed.

" The end of law is not to abolish or restrain but to preserve and enlarge freedom. The legitimate power is required to govern by promulgated laws established for the common good alone and resting ultimately on the consent and the authority of the people, from which law, is no one exempt — not even the legislators".

The sanctity of law can be maintained only so long as it is the expression of the will of the people. When it becomes a mere instrument in the hands of an oppressing class it loses its sanctity and significance, for the fundamental preliminary for the administration of justice is the elimination of every intrest. As soon as the law seizes to correspond to the popular social needs, it becomes the means for perpetration of injustice and tyrany. The maintaining of such a law is nothing but a hypocritical assertion of a special intrest against the common intrest.

The laws of the present Govt. exist for the interest of the alien rulers against of the intrest of our people, and as such, they have no moral binding whatsoever.

PTO.

It is therefore incumbent duty of all Indians to defy and disobey these laws. The British law courts as part and parcel of the machinery of exploitation cannot administer justice — especially in political cases where there is a clash between the intrests of the Govt and the people.
We know that these courts are nothing but the stages for the performance of mockery of justice.

For these reasons we decline to be a party to this farcical show and henceforth we shall not take any part in the proceedings of this case.

Yours

This statement was said to be made on behalf of —
J N Sanyal
Mahabir Singh
B K Datt
Dr G P Trigham
Kundan Lal

5 5/30 ...

Let this be placed on record but no copies are to be given as the document contain undesirable matter.

Exhibit P.E.X/3.

THE

HINDUSTAN SOCIALIST REPUBLICAN ARMY.

Notice.

"It takes a loud voice to make the deaf hear", with these immortal words uttered on a similar occasion by Villant a French Anarchist Martyr, do we strongly justify this act of ours.

Without repeating the humiliating history of the past ten years of the working of the reforms, and without mentioning the insults hurled down upon the head of the Indian Nation through this house - the so called Indian Parliament - we want to point out, that while the people are expecting some more crumbles of reforms from the Simon Commission and are even quarelling over the distribution of the expected bones, the Government is thrusting upon new repressive measures like those of the Public Safety and the Trades Disputes Bills, while reserving the Press Sedition Bill for the next session. The indiscriminate arrests of the Labour leaders working in the open field, clearly indicates whither the wind blows.

In these extremely provocative circumstances the HINDUSTAN SOCIALIST REPUBLICAN ASSOCIATION, in all seriousness, realizing its full responsibility had decided and ordered its Army to do this particular action so that a stop be put to this humiliating farce and to let the alien Bureaucratic exploiters do what they wish, but to make them to come before the public eye in their naked form.

Let the representatives of the people return to their constituencies and prepare the masses for the coming Revolution and let the Government know that while protesting against the Public Safety and Trades Disputes Bills and the callous murder of Lala Lajpat Rai

Above, opposite: The Hindustan Socialist Republican Army, the organisation through which Bhagat Singh worked, and the violent wing of the Hindustan Socialist Republican Association, protesting on 4 June 1929 at how 'the Government is thrusting upon [us] new oppressive measures like those of the Public Safety and Trades Disputes Bills, while reserving the Press Sedition Bill for the next session' and how such repression has led to 'the callous murder of Lala Lajpat Rai on behalf of the masses'. It remains remarkable, however, that while asking that the representatives of the people 'prepare the masses for the coming revolution' they still go on to add the qualification that 'we are sorry to admit [that] we who attach so great a sanctity to human life, we who dream of a glorious future, when man will be enjoying perfect peace and full liberty, have been forced to shed human blood'. This is the clearest evidence that even at the height of extreme provocation, and whilst calling for violent revolution, these young men did not wish to ignore the ideals that they lived by of the sanctity of human life and perfect peace and full liberty. Previously unpublished.

Rai on behalf of the helpless Indian masses: we want to emphasize the lesson often repeated by the history, that IT IS EASY TO KILL INDIVIDUALS BUT YOU CANNOT KILL THE IDEAS. GREAT EMPIRE CRUMBLED WHILE THE IDEAS SURVIVED. BOURBOHS AND CZARS FELL WHILE THE REVOLUTIONS MARCHED TRIUMPHANTLY AHEAD.

We are sorry to admit we who attach so great a sanctity to human life, we who dream of a very glorious future, when man will be enjoying perfect peace and full liberty, have been forced to shed human blood. But the sacrifice of individuals at the altar of the Great Revolution that will bring freedom to all rendering the exploitation of man by man impossible, is inevitable.

LONG LIVE THE REVOLUTION.

Sd/- Balraj,

Dated________192 Commander-in-Chief.

Signature of A.D.M. d/ 8-5-29

Transferred to Sessions file.

Sd/- ~~Th.~~ ([illegible])

Sessions Judge, Delhi.

4-6-29.

Read out, admitted in evidence and added to Special Tribunal Lahore Conspiracy Case file.

~~Sd/-~~ J.Coldstream,

Judge,
Special Tribunal.
17-6-30.

Staroo No. 85.—G. D.]

Form No. $\frac{\text{C. O. } 22.}{\text{H. C.—G. D. } A.}$

INDEX.

Sub-head No. *A.*

File No. *A1.*

From or to whom.	No.	Date.	Brief abstract of contents.	Page.
both B.I.	5	5.5.30	Inquiries of the facilities given to accd; re: their interview with their relations—	1—2
to C. Jel	6	— do.	— Do— - Do. - Do.	3—4
dated 5th May 1930			of President of the Tribunal refusing interview of the accd: with their relations in court precincts.	5—6
dated 5th May 30			of President of the Tribunal refusing the application of defence committee to sit in the body of the Court.	7—8.

The file on facilities in the Lahore Archives confirms that on the first day of the sitting of the Special Tribunal, the president refused Bhagat Singh's request of the same day for interviews with his relatives, as well as refusing the application by the Defence Committee to sit in during the proceedings. Previously unpublished.

Bhagat Singh and others - - - - - - - *Petitioners*

v.

The King-Emperor - - - - - - - *Respondent*

FROM

THE COURT OF THE LAHORE CONSPIRACY CASE TRIBUNAL.

———

REASONS FOR THE REPORT OF THE LORDS OF THE JUDICIAL COMMITTEE OF THE PRIVY COUNCIL ON PETITION FOR SPECIAL LEAVE TO APPEAL, DELIVERED THE 27TH FEBRUARY, 1931.

———

Present at the Hearing :

VISCOUNT DUNEDIN.
LORD THANKERTON.
LORD RUSSELL OF KILLOWEN.
SIR GEORGE LOWNDES.
SIR DINSHAH MULLA.

[*Delivered by* VISCOUNT DUNEDIN.]

———

This case does not fall within the strict rule that has been again and again laid down that this Board does not and will not act as a tribunal of criminal appeal, because here the objection, if it were good, would go to the root of the jurisdiction. But it is subject to the ordinary criterion which is applied to all petitions for special leave to appeal, to wit, that leave will not be granted where upon the face of the application it is plain that on the merits it is bound to fail.

Now the only case that is made here is that section 72 of the Government of India Act did not authorise the Governor-General to make the order he did constituting a special tribunal for the trial of the offenders who, having been convicted, are now petitioners here. The 72nd section is as follows :—

"72. The Governor-General may in cases of emergency make and promulgate Ordinances for the peace and good government of British India or any part thereof, and any Ordinance so made shall for the space of not

[26]   (B 306—4494)T

Above and overleaf: The remarkably short judgment of the five-member Board of the Privy Council, cursorily dismissing the petition of the accused against the decision of the Special Tribunal in Lahore.

2

more than six months from its promulgation, have the like force of law as an Act passed by the Indian Legislature; but the power of making Ordinances under this section is subject to the like restrictions, as the power of the Indian Legislature to make laws; and any Ordinance made under this section is subject to the like disallowance as an Act passed by the Indian Legislature and may be controlled or superseded by any such Act."

The petitioners ask this Board to find that a state of emergency did not exist. That raises directly the question who is to be the judge of whether a state of emergency exists. A state of emergency is something that does not permit of any exact definition:—It connotes a state of matters calling for drastic action which is to be judged as such by someone. It is more than obvious that that someone must be the Governor-General and he alone. Any other view would render utterly inept the whole provision. Emergency demands immediate action, and that action is prescribed to be taken by the Governor-General. It is he alone who can promulgate the ordinance.

Yet, if the view urged by the petitioners is right, the judgment of the Governor-General could be upset either (a) by this Board declaring that once the ordinance was challenged in proceedings by way of habeas corpus the Crown ought to prove affirmatively before a Court that a state of emergency existed, or (b) by a finding of this Board—after a contentious and protracted enquiry—that no state of emergency existed, and that the ordinance with all that followed on it was illegal.

In fact, the contention is so completely without foundation on the face of it that it would be idle to allow an appeal to argue about it.

It was next said that the ordinance did not conduce to the peace and good government of British India. The same remark applies. The Governor-General is also the judge of that. The power given by Section 72 is an absolute power, without any limits prescribed, except only that it cannot do what the Indian legislature would be unable to do, although it is made clear that it is only to be used in extreme cases of necessity where the good government of India demands it.

It was urged that there was repugnancy between the ordinance as passed and the constitution of the High Court of Lahore, and that the terms of Section 84 (1) make void the ordinance because of such repugnancy. But, as soon as it is admitted, as Counsel candidly did admit, that an Act might be passed by the Indian legislature under the powers of Section 65 in the same terms as the ordinance the point as to repugnancy vanishes.

Their Lordships must add that, although the Governor-General thought fit to expound the reasons which induced him to promulgate this ordinance, this was not in their Lordships' opinion in any way incumbent on him as a matter of law.

Their Lordships, for these reasons, have humbly advised His Majesty that this petition should be dismissed.

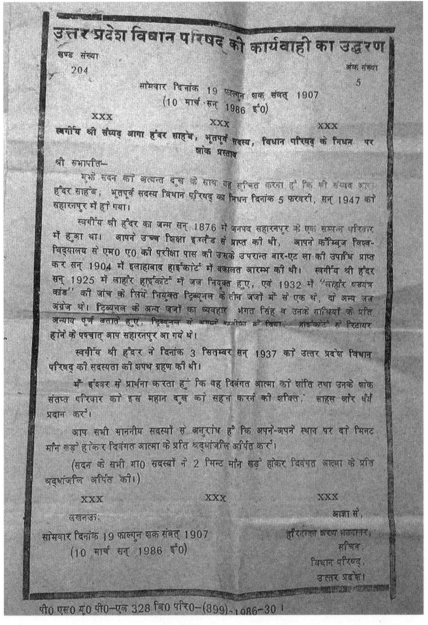

उत्तर प्रदेश विधान परिषद् की कार्यवाही का उद्धरण

खण्ड संख्या
204

ग्रंथ संख्या
5

सोमवार दिनांक 19 फाल्गुन शक संवत् 1907
(10 मार्च सन् 1986 ई0)

xxx   xxx   xxx

स्वर्गीय श्री सैय्यद आगा हैदर साहब, भूतपूर्व सदस्य, विधान परिषद् के निधन पर
शोक प्रस्ताव

श्री सभापति—

मुझे सदन को अत्यन्त दुख के साथ यह सूचित करना है कि श्री सैय्यद आगा
हैदर साहब, भूतपूर्व सदस्य विधान परिषद् का निधन दिनांक 5 फरवरी, सन् 1947 को
सहारनपुर में हो गया।

स्वर्गीय श्री हैदर का जन्म सन् 1876 में जनपद सहारनपुर के एक सम्पन्न परिवार
में हुआ था। आपने उच्च शिक्षा इंग्लैंड से प्राप्त की थी, आपने कैम्ब्रिज विश्व-
विद्यालय से एम0 ए0 की परीक्षा पास की उसके उपरान्त बार-एट ला की उपाधि प्राप्त
कर सन् 1904 में इलाहाबाद हाईकोर्ट में वकालत आरम्भ की थी। स्वर्गीय श्री हैदर
सन् 1925 में लाहौर हाईकोर्ट में जज नियुक्त हुए, एवं 1932 में 'लाहौर एडयंत्र
कांड'' की जांच के लिये नियुक्त ट्रिब्यूनल के तीन जजों में से एक थे, दो अन्य जज
अंग्रेज थे। ट्रिब्यूनल के अन्य जजों का व्यवहार भगत सिंह व उनके साथियों के प्रति
अन्याय पूर्ण बताते हुए, ट्रिब्यूनल से त्यागपत्र दे दिया। हाईकोर्ट से रिटायर
होने के पश्चात् आप सहारनपुर आ गये थे।

स्वर्गीय श्री हैदर ने दिनांक 3 सितम्बर सन् 1937 को उत्तर प्रदेश विधान
परिषद् की सदस्यता की शपथ ग्रहण की थी।

मैं ईश्वर से प्रार्थना करता हूं कि वह दिवंगत आत्मा को शांति तथा उनके शोक
संतप्त परिवार को इस महान दुख को सहन करने की शक्ति, साहस और धैर्य
प्रदान करें।

आप सभी माननीय सदस्यों से अनुरोध है कि अपने-अपने स्थान पर दो मिनट
मौन खड़े होकर दिवंगत आत्मा के प्रति श्रद्धांजलि अर्पित करें।

(सदन के सभी मा0 सदस्यों ने 2 मिनट मौन खड़े होकर दिवंगत आत्मा के प्रति
श्रद्धांजलि अर्पित की।)

xxx   xxx   xxx

लखनऊः

सोमवार दिनांक 19 फाल्गुन शक संवत् 1907
(10 मार्च सन् 1986 ई0)

आज्ञा से,

हरिरंजन शरण भटनागर,
सचिव,
विधान परिषद्,
उत्तर प्रदेश।

पी0 एस0 द्व0 पी0—एल 328 वि0 परि0—(899)-1086-30 ।

Even as late as 1986 a two-minute silence was being observed in the Uttar Pradesh
Legislative Council in memory of Justice Agha Haider, who had taken an oath as its
member on 3 September 1937. As this previously unpublished notice in Hindi shows,
he was born in 1876 and died in Saharanpur on 5 February 1947, having graduated
from Cambridge University in order to begin his practising career at the Allahabad
High Court in 1904. This notice confirms how he served as a Lahore High Court
judge from 1925 to 1932, and sat on the Lahore Conspiracy Case, with two British
judges, before resigning on account of the 'unjust behaviour of the other judges of
the Tribunal towards Bhagat Singh and his companions'.

Notes

Prologue

1. The observation was made by William Dalrymple at the Military Literature Festival in Chandigarh, India, following a two-day festival on the Anglo-Sikh wars in India in December 2017. See, 'Had generals not betrayed Sikh army, British would have left in 1857... There would be no Pakistan', *The Hindustan Times*, 10 December 2017. (Available at https://www.hindustantimes.com/punjab/had-generals-not-betrayed-sikh-army-british-would-have-left-in-1857/story-rVmg6uc7bHh4MQaYEiM3LL.html)
2. Intikhab Hanif, 'Archives of Bhagat Singh case trial to be exhibited', *Dawn*, 25 March 2018 (Available at https://www.dawn.com/news/amp/1397297)
3. Ibid.

Chapter 1: Coercive Colonial Legalism

1. Manmath Gupta in *History of Indian Revolutionary Movement* (Somaiya Publications, 1972) p. 126, confirms that when he went to the place of the cremation some thirty years later old villagers were able to show him precisely the spot where the pyre was lit.
2. Ibid.
3. 'Labour Government Executes 3 India Rebels Frame-Up Revolutionaries for British Imperialism', in Verma (ed.), *Bhagat Singh: on the path of Liberation*, pp. 181-2; cited in Kama Maclean, *A Revolutionary History of Interwar India: Violence, Image, Voice and Text* (Hurst & Co, London, 2015), p. 37
4. (1931) 33 BOMLR 950
5. See, S. Irfan Habib, *To Make the Deaf Hear: Ideology and Programme of Bhagat Singh and His Comrades* (Three Essays Collective, 3rd edn, 2015)
6. The report appeared in full in *The Tribune*, 21 June 1930.

7. Chaman Lal, *Bhagat Singh – The Jail Notebook and Other Writings* (LeftWord, 2007), p. 24

8. Binda Preet Sahni, 'Effects of Emergency Law in India 1915-1931', *Studies on Asia* (Series IV, Vol. 2, No. 2, Oct. 2012, pp. 146–179), p. 150

9. A. G. Noorani, *The Trial of Bhagat Singh* (OUP, sixth imp., 2010), app. IX

10. *The Tribune*, 4 October 1931, p. 7

11. Shiri Ram Bakshi, *Revolutionaries and the British Raj* (Atlantic Publishers, 1988), p. 88

12. F. S. Aijazuddin, 'Seeing Orange', *Dawn*, 19 October 2017 (available at https://www.dawn.com/news/1364733/seeing-orange)

13. Frantz Fanon, *The Wretched of the Earth* (1961), wherein Fanon, one of the twentieth century's most important theorists of revolution, colonialism, and racial difference, gives brilliant analysis of the psychology of the colonized and their path to liberation.

14. Chaman Lal, *Bhagat Singh – The Jail Notebook and Other Writings* (LeftWord, 2007), p. 22

15. Ibid, p. 133

16. Joseph Harker, '"Black Lives Matter" risks becoming an empty slogan. It's not enough to defeat racism', *The Guardian*, 11 June 2020 (available at https://www.theguardian.com/commentisfree/2020/jun/11/black-lives-matter-racism-bristol-colston)

17. Kim Wagner, 'Savage Warfare: Violence and the Rule of Colonial Difference in Early British Counterinsurgency', *History Workshop Journal* (Vol. 85, 1 April 2018, pp. 217–237), p. 218 (available at https://doi.org/10.1093/hwj/dbx053). See also Jordanna Bailkin, 'The Boot and the Spleen: When Was Murder Possible in British India?', *Comparative Studies in Society and History* (Vol. 48, No. 2, 2006); Taylor Sherman, *State Violence and Punishment in India, 1919-1956* (Taylor & Francis, 2010); Elizabeth Kolsky, *Colonial Justice in British India: White Violence and the Rule of Law* (Cambridge University Press, 2011); Martin Thomas, *Violence and the Colonial Order: Police, Workers and Protest in the European Colonial Empires, 1918–1940* (Cambridge University Press, 2012); William Gallois, *A History of Violence in the early Algerian Colony* (Palgrave, 2013)

18. Wagner, op. cit., pp. 217–218

19. Ibid, p. 231

20. *Bhagat Singh v. The King-Emperor* (1931) 33 BOMLR 950. Indeed, Kim Wagner cites legal sources himself (at fn. 83) to demonstrate the point. Mark Condos, 'Licence to Kill: the Murderous Outrages Act and the Rule of Law in Colonial India, 1867-1925', *Modern Asian Studies* (June 2015, pp. 479–517); Elizabeth Kolsky, 'The Colonial Rule of Law and the Legal Regime of Exception: Frontier "Fanaticism" and State Violence in British India', *American Historical Review* (Vol. 120. No. 4, 2015, pp. 1218–46)

21. Durba Ghosh, *Gentlemanly Terrorists: Political Violence and the Colonial State in India, 1919–1947* (Cambridge University Press, 2017), p. 248

22. Ibid, p. 253

23. See Sabrang (available at https://www.sabrangindia.in/ann/muslims-who-gave-india-its-nationalistic-slogans_. See also S. Irfan Habib, 'Nothing Indian about "Bharat Mata Ki Jai", says historian Irfan Habib at JNU', *India.Com*, 29 March 2016 (available at https://www.india.com/news/india/nothing-indian-about-bharat-mata-ki-jai-says-historian-irrfan-habib-at-jnu-1065066/)

24. Kuldip Nayar, *The Martyr, Bhagat Singh – Experiments in Revolution* (Har-Anand Publications, 2000), p. 6

25. Ibid., p. 7

26. Ibid.

27. Ibid., pp. 7–8

28. Choodie Shivaram, 'How the National Archives of India is actually destroying History', *The Wire*, 24 May 2017 (available at https://thewire.in/history/national-archives-of-india)

29. Chaman Lal, 'Rare documents on Bhagat Singh's trial and life in jail', *The Hindu,* 15 August 2011 (available at https://www.thehindu.com/opinion/op-ed/rare-documents-on-bhagat-singhs-trial-and-life-in-jail/article2356959.ece)

30. Kama Maclean, *A Revolutionary History of Interwar India: Violence, Image, Voice and Text* (Hurst & Co, 2015), p. 45

31. A. G. Noorani, *The Trial of Bhagat Singh* (OUP, sixth imp., 2010), p. 95

32. Ibid., p. 76

33. *The Tribune*, 4 September 1929. Also see Noorani, op. cit., app. III

34. A. G. Noorani, *The Trial of Bhagat Singh* (OUP, sixth imp., 2010), pp. 76–77

35. Binda Preet Sahni, 'Effects of Emergency Law in India 1915–1931', *Studies on Asia* (Series IV, Vol. 2, No. 2, Oct. 2012, pp. 146–179), p. 150

36. Ibid., p.148

37. The Government of India Acts were actually a long succession of Acts enacted by the British Parliament between 1773 and 1935. Their purpose was to regulate the government of India. Of these the first seven Acts were actually East India Company Acts, being passed in 1773, 1780, 1784, 1786, 1793, and 1830. The remaining Acts thereafter were properly called Government of India Acts, and were dated 1833, 1853, 1858, 1919, and 1935. The relevant Act at the time of Bhagat Singh's trial was that of 1919.

38. Defence of India (Criminal Law Amendment) Act, 1915 (Act IV of 1915) or 'An Act to provide for special measures to secure the public safety and the defence of British India and for more speedy trial of certain offences'.

39. Rowlatt Act (Act No. XI of 1919)

40. The three trials in what became known as the Bhagat Singh litigation were (i) the Delhi Assembly Bomb Case (ii) the Second Lahore Conspiracy Case, and (iii) *Bhagat Singh v. The King-Emperor* dated 27 February 1931.

41. Binda Preet Sahni, 'Effects of Emergency Law in India 1915–1931', *Studies on Asia* (Series IV, Vol. 2, No. 2, Oct. 2012, pp. 146–179), p.149

Chapter 2: The Slipper and the Magistrate

1. Kama Maclean, *A Revolutionary History of Interwar India: Violence, Image, Voice and Text* (Hurst & Co, 2015), p. 36
2. Neeti Nair, 'Bhagat Singh as "Satyagrahi": The Limits to Non-Violence in Late Colonial India', *Modern Asian Studies* (Vol. 43, Issue 3, 2009, pp. 649–681), p. 649
3. Kama Maclean, *A Revolutionary History of Interwar India*, p. 37
4. Chris Moffat, *India's Revolutionary Inheritance* (CUP, 2019), p. 92
5. *India Law Journal*, 2007 (available at http://www.indialawjournal.org/archives/volume1/issue_3/bhagat_singh.html)
6. *The Tribune*, 26 September 1929, p. 3
7. Noorani, *The Trial of Bhagat Singh* (OUP, sixth imp., 2010), p. 99
8. *The Tribune*, 26 September 1929, p. 3
9. *The Tribune*, 6 October 1929, p. 1
10. *The Tribune*, 22 October 1929, p. 2
11. *The Tribune*, 22 October 1929, pp. 9–10
12. *The Tribune*, 22 October 1929, p. 3
13. Steven Lee Myers and Alissa J. Rubin, 'Iraqi Journalist Hurls shoes at Bush and denounces him on TV as a "Dog"', *The New York Times*, 14 December 2008 (available at https://www.nytimes.com/2008/12/15/world/middleeast/15prexy.html)
14. Bethan McKernan, 'Journalist who threw shoes at George W Bush runs for office in Iraqi election', *The Independent*, 2 May 2018 (available at https://www.independent.co.uk/news/world/middle-east/muntazer-saidi-george-w-bush-throws-shoes-iraq-elections-politics-a8333236.html)
15 Alan Duke, *CNN*, 7 February 2013 (available at https://www.cnn.com/2013/02/06/world/meast/shoe-throwing-significance/index.html)
16. *The Tribune*, 25 October 1929, pp. 1–7

Chapter 3: The Hunger Strike

1. *The Tribune*, 26 October 1929, pp. 1–2
2. Ibid.
3. *The Tribune*, 11 November 1929, p. 9
4. *The Tribune*, 9 November 1929, p.1–2
5. B. B. Misra, *The Indian Middle Classes: Their Growth in Modern Times* (Oxford University Press, 1961), p. 276
6. *The Tribune* 26 January 1930, p. 2
7. Gurdev Singh Deol, *Shaheed-e-azam Sardar Bhagat Singh* (Deep Prakashan, 1978), p. 75
8. Kamlesh Mohan, *Militant nationalism in the Punjab, 1919–1935* (Manohar, 1985), p. 363
9. *The Tribune*, 12 February 1930
10. *The Tribune*, 30 January 1930
11. *The Tribune*, 12 February 1930

12. *The Tribune*, 21 February 1930
13. Ibid.
14. Ajoy Ghosh, *Bhagat Singh and His Comrades: A Page from Our Revolutionary History* (1945), p. 16

Chapter 4: Inquisition by Edict

1. See Stephen Legg, *Dyarchy: Democracy, Autocracy, and the Scalar Sovereignty of Inter-war India* (available at http://eprints.nottingham.ac.uk/28973/1/LEGG%20DYARCHY%20ONLINE.pdf)
2. His argument is that the British divided up its empire into two types of dominions. There were dominions for self-government, such as Australia and Canada, and there were dominions for 'occupations of use', which were to be 'disposed of when they no longer served their purpose' – but the uniqueness of India lay in the fact India 'fitted into neither category. It would neither be abandoned nor would it move towards self-government'. See Walter Reid, *Keeping the Jewel in the Crown: The British Betrayal of India* (Birlinn Press, 2016)
3. See *Constituent Assembly Debates* (available at https://www.constitutionofindia.net/historical_constitutions/government_of_india_act__1919_1st%20January%201919)
4. Charles Allen, *Plain Tales from the Raj* (Andre Deutsch, 1975)
5. Ajoy Ghosh, *Bhagat Singh and His Comrades: A Page from Our Revolutionary History* (Bombay, 1945), p. 16
6. See Section 69 of the Government of India Act 1919.
7. Lahore Ordinance No. III of 1930, §3
8. Ibid., §4
9. Ibid., §5(2)
10. Ibid., §6(1)
11. Ibid., §6(2)
12. Ibid., §6(3)
13. Ibid., §7
14. Ibid., §8
15. Ibid., §9 (1)
16. Ibid., §9 (3)
17. Ibid., §11
18. *The Tribune*, 6 May 1930 (see Editorial)
19. A. G. Noorani, *The Trial of Bhagat Singh* (OUP, sixth imp., 2010), pp. 133–134, quoting from Rahbar pp. 176–177
20. See S. Gopal, *Jawaharlal Nehru: A Biography, Vol. 1, 1889–1947* (Oxford University Press, 1976), p. 128
21. Under Article 7 of the European Convention of Human Rights ('EctHR') 'No one shall be held guilty of any criminal offence on account of any act or omission which did not constitute a criminal offence under national or international law at the time when it was committed.' Britain's Human Rights Act 1998, which is modelled on the EctHR, adopts this exact language in Article 5(1) of its provisions.

22. The Criminal Procedure Code 1898 (available at http://bdlaws.minlaw. gov.bd/print_sections_all.php?id=75)
23. *Emperor v. Lakshman Chavji Narangikar* (1931) 33 BOMLR 675, where the Bench consisted of Justices Madgavkar, Patkar, and Murphy
24. Ibid., para 12
25. Ibid., para 13
26. Here Justice Madgavkar was referring directly to the case of *King-Emperor v. Parbhushankar* (1901) I.L.R. 28 BOM 680, s.c. 3 BOM, L.R. 278
27. Ibid., para 17

Chapter 5: The Lahore Bar Reacts

1. The report appeared in full in *The Tribune*, 21 June 1930.
2. These were G. C. Narang, M. Sleem, J. N. Aggarwal, Mehar Chand Mahajan, M. Barkat Ali, and Moti Sagar. Each of them also then appeared in the Lahore High Court, though J. N. Aggarwal spearheaded the arguments. The Crown was represented by N. N. Sarkar, the Advocate-General of Bengal.
3. *Des Raj v. Emperor, All Indian Reporter*, 1930, Lahore, at 781. Also, 126 Ind. Cas. 177: 31 P.L.R. 677: 31 Cr. L.J. 987: Ind. Rul. (1930) Lah. 705
4. *Chanappa Shantirappa And Ors. v. Emperor* 129 *Ind Cas* 596 (available at https://indiankanoon.org/doc/1562258/), para 57
5. Ibid., para 42
6. Ibid.
7. Ibid., para 25
8. Ibid., para 55
9. Ibid., para 58
10. Ibid., para 7
11. Ibid., para 8
12. Ibid., para 9
13. Ibid., para 17
14. Ibid., para 27
15. *Phillips v. Eyre* (1870) 6 Q.B. 1
16. *Ex parte, D.F. Marais* (1902) A.C. 109
17. *Tilonko v. Attorney-General of Natal* (1907) A.C. 93
18. Ibid., para 31
19. Ibid., para 33
20. Ibid., para 35
21. Ibid., para 35
22. Ibid., para 36
23. Ibid., para 43
24. Ibid., para 44
25. A. G. Noorani, *The Trial of Bhagat Singh* (OUP, sixth imp., 2010), p. 161
26. Ibid., p. 162
27. Ibid.

Chapter 6: 'Inquilabi' Justice Agha Haider

1. SR17 at the Lahore Archives
2. Malvinder Jit Singh Warraich, *Bhagat Singh: The Eternal Rebel* (second edn, Unistar, 2014), p. 200–201
3. SR 21 at the Lahore Archives
4. Folio 23. The letter was signed off on 5 May 1930 by J. N. Sanyal, Mahabir Singh, B. K. Nath, D. G. Nigham, Kundan Lal, etc.
5. *The Tribune*, 14 May 1930
6. This is directly from page 38 of the Proceedings of the Lahore Conspiracy Case (PLCC).
7. Quoted from Chris Moffat, *India's Revolutionary Inheritance* (Cambridge University Press, 2018), p. 95, who refers to a letter from H. G. Haig, 14 February 1930, in NAI Home Office-Pol F. No. 172/1930. Chief of the Intelligence Bureau in question was David Petrie.
8. *The Tribune*, 6 May 1930
9. PLCC for 13 May 1930
10. Ibid., p. 202
11. *The Tribune*, 3 June 1930, p. 7
12. A. G. Noorani, 'Product of a system', *Dawn*, 27 January 2018 (available at https://www.dawn.com/news/1385499)
13. A. G. Noorani, *The Trial of Bhagat Singh* (OUP, sixth imp., 2010), p. 157, draws in this regard from Deol, *Shaheed-e-azam Sardar Bhagat Singh*, p. 76 and Mohan, *Militant nationalism in the Punjab, 1919–1935*, p. 368
14. *The Indian Express*, 19 June 2002
15. Available at https://www.exoticindiaart.com/book/details/trail-of-bhagat-singh-polotics-of-justice-NAH507/
16. Mark Drumbl, 'Judge Pal with Jefferson Davis in Tokyo', *Opinio Juris*, 23 March 2019 (available at https://opiniojuris.org/2019/03/23/judge-pal-with-jefferson-davis-in-tokyo/)

Chapter 7: Trial without the Accused

1. §4 of statement
2. A. G. Noorani, *The Trial of Bhagat Singh* (OUP, sixth imp., 2010), p. 165
3. *The Tribune*, 25 June 1930, p. 7
4. PLCC, p. 420
5. On the other hand, Ganda Singh, the head constable, and Naib Singh, a police constable, did give more persuasive evidence; see *The Tribune*, 26 June 1930, p. 7.
6. *The Tribune*, 26 June 1930, p. 7
7. Petition at para 11
8. A. G. Noorani, p. 172
9. Flaux LJ in *Begum v. Special Immigration Appeals Commission & Ors* [2020] EWCA Civ 918, para. 113
10. Ibid., pp. 302–305
11. *The Tribune*, 4 October 1930

12. S. Gopal, *Jawaharlal Nehru: A Biography, Vol. 1, 1889–1947* (Oxford University Press, 1976), pp. 394–95
13. I am grateful to Ms Sunaina Suneja, granddaughter of Amolak Ram Kapoor, for this information.
14. Khurshid Mahmud Kasuri, *Neither a Hawk Nor A Dove: An Insider's Account of Pakistan's Foreign Relations* (Oxford University Press, 2015), p. 80
15. D. N. Pritt, *The Autobiography of D. N. Pritt* (Lawrence & Wishart, 1965)

Chapter 8: Heresies of the Raj

1. Ajoy Ghosh, *Bhagat Singh and His Comrades: A Page from Our Revolutionary History* (1945), p. 16
2. *The Tribune*, 6 October 1929; A. G. Noorani, *The Trial of Bhagat Singh* (OUP, sixth imp., 2010), p. 189
3. A. G. Noorani, 'Product of a system', *Dawn*, 27 January 2018 (available at https://www.dawn.com/news/1385499)
4. PLCC, p. 14
5. *The Tribune*, 26 June 1930, p. 7
6. S. Irfan Habib, *To Make the Deaf Hear* (Three Essays Collective, third edn, 2015), p. xiv
7. I am grateful to Shamoon Hashmi for having first alerted me to this during his visit to London. He also provided me with photographs of Agha Haider's family.
8. M. S. Waraich, R. Mann and H. Jain, *The Hanging of Bhagat Singh (vol.2- A) Select Tribunal Proceedings – With Sukhdev's Remarks* (Unistar, 2010), p. xxvi
9. A. G. Noorani, *The Trial of Bhagat Singh*, p. 144
10. Ibid., p. 145
11. Ibid.
12. Ibid.
13. Transcript of Judgment, p. 27
14. Ibid., p. 76
15. Ibid., p. 56
16. For a detailed exposition, see M. S. Waraich, R. Mann and H. Jain, *The Hanging of Bhagat Singh*, pp. 256–267
17. Transcript of Judgment, pp. 215–233
18. Ibid., pp. 157–176
19. 'After Hanging, Rewards', *The Tribune*, 25 March 2017 (available at https://www.tribuneindia.com/news/archive/comment/after-hanging-rewards-381758)
20. A. G. Noorani, *The Trial of Bhagat Singh*, p. 186

Chapter 9: Priviligium in the Privy Council

1. Louis Jacques Blom-Cooper, Gavin Drewery, and Charles Blake, *Law and the Spirit of Inquiry: Essays in honour of Sir Louis Blom-Cooper* (Marinus Nijthoff Publishers, 1993), p. 189

2. Dudley Thompson & Magaret Cezair-Thompson, *From Kingston to Kenya: The Making of a Pan-Africanist Lawyer* (The Majority Press), pp. 99–100
3. Ibid.
4. For a discussion, see John Drysdale, *Singapore Struggle for Success* (Heritage Classics, 1984)
5. Blom-Cooper, Drewery, and Blake, *Law and the Spirit of Inquiry*, p. 189
6. 'D. N. Pritt, British Lawyer, Dies; Defended Ho Chi Minh, Kenyatta', *The New York Times*, 24 May 1972 (available at https://www.nytimes.com/1972/05/24/archives/-n-pritt-british-lawyer-dies-defended-hochiminhkenyatta.html)
7. Lord Bingham, 'The Rule of Law', *Cambridge Law Journal* (Vol. 66, No. 1, March 2007, pp. 67–85), pp. 70–71
8. Ibid., p. 73
9. For a discussion, see Ian Harden and Normal Lewis, *The Noble Lie: The British Constitution & the Rule of Law* (Hutchinson Press, 1988)
10. For a fuller discussion, see John Hasnas, 'The Myth of the Rule of Law', *Wisconsin Law Review* (Vol. 199, 1995), who has argued that the rule of law is a myth perpetrated by governments to make their populations more compliant: 'The fact is that there is no such thing as a government of law and not people. The law is an amalgam of contradictory rules and counter-rules expressed in inherently vague language that can yield a legitimate legal argument for any desired conclusion. For this reason, as long as the law remains a state monopoly, it will always reflect the political ideology of those invested with decision making power.' (Available at http://faculty.msb.edu/hasnasj/GTWebSite/MythWeb.htm)
11. *Liversidge v Anderson* [1941] UKHL 1
12. Lord Bingham, 'The Rule of Law and the Sovereignty of Parliament', *Kings Law Journal* (Vol. 19, pp. 234–223), p. 225
13. David Cole, *Enemy Aliens* (New York, 2003), p. 85
14. By Section 65(1) of the Government of India Act, the Governor-General in Legislative Council was given power to make laws for all persons, for all courts, and for all places and things, within British India. By Section 72 he was also given power for promulgating ordinances in cases of emergency.
15. See, for instance, Satvinder S. Juss, 'Belhaj, justiciability, and the "Silhouette-Like" Act of State Doctrine', *Public Law* (Issue 1, 2019), pp. 16–27.
16. The passages cited are also set out in A. G. Noorani, *The Trial of Bhagat Singh* (OUP, sixth imp., 2010), p. 196.
17. Historically it was possible, under a procedure known as a bill of Attainder, to 'attaint' a person without a judicial trial, through a procedure initiated in Parliament, which declared guilt and imposed punishment. Although the system was well established by the fifteenth century, it was open to flagrant abuses of due process. Rival factions used them with abandon to eliminate the figureheads of the opposing side during the Wars of the Roses between 1455 and 1485, and King Henry VIII persuaded Parliament to pass such bills against his own ministers whom he could no longer trust. Unsurprisingly, Bills of attainder were abhorred. They deprived the accused of a fair trial. They

were also typically *ex post facto*. 'Impeachment', after all, was still a judicial proceeding in the House of Lords. It was affected by charges brought by the House of Commons. But a bill of Attainder was simply a legislative act. All it needed was adoption by both chambers with the formal consent of the king. It violated not only the precepts of due process but also the principle that a law should address a particular form of behaviour. It should not address a specific individual or a group.

Chapter 10: Repugnant Law

1. The Government of India Act 1919, Section 65(1). The Indian legislature has power to make laws (d) for the government officers, soldiers, airmen and followers in his majesty's Indian forces, wherever they are serving.
2. Kuldip Nayar, *The Martyr: Bhagat Singh – Experiments in Revolution* (Har-Anand Publications, 2000), p. 8
3. A. G. Noorani, *The Trial of Bhagat Singh* (OUP, sixth imp., 2010), c. 12
4. Ibid., p. 217
5. *Eshugbayi Eleko v. Officer Administering the Government of Nigeria* [1931] UKPC 37, [1931] AC 662 (24 March 1931) (available at http://www.bailii.org/uk/cases/UKPC/1931/1931_37.html)
6. Per Lord Wilberforce in *Zamir v. Secretary of State for the Home Department* [1980] UKHL 14 (17 July 1980), para 19
7. Brooke LJ cited the judgment in *D v. Home Office* [2006] 1 WLR, para 69.
8. *AN v. Secretary of State for the Home Department* [2010] EWCA Civ 869, para 33 (available at http://www.bailii.org/ew/cases/EWCA/Civ/2010/869.html)
9. *Eshugbayi Eleko v. Officer Administering the Government of Nigeria* [1931] UKPC 37, [1931] AC 662 (24 March 1931) (available at http://www.bailii.org/uk/cases/UKPC/1931/1931_37.html)
10. *Bhagat Singh and others (Reasons) v. The King-Emperor (Lahore)* [1931] UKPC 26 (27 February 1931) (available at http://www.bailii.org/uk/cases/UKPC/1931/1931_26.html)

Chapter 11: Pritt Vindicated

1. National Archives of India, File 13/12/1931, Home Department, Political
2. A. G. Noorani, *The Trial of Bhagat Singh* (OUP, sixth imp., 2010), p. 161
3. Ibid., p. 162
4. Ibid.
5. *Liversidge v. Anderson* [1942] AC 206
6. Lord Bingham, 'The Case of Liversidge v. Anderson: The Rule of Law Amid the Clash of Arms', *The International Lawyer* (Vol. 43, No. 1, Spring 2009), pp. 33–38
7. Lord Atkin, *Liversidge v. Anderson* [1942] AC 206, p. 244
8. Ibid., p. 245

9. *Bhagat Singh v. The King-Emperor* L.R. 58 I.A. 169
10. *Stephen Kalong Ningkan v. Government of Malaysia* [1968] 1 M.L.J. 119
11. The other decision was *The King-Emperor v. Beoari Lal Sarma & Ors* [1945] A.C. 14
12. Visu Sinnaduria, 'Proclamation of Emergency – Reviewable?', *Malaya Law Review* (Vol. 10, No. 1, July 1968, pp. 130–133), p. 131
13. *Secretary of State for the Foreign & Commonwealth Affairs v Bancoult, R (on the application of)* [2007] EWCA Civ 498 (23 May 2007) (available at http://www.bailii.org/ew/cases/EWCA/Civ/2007/498.html)
14. Satvinder Juss, 'Bancoult & and The Royal Prerogative in Colonial Constitutional Law' in Juss & Sunkin, *Landmark Cases in Public Law* (Hart, 2017, pp. 239–270), p. 242
15. *Secretary of State for the Foreign & Commonwealth Affairs v Bancoult, R (on the application of)* [2007] EWCA Civ 498 (23 May 2007), para 46
16. Ibid.
17. Ibid., para 48
18. Ibid., para 51
19. *Bancoult* (No. 1) [2001] QB 1067 at para 57
20. Section 2 provides, '*Any Colonial Law which is or shall be in any respect repugnant to the Provisions of any Act of Parliament extending to the Colony to which such Law may relate,* or repugnant to any Order or Regulation made under Authority of such Act of Parliament, or having in the Colony the Force and Effect of such Act, shall be read subject such Act, Order, or Regulation, and *shall, to the Extent of such Repugnancy, but not otherwise, be and remain absolutely void and inoperative.*' (Emphases added in judgment.) Per Lord Hoffman at para 36 of *Bancoult, R (On The Application of) v Secretary of State For Foreign and Commonwealth Affairs* [2008] UKHL 61, para 38 (available at http://www.bailii.org/uk/cases/UKHL/2008/61.html)
21. Section 3 provides, 'No Colonial Law shall be or be deemed to have been void or inoperative on the Ground of Repugnancy to the Law of England, *unless the same shall be repugnant to the Provisions of some such Act of Parliament*, Order, or Regulation as aforesaid.' (Emphases added in judgment.) Ibid.
22. Ibid, paras 37–38
23. Ibid.
24. M. Elliott and A. Perreau-Saussine, 'Pyrrhic Public Law: Bancoult and the sources, status and content of common law limitations on prerogative power', *Public Law* (October 2009), pp. 710–711, referring to *GCHQ* [1985] AC 374, pp. 417–418, reminding us that Roskill was quoting from Atkin's speech, rendered in a different context, in *United Australia Ltd v. Barclays Bank Ltd* [1941] AC 1 HL, p. 29.
25. *Bancoult* (no 2) [2008] UKHL 61; [2009] 1 AC 453, para 71
26. Ibid., para 157
27. Ibid., para 47
28. Ibid., para 109

29. Ibid., para 131
30. Ibid., paras 109 and 131 (where Lord Rodger did not accept the contention that 'that judicial review of an order in council would trespass against the rule that prerogative orders are regularly made against Ministers in their official capacity, but never against the Crown' and where Lord Carswell noted that 'it must be borne in mind that it is the *Wednesbury* standard which must be applied to the Secretary of State's decision to have the Orders in Council enacted'.
31. Ibid., para 75
32. *Bancoult, R (on the application of) v. Secretary of State for Foreign and Commonwealth Affairs* (no 2) [2016] UKSC 35, para 117
33. Ibid., para 118
34. T. Frost and C. Murray, 'The Chagos Island cases: the empire strikes back', *Northern Ireland Legal Quarterly* (Vol. 66, No. 3, 2015, pp. 263–288), pp. 287. Referred to by Lady Hale in her dissenting judgment in *Bancoult, R (on the application of) v Secretary of State for Foreign and Commonwealth Affairs* (No 2) [2016] UKSC 35, para 188.
35. Ibid., p. 266
36. *Bancoult, R (on the application of) v. Secretary of State for Foreign and Commonwealth Affairs* (no 2) [2016] UKSC 35, para 193

Select Bibliography

Books

Anand, Anita, *The Patient Assassin: A True Tale of Massacre, Revenge and the Raj* (London: Simon & Schuster, 2019)

Bakshi, Shiri Ram, *Revolutionaries and the British Raj* (Atlantic Publishers, 1988)

Bose, Sisir K. and Bose, Sugata, *The Indian Struggle 1920-1942* (Netaji: Collected Works, vol. 2) (OUP, 15th Impression, 2015)

Condos, Mark, *The Insecurity State* (CUP, 2017)

Deol, Gurdev Singh, *Shaheed Bhagat Singh: A Biography* (Patiala: Punjabi University, 2nd ed., 1985)

Dutta, V. N., *Gandhi and Bhagat Singh* (Delhi: Rupa & Co., 2008)

Ghosh, Durba, *Gentlemanly Terrorists: Political Violence and the Colonial State in India 1919-1947* (CUP, 2017)

Gupta, Mamta, *History of Indian Revolutionary Movement* (Somaiya Publications, 1972)

Habib, Irfan, *To Make the Deaf Hear: Ideology and Programme of Bhagat Singh and His Comrades* (New Delhi: Three Essays Collective, 3rd edn, 2015)

Lal, Chaman, *Understanding Bhagat Singh* (Aakar Books, 2013)

Lal, Chaman, *The Bhagat Singh Reader* (Harper Collins India, 2019)

Maclean, Kama, *A Revolutionary History of Interwar India: Violence, Image, Voice and Text* (Hurst & Co, London, 2015)

Majumdar, R. C., 'Foreword' in Uma Mukherjee, *Two Great Indian Revolutionaries: Rash Behari and Jyotindra Nath Banerjee* (Calcutta: Firma K.L. Mukhopadhyay, 1966)

Moffatt, Chris, *India's Revolutionary Inheritance* (CUP, 2019)

Nayar, Kuldip, *The Martyr, Bhagat Singh – Experiments in Revolution* (New Delhi: Har-Anand Publications, 2000)

Noorani, A. G., *The Trial of Bhagat Singh* (OUP, 6th Impression, 2010)

Ray, Asok Kumar, *Revolutionary Parties of Bengal: Dacca Anushilan, New Violence, and Jugantar, 1919-1930* (Kolkata: Papyrus Books, 2013)

Sherman, Taylor C., *State Violence & Punishment India* (Royal Asiatic Society Books, Routledge, 2010)

Wagner, Kim A., *Amritsar 1991: An Empire of Fear & the Making of a Massacre* (Princeton Univ. Press, 2019)

Waraich, M. S., Mann, R. and Jain, H., *Select Tribunal Proceedings, With Sukhdev's Remarks* (Chandigarh: Unistar, 2010)

Warraich, M. S., *Bhagat Singh: The Eternal Rebel* (Ministry of Information & Broadcasting, 2nd Edn, 2014)

Articles

Elam, Daniel, 'The "arch priestess of anarchy" visits Lahore: violence, love and the worldliness of revolutionary texts', *Postcolonial Studies* (Vol. 16, No. 2, 2013), pp. 140–154

Killey, Ian D., '"Peace, Order and Good Government": A Limitation on Legislative Competence', *Melbourne University Law Review* (Vol. 17, June 1989), pp. 24–55

Moffat, Chris, 'Experiment in Political Truth', *Postcolonial Studies* (Vol. 16, No. 2, 2013), pp. 185–201

Nair, Neeti, 'Bhagat Singh as "Satyagrahi": The Limits to Non-Violence in Late Colonial India', *Modern Asian Studies* (Vol. 43, Issue 3, 2009), pp. 649–681

Pinney, Christopher, 'The Body and the Bomb: Technologies of Modernity in Colonial India', in Richard Davies (ed.), *Picturing the Nation: Iconographies of Modern India* (New Delhi: Orient Longman, 2007)

Sahni, Binda Preet, 'Effects of Emergency Law in India 1915–1931', *Studies on Asia* (Series IV, Vol. 2, No. 2, Oct. 2012), pp. 146–179

Sherman, Taylor C., 'Tensions of colonial punishment: perspectives on recent developments in the study of coercive networks in Asia, Africa and the Caribbean', *History Compass* (Vol. 7, No. 3, 2009), pp. 659–677

Sherman, Taylor C., 'State Practice, Nationalist Politics and the Hunger Strikes of the Lahore Conspiracy Case Prisoners, 1929–39', *Cultural and Social History* (Vol. 5, No. 4, 2008), pp. 497–508

Singh, Pritam, 'Why the story of Bhagat Singh Remains on the Margins', *South Asia Citizens Web* (4 September 2008)

Wagner, Kim, 'Savage Warfare: Violence and the Rule of Colonial Difference in Early British Counterinsurgency', *History Workshop Journal* (Vol. 85, 2018), pp. 217–237

Acknowledgements

Numerous debts, and some too considerable to record here, have been incurred by the author during the research and writing of this book. Whether the effort was worth it remains to be seen. Oscar Wilde once said, 'There is no such thing as a moral or an immoral book. Books are well written, or badly written.' Whether this one passes his test is up to the reader, of whom I have no doubt there will be many given the subject matter. If Edward Said was right that history is written by those who win and those who dominate, then this is a book about those who did not win and did not dominate. The story that is told may therefore struggle for recognition. The hope is that this may one day become the dominant tale of an independence movement which, with the passage of time, has all but soured today.

In recording my gratitude, I would like to single out for praise a number of people without whose assistance this book would never have seen the light of day. I am especially grateful to the urbane and sophisticated Syed Fakir S. Aijazuddin, the direct linear descendant, in the seventh generation, of Syed Fakir Nuruddin, who was one of the three 'Fakir' brothers who loyally and steadfastly served as chief ministers in the court of Maharajah Ranjit Singh, the 'Lion of Punjab'. They did so unflinchingly right to the very end, in the mid-nineteenth century, in a tumultuous time until finally the British Raj took over. I am no less grateful to Mr Mohammed Abbas Chugtai, whom I regard as the 'Lion of Lahore' when it comes to the staunch preservation of priceless manuscripts in his care as the Director of the Punjab Archives Department in Lahore, Pakistan, where the research for this book was undertaken in almost its entirety. Watching Mr Chughtai work in his office is to witness a daily wonder. It is due to his assiduous efforts that access to the archives has been made possible.

Acknowledgements

The well-organised and well-preserved Lahore Archives are one of the hidden gems of Lahore, and deserve to be better known. Indeed, huge amounts of forgotten material has been diligently catalogued and indexed here. In this regard, praise must also go to the deputy director, Research Officer Saida Asghar Ali, who assists in this endeavour.

I am indebted to Furrukh A. Khan and his family, in whose house I stayed in LUMS for the time I worked in the Lahore Archives. Every evening was a festival of delights, with musical concerts and good food to follow, over stimulating intellectual discussion in the cloisters of this venerable institution. My appreciation is also due to Ms Sadia Bari for taking me to see Begum Nafisa Khalid in Gujranwala and for the hospitality I received in both houses there.

The people who first introduced me to the Lahore Archives were Professor Daniel Elam at the Department of Comparative Literature at the University of Hong Kong and Dr Chris Moffat of Queen Mary University of London, who had already undertaken cutting-edge work in this field. To Faraz Hashmi, who works for the BBC Urdu Service in London, I am beholden for the translation of Urdu documents from the Anarkali Police Station dated to 1928–1929 in the aftermath of the murder of J. P. Saunders, which triggered the events which led to the execution that is recounted in these pages. Given the archaic nature of language in these documents, their translation by Mr Hashmi was no mean achievement, and he undertook his task with aplomb.

I have been blessed over the years with the affection of former students Faisal Mahmod Khan and Hasan Mann, who always look after me in Pakistan whenever I wish to visit. Zahid Hafeez Chaudhri, a former Deputy High Commissioner of Pakistan in London, and now Director General at the Ministry of Foreign Affairs in Islamabad, has always been ready to assist with a visa. In India, it is to Sunaina Suneja that I owe special heartfelt thanks for sending me diary copies and a photograph of Shri Amolak Ram, the legendary lawyer who represented Bhagat Singh and never forgot his roots. His valiant role in Bhagat Singh's defence, together with many other lawyers, has yet to be fully recognised and honoured.

A range of accomplished scholars already established in the field have given generously of their time. I must single out Professor Kim Wagner and Dr Mark Condos of King's College London, Professor Kama Maclean of the University of New South Wales, Professor Pritam Singh of Oxford University, Dr Taylor Sherman of the London School of Economics, and Professor Ishtiaq Ahmed of Stockholm University. However, no study on

Bhagat Singh can be complete without paying homage to the pioneering work of Professors Chaman Lal and Malwinderjit Singh in India (the latter having met with the mother of Bhagat Singh in the 1960s). Both are lifelong devotees of the forgotten revolutionary struggle for Indian independence, and both have given me every encouragement and support.

Sadly, I cannot bestow the same praise on the National Archives of India in New Delhi, where I was asked by the Assistant Director of Research, Jaya Prabha Ravindran, to leave on the second day of my planned ten-day visit, on 19 December 2017, on grounds that I was an NRI (a 'non-resident Indian') who was benefitting from indigenous sources which were not my due. I hope this extraordinary dereliction will be remedied when other foreign scholars visit what is otherwise an exceedingly fine repository of archival materials. To quote Choodie Shivaram in *The Wire*, it is heartbreaking that, while 'the heritage Lutyens building houses priceless historical documents … accessing files at NAI is an intimidating experience' and 'scholars complain that often files they want are not given to them under one pretext or another'.

In the United Kingdom, I remain awestruck by the research facilities provided to me by the British Library in London. No effort in that Mecca for researchers is spared by its officials, who provide every possible assistance to all scholars who come in search of materials. It is a model which should be emulated worldwide. They have given me permission to publish some images of documents from the British Library for which I will be forever grateful. Knowledge, unlike many other commodities, is one thing which does not diminish, but only increases, the more it is disseminated.

Back in London, my thanks go to Pervaiz Alam, the Director of Cine Ink Ltd UK, for interviewing me on Bhagat Singh long before I had completed this manuscript (https://www.youtube.com/watch?v=xcUHtuzNBp4) and for spurring me on. To Ghogi I give credit for sustained strategic support, without which I could not have managed. Last but not least, at Amberley Publishing I am obliged to Nick Hayward and Shaun Barrington, but most of all to Alex Bennett, who took a 'hands-on' approach to the manuscript and provided the kind of meticulous care and attention that must stand as a textbook example of what the role of an editor should be. I am grateful to them all for their unwavering enthusiasm and felicity in timeously bringing this work to fruition in the difficult circumstances of the coronavirus pandemic which befell us all in 2020.

Satvinder S. Juss
Chet (Punjabi New Year) 2020

Index